William Taylor

Model Preacher

comprised in a series of letters illustrating the best mode of preaching the gospel

William Taylor

Model Preacher

comprised in a series of letters illustrating the best mode of preaching the gospel

ISBN/EAN: 9783337284923

Printed in Europe, USA, Canada, Australia, Japan

Cover: Foto ©Lupo / pixelio.de

More available books at **www.hansebooks.com**

THE MODEL PREACHER:

COMPRISED IN

A SERIES OF LETTERS

ILLUSTRATING

THE BEST MODE OF PREACHING THE GOSPEL.

BY

REV. WILLIAM TAYLOR,
OF THE CALIFORNIA CONFERENCE,

AUTHOR OF "SEVEN YEARS' STREET PREACHING IN SAN FRANCISCO," "CALIFORNIA LIFE ILLUSTRATED," "ADDRESS TO YOUNG AMERICA," ETC.

He that winneth souls is wise.—SOLOMON.

Study to show thyself approved unto God, a workman that needeth not to be ashamed, rightly dividing the word of truth.—ST. PAUL.

Five Thousand Printed.

CINCINNATI:
PUBLISHED BY SWORMSTEDT & POE,
FOR THE AUTHOR.

R. P. THOMPSON, PRINTER.
1860.

Entered, according to Act of Congress, in the year 1859,

BY D. L. ROSS,

In the Clerk's Office of the District Court for the Southern District of Ohio.

PREFACE.

In writing to my young brother, Archibald Taylor—who is a traveling preacher in Oregon—on the subject of the most efficient mode of preaching the Gospel, I conceived the idea of copying and publishing my letters, for the benefit of other young preachers and the public at large. As the result of that conception, I now respectfully submit to ministers and people "THE MODEL PREACHER."

THE AUTHOR.

CINCINNATI, AUGUST 15, 1859.

CONTENTS.

LETTER I.
ARRESTING ATTENTION.

FIRST thing necessary to effective preaching—Every man, woman, and child preoccupied—Horses, hogs, and cattle in church—A friend trying to give attention—Criticisms—Speculations—Love-glances—Taking patterns, and pricing goods in church—Boys in Jones's orchard—Jimmy in the well—Gathering in the wanderings of their minds—Frank Dodge in church—Firstly—Secondly—Thirdly—Benediction—Joyful tidings—Little Charlie—Buried alive in a California ranche—Took his lumber-yard to church—Lady passenger—Her troubles—The skunk—Not the animal for the pulpit..PAGES 11–25

LETTER II.
SURPRISES.

How to arrest attention—Surprise power illustrated—California conference surprised—The dodge of the dog—Dreadful surprise in Stamford, Connecticut—Dog diving for a child—Dr. Wit—Surprises adapted to an essential law of humanity—Plays of children—Advice of a minister—A more excellent way—Demands of this law illustrated—The caged eagle—Dignity of humanity—United in marriage bonds with divinity—Orang-outang—Last words of Jesus—Caged eagle out and gone—Pursuit of happiness—How does God regard this law of our being?............26–43

LETTER III.
SURPRISE POWER—CONTINUED.

Surprises of God's books—Nature—Providence—Inspired word—How God makes the landscape—Varieties of nature—One of God's rivers—Surprise power of the Bible—Abraham—Joseph in Egypt—Joseph Gennella—How Bible writers tell it—Model of Moses stolen—Forged copy-right of the devil—The old squatter and monopolizer—Satan professed religion and remodeled the Church—His claims to the best music ignored—His stratagem to defeat the ends of Gospel preaching..PAGES 44–73

LETTER IV.

SURPRISES APPROPRIATE TO THE PULPIT.

Seven varieties inappropriate—Dow climbing a sapling—Introduction to a sermon on swearing—Egyptian legend—Fork for a pack-saddle—Striking a match—False alarm—Dow's colored angel—Running on a rainbow with a basketful of stars—Riding on a streak of lightning—The devil's drag-net—The unterrified preacher—"Grasping at the stars and sticking in the mud"—Flight to the dome of heaven—Virgin of truth murdered—Surprises appropriate to the pulpit—Two varieties—Inherent surprise power of truth—Novelty of a new Gospel—How Jesus did—Surprise notes—Shadow without the substance...74–92

LETTER V.

THE MODEL PREACHER.

A model preacher by Cox—How *the* model preacher did it—Five leading characteristics of his preaching.................................93–102

LETTER VI.

CLEARNESS.

Subject defined and illustrated—Ministerial duty defined by St. Paul—Young embassadors in the wilderness—The preacher reading Caughey's sermon to his people—St. Paul and the jailer—How the leper was cured...103–116

LETTER VII.

CLEARNESS—CONTINUED.

Hospital for the cure of souls—The greatest practical error in the Church—Perplexities of brother W.—How to get out of the labyrinth—Walking in the light...117–128

LETTER VIII.

EARNESTNESS.

Gospel philanthropy—Man in Niagara—How he got out—Gospel patriotism—Patriot's creed—Arnold Winkelried—Patriotism of Jesus—Of the martyrs—"Baptized for the dead"—Nathan Coffin—Arnold and Judas, the traitors—Drummed out of camp—George Washington on his knees—General Joshua—Patriots of the Revolution—Jonathan routing the Philistines—Patriots of Jesus ....PAGES 129-149

LETTER IX.

NATURALNESS.

Subject stated and illustrated—Eight causes of unnaturalness in the pulpit—Test of an unnatural style—Naturalness of the model preacher—Variety of the heart's emotions, and intonations of the voice—"Don't spoil the pump"—Pronunciation—Emphasis—Rule for imparting thought and emotion—"No such thing as naturalness"—Where to find it—Little orators—Dignity of the pulpit—Solemnity of the Gospel—Solemn things, not "big words"—The lost boy—"Lizzie in the well!"—Child rescued from a burning house—The Shunamite's son—President Robinson—Rev. J. Poisel—Lost son found—Terrible railroad accident—Battle of Solferino..150-175

LETTER X.

LITERALNESS.

Literal facts and figures—Four-fold end of literalness stated and illustrated—Rule for selecting illustrative incidents—Test by which to prove their power—Rule for limiting their exciting effect—"Shouting over the wrong heaven"—Laughing in Church—A doctor of divinity smiled under preaching—A preacher abused—Uses and abuses of tears and smiles—Examples of laughing in the Bible—Literalness of scientific teaching..............................176-193

LETTER XI.

APPROPRIATENESS.

Subject defined and illustrated—Perfect adaptation of Gospel truth to humanity—Armstrong behind the door—Can't drive souls to

Christ—Three rules for winning souls to Christ—Application of the first rule illustrated—Points of agreement—Chords and discords—Leader of the mob appointed to keep order—Effect of this rule at a camp meeting—How its opposite worked at a camp meeting—A Virginia sheriff arrested—The thing that settled John Carlisle—How Ben. Currier was served..................................PAGES 194–212

LETTER XII.

APPROPRIATENESS—CONTINUED.

First street preaching in San Francisco—The gambler's funeral—Fighting preachers—How to manage men, dogs, and bulls—St. Paul's example—Wesley mobbed—Whitefield in Moorfields—Charles Wesley—Beginning on the points of disagreement—Its effects—Rarey on horse-taming—Effect of this law on prisoners—Two theories authorizing Gospel polemics—"Anathema maranatha"—Law of sympathy defended—Nathan and David—St. Paul's mode—St. Stephen's last sermon.........................213–235

LETTER XIII.

APPROPRIATENESS—CONTINUED.

Three rules for winning souls restated, and last two illustrated—"The wretched man"—A variety of poor comforters—Out of jail and happy—Springs of Jericho healed—"A good tree"—Discussion with aunt Helen—One-idealism—Commenced on the inside of the colored brother...236–250

LETTER XIV.

THE MASTER'S MODEL.

Characteristics restated and tested by the pattern shown in the mount—The Gospel arch—Examples of Divine and apostolic preaching—Jesus and the lawyer—Peter preaching in Solomon's porch—Peter and John before the council—Apostolic prayer meeting—Dr. Luke's revival notice—Brother Ratcliff—Wide application and definite results of "the model"—Examples of its efficiency—Whitefield, Wesley, Summerfield, Spurgeon, Caughey, Beecher, J. B. Gough—The model not confined to the pulpit—How the infidel was led to Christ—How "Bud Thomas" fixed the lawyer—Three deductions...251–274

LETTER XV.

PULPIT ORATORS.

Did they conform to the Master's model?—Chrysostom—Specimen of his preaching—Bishop Latimer—His "sermon of the plow"—Chillingworth—The "form of godliness without its power"—John Bunyan—Sermon "on the barren fig-tree"—George Whitefield—Specimens of his preaching—Christmas Evans on "the fall and recovery of man"—Spurgeon's preaching—Caughey on "the omnipotence of faith".. PAGES 275-372

LETTER XVI.

PULPIT ORATORS—CONTINUED.

The degree of their conformity to the model of the great Teacher—Chalmers—British Standard on extempore preaching—Our fathers in the Gospel compared with their sons—Jonathan Edwards—Jesse Lee—Dr. Fisk—Cookman—Dr. Olin—Bishop M'Kendree—Wm. B. Christie—Russel Bigelow—John Strange—John Collins—Valentine Cook—Dr. Durbin—Bishop Simpson—Mighty men of "one talent"..373-384

LETTER XVII.

MISCELLANEOUS SUGGESTIONS.

Pulpit encyclopedias—Reading sermons—Plagiarism—The man who stole a sermon—Mixing with politics—How to treat the body—Physical "preparation for the Sabbath"—Attitude in prayer—How to speak with ease—"Blue Monday"—Stimulants—Various kinds—Recipe for wholesome stimulus—Long sermons—Sir John Scarlett—Exordiums—Virgin gold from the mines.....385-403

THE MODEL PREACHER.

LETTER I.

ARRESTING ATTENTION.

My Dear Brother,—To preach the Gospel effectively, you must first arrest the attention of your hearers. The mind of every man, woman, or child you meet in the country or in the city is preoccupied, either revolving some theme, or, more probably, indulging a reverie.

The same is true, also, of every person who comes to hear you preach. Every memory and imagination constitute the scene of a vast panoramic display of images and associations as wide as the world. If, like the prophet Ezekiel in the ancient temple of Israel, you could "dig a hole through the wall," and look into the secret chambers of the souls of your hearers, you would see, right there in the Lord's house, farms and farming implements; horses, hogs, and cattle; lumber yards and merchandise of every kind; railroads and canals; bank stocks; commercial contracts; deeds and bonds; houses of every style of architecture, household furniture, and instruments of music; an association of old friends and new ones, engaged in public discussions and private confabs on all the exciting subjects of the times. In many minds you would see a train of gloomy associations—mistakes, forgets, mishaps, and wrongs unredressed. All these images, and a thousand more, preoccupy the minds of your hearers, and hold their preoccupancy, passing in and out in almost endless succession and variety.

Now, sir, it avails nothing for you to arise before such an assembly and say, "Please to give me your attention." They can't do it. Not one in a thousand has sufficient mental discipline to give you undivided attention, till you arrest it by some power stronger than the sparkling reverie tide which bears him along so gently, as scarcely to awake his consciousness of the fact. High intellectual development and piety on the part of your hearers, do not enable them to give you their attention unless you arrest it.

Your friend selects a good position in the audience room, from which he can see every gesture and catch every flash of your eye, determining to give you undivided attention. Just as he gets himself well fixed for receiving and digesting every word of truth you may dispense, his attention is arrested by the opening of the door behind him; he involuntarily turns his head toward the fellow-worshiper, as he walks up the aisle looking for a seat, and says to himself: "That man looks very much like an old friend of mine—my old friend. He went to Chicago and bought land—increased in value—sold it for one thousand dollars per acre—went to California—wrought in the mines—made a pile—went to trading and lost it—made another raise and went to Oregon—was in the Indian wars there—came very near losing his life—went to Australia—was shipwrecked on his voyage, and came very near going under. I wish I could hear what has become of him. Fudge! What am I thinking about? I've lost a part of the sermon."

He then tries to gather up and connect the loose ends of the chain of your discourse, riven and cast out of his mind by the ghostly image of his old friend, and now he is intent on hearing you through without interruption. Eyes and ears open, sir, to receive some stirring truth that will wake the sympathies of his soul. Following along in the path you have marked out for his thoughts, he hears you say: "Some fastidious persons are like the old Pharisees, of whom our blessed Savior said, 'Ye strain at a gnat and swallow a camel.'"

"Yes," says he to himself, "the boys at school used to read it, 'Strain at a gate and swallow a sawmill.' A great set of boys! Bill Moore married his cousin. Bart got drowned, poor fellow! Andy Snider went to Shenandoah and learned the blacksmith trade. Bob M'Cown is a poor old bachelor," etc. He chases those boys nearly all over creation before he wakes up, arrests his reverie, and comes back to the subject of discourse. Now, sir, he's your friend, and doing his best to give you his attention.

Around him are others who don't care much whether they hear you or not. There sits the architect criticising, not your sermon, but the style of your church.

In the next seat is the physiognomist, scanning the faces of his neighbors, and by his side the phrenologist, counting the bumps on their heads.

Further back is the young lover, casting his glances toward the other side of the church.

Up in the amen corner sit the good old fathers, looking up at you with longing eyes and thirsty souls, thinking about the good times they had, long ago, when old father Miller traveled the circuit.

The good sisters on the other side are as variously and fully engaged; some examining bonnets and ribbons, some taking patterns of the new style of dress, some pricing goods.

The mother imagines she sees her boys in neighbor Jones's orchard stealing apples, which excites her holy horror; another just remembers that she forgot to return the clothes-line she borrowed last week, and regrets it.

Another wonders if poor little Jimmy might n't get into the well before she gets back; another is wondering who did up your linen, saying to herself, "It's a pity our preacher can't find somebody who can do up a bosom for him."

Others are praying, and trying to get their "spiritual strength renewed," but in spite of their efforts to "gather in the wanderings of their minds," and to have their souls watered under the "droppings of the sanctuary," their roving thoughts will run to and fro in the earth, while you are proclaiming the tidings of mercy to guilty souls.

They are there to hear the tidings, and waiting to be arrested and interested. Some, to be sure, care not for you nor your message, but you have them within range of your Gospel gun, and ought to draw a bead on them and fetch them down, as Daniel Boone did his coon.

Frank Dodge once said in my hearing: "The best time I can get for maturing a commercial scheme, or planning a sea voyage, is at church while the preacher is preaching. Away from the care and bustle of business, under the soothing sounds of the Gospel, I have nothing to disturb my meditations."

Now, my brother, don't suppose that these cases of inattention I have enumerated are rare cases. I have only given you a glimpse at the mental workings, or rather wanderings of every congregation you address, and of every congregation that assembles any where, till their attention is arrested. Not all indulging in "vain thoughts," to be sure, for many are thinking of God, and in "his law do they meditate day and night." All occupied with their own favorite themes and thoughts, but none closely following the train of your thoughts, till you take them captive and draw them after you by the power of truth and sympathy.

You have no right to complain of their inattention, and it will do no good to scold them about it. It is your business to arrest them, knock their thoughts and reveries into pi, and sweeping them away, insert your theme in their minds and hearts. To do this, you must wake them up, stir the sympathies of their souls, and thrill them, by all sorts of unanticipated means, with the joyful tidings of sovereign mercy, or the thundering peals of coming retribution.

Do you imagine, my brother, that any commonplace performance will effect all this? Just try your hand and see. Select a good text—give to your audience, by way of introduction, a brief history of the author, and the circumstances under which he wrote it. Then tell them how you are going to treat the subject. Announce your divisions in advance, I, II, III, and IV. State your subdivisions and propositions, and argue them out by a process of abstract reasoning; prove your positions by judicious selections from the Scriptures, "as saith the prophet," or as "the apostle says." Let the people see that you are not a mere talker, but a first-class sermonizer. You will thus command their respect and confidence as a theologian. An occasional quotation from "Young's Night Thoughts," or "Pollok's Course of Time," will add interest and beauty to your sermon. Do n't waste the precious time necessary to bring out the logical deductions of your propositions in telling anecdotes. That would lower your ministerial dignity. Do n't descend to personalities in your delineations of character, for some of your hearers will think you designed it for them, and will take offense. When through with your general divisions, and their appropriate subdivisions, then give a brief synopsis of the whole, and close with three or four additional divisions, by way of application.

Peep into the pulpit encyclopedias of this enlightened age, and see if the model I have given you an't according to Gunter. Follow it as closely as possible, and I'll warrant your congregation a good time for an undisturbed reverie, or any mental speculation into which their desires and habits may lead them; or a nap of sleep, according to their taste, till arrested by the joyful sound of "receive the benediction," and then they'll feel as did my little Charlie on one occasion. I was leading my little boy through the wild-wood, one bright spring morning, and said to him, "Charlie, wouldn't you like to kneel down with pa in this pretty grove, and pray?"

"Yes, sir! Here's a good place, pa."

When I got through with my devotions, I said to him, "Charlie, have you prayed any?"

"No, sir; but I kneeled down all the time."

"Don't you want to pray?"

"Yes, sir; won't you tell me how to pray, pa?"

"Yes, my dear boy, the Lord is listening, and I'll tell you what to say to him."

The little fellow then repeated after me a prayer, adapted to his years, with great seriousness, till we came to that solemn word, Amen, which he pronounced as the first of a list of about ten other words in a single breath; in the mean time springing to his feet, and running a rod after his dog: "Amen, where's my hat? here Trip, here Trip, here Trip," and away he ran, in a chase after his little dog.

Before you have reached the closing amen of your benediction, half the men in the house have seized their hats, and stand ready for a move in double quick time toward the roast turkey, or other welcome sights awaiting them in the wide world without. As they press their way along the sidewalk, you may overhear the question, "Well, brother, how did you like the sermon to-day?" "O, very well. It was a good, sound, doctrinal sermon. Brother Taylor is a good preacher." "Yes, an excellent sermonizer."

I have tried in a variety of ways fully to know the difficult, but important task of arresting attention.

I remember once, when collecting money for the erection of a church, I called on a gentleman, and to arrest his attention to the important object of my call, I took him by the arm, saying, "See here, my dear friend, I am engaged in building a church in the southern part of the city. There is no church in all that region; and you are fully aware, doubtless, of the importance of having one there. You are largely interested in real estate in that part of the city, I learn, and you are no doubt as anxious as any one to have the right class of persons to settle there and build up good society, which you know is out of the question without the attraction of a good church. I think it would be a good investment for you to give to my cause five hundred dollars." The man looked at me with such apparent earnestness that I said to myself, "Ah, I've got him; he'll give me a couple of hundred any how." But, when I closed my speech, he said, "What is it you want the money for, sir?" My speech had gone for nothing. The man was away from home; I had failed to wake him up. He had simply got an impression, by some means, that I wanted to bore him for money.

This absent-mindedness, or preoccupancy of the mind, to which all are subject, often leads to an entire misapprehension of what you say in the pulpit and out of it. And hence the misstatement of facts which often occurs.

In crossing the Bay of San Francisco, on one occasion, I saw an old lady with a very sad countenance. Her sorrowful appearance excited my sympathy, and led me to say to myself, "Poor old lady! I wonder if her name is written in the Book of life." "Dear old mother, she'll soon be in her grave, and I'm afraid she is not ready." I took a seat by her side, and after a few kind inquiries about her health and well-being, drew her out into a free and familiar conversation. She told me the sad tale of her sorrows. Said she, "I bought a ranch over the Bay, and paid my money for it, and have spent a great deal of money in improving it, and thought I had a good quiet home where I might spend my days in peace. But I learn that the Peralto title has been confirmed. My title is not the Peralto title, and I'm afraid I shall lose my place, and all the money I have spent on it, and I don't know what I shall do."

I sympathized with her most sincerely, and tried to comfort with the hope that if her title was found invalid, that having bought in good faith, I thought she could at least compromise with Peralto, so as to get pay for her improvements.

I then tried to direct her attention to the more important interests of her soul, saying, "Mother, it is very hard that you should lose your ranch, but it is your privilege to obtain a sure title to a much better place, an inheritance in heaven. I hope you will see well to that."

"I thought I did see well to it," she replied; "I had the title examined by a lawyer who I thought ought to know all about it. It seemed to be a sure title, and I paid my money for it; but now it seems to be good for nothing, and my money is gone."

I saw at once that I had overshot the mark—had missed her entirely. After a little talk further about the ranch, I tried again to arrest her soul, which I found was not only "cleaving to the dust," as says the Psalmist, but buried up in a California ranch, expecting to be dug out by a hated old Spaniard who held the adverse title.

"Mother," said I, "it will grieve me much to hear of your losing your place, but you are now far advanced in life. Your gray hairs and trembling limbs indicate to me that you are near the grave. You have but a few years at most to live on your place, if you succeed in holding it; and then, if you have no title to a home in heaven, what will you do? It is bad enough to lose your money, but it will be ten thousand fold worse to lose your soul. I hope now, my dear mother, that you will seek Jesus, and obtain the remission of your sins, and a sure title to heaven—a warrantee deed to an inheritance incorruptible, undefiled, and that fadeth not away."

She looked very serious, and seemed to be pondering the weighty considerations I had pressed upon her attention, when, after a moment's pause, she replied, "Well, I do n't know about it. I 've heard of those warrantee deeds, but I do n't believe they are good for any thing in California. I believe the Spanish grants just about cover the whole country, all at least that is worth any thing." Failed again. There was such an attraction of gravitation chaining her soul, that I could not arrest her attention with any thing higher than a ranch.

I have often met with similar cases—persons whose minds were so enervated and corroded by some misfortune, real or imaginary, that I could not approach them from any point, or with any subject, without seeming to wake up all the melancholy ghosts which had haunted them during the storm of their misfortunes; and yet they were sensible, and hospitable, and able to attend to all the ordinary duties of life.

A good Christian brother in Evansville, Indiana, told me the other day, that while engaged in the lumber business in Louisville, Kentucky, a few years ago, his business at one time became a little tangled and complicated; and, on Sabbath morning, when he was trying to commune with God, his mind was so filled with rafts of logs and lumber, that he left home, and went across to New Albany, to spend the Sabbath, just to try to get his mind loose from the harassing cares and incumbrances that crowded and fettered his soul. Said he, "My rafts and lumber yard and account books followed me across the Ohio, and through the streets of New Albany, and into the house of the Lord; and I could not cut myself loose from them till the preacher, a messenger from God to my soul, arrested my attention, and broke the spell. The Lord abundantly blessed my soul that day, and I returned home rejoicing."

O how many struggles with worldly thoughts and associations I have had, and have often longed for the preacher to help me wake my soul, and bring it up by the grace of Jesus to a higher and holier atmosphere! Mere abstract reasoning, however sound and logical, won't do it. A commonplace statementary sermon, however orthodox, won't raise a ripple, much less stir the hidden depths of the soul.

Some months ago, traveling in a stage-coach to a

session of the Erie conference in Meadville, Penn., we stopped about day-dawn and took a lady passenger aboard. She had a child in her arms, and was accompanied by a little girl. As she entered the coach I heard her say in a complaining tone, "I do n't like this way of jumping up before day, and starting off without my breakfast." I saw that her spirit was troubled, and thought I would try to compose and cheer her, if opportunity offered for an acquaintance, for she was a very nice-looking lady. Soon as she got seated, and the stage started off, she said to the little girl, "There now, Gertrude, we forgot the baby's vail. Poor little thing, it will take its death of cold.

"I must have these curtains down."

"If you please, madam," I remarked, "I will button them down for you."

"Thank you, sir."

"This is quite a cold morning for July," said I.

"Yes, sir, quite cold; I fear my poor babe will be sick from going out so early.

"Gertrude, did you bring the baby's cordial?"

"Yes, ma'am."

"Rough traveling over these hills, madam," said I.

"Yes, sir, pretty rough."

"Look out there, Gertrude, you'll let that phial fall, and spill that medicine."

"How far is it, madam, to Meadville?" I inquired; not that I cared, but I wanted to get her attention from her corroding cares.

"I believe they call it eleven miles," she replied.

"There now, Gertrude, we forgot that oil and the brushes. Why didn't you think of that?"

"Well, I forgot," said Gerty.

"That's a very nice little baby, ma'am, I said." "He has his mother's eyes, has n't he?"

She smiled, as she remarked, "It is a very good baby;" and thought I, "By that hook I can fetch her mind up from the gloomy channels in which it has been flowing this morning." But I failed on that as I had done before.

"Gerty," said she, "did you find the key of the cellar door yesterday evening?"

"Yes, ma'am."

"Did you lock the door?"

"Yes, ma'am."

"Have you had a visitation of the prevailing revival spirit of the times in this region, this season?"

"Yes, sir," she replied, "a great many have joined Church during the past winter."

"There now, Gertrude, upon my word, we forgot to return Mrs. Johnson's irons. What will that woman think of us? We promised to return her irons yesterday, and now we have come off, and left them locked up in the house. I wish you had thought of that; you knew I had so much on my mind I couldn't think of every thing.

"Driver, when does the stage return?"

"It leaves Meadville this evening at six o'clock, ma'am." "Well, I must write a letter, and send it down this evening, and have Mrs. Johnson's irons sent home."

I thought to myself, "Martha, Martha, thou art careful about many things." Just so with nearly all who come to hear me preach. They treat me respectfully, hear my words; but how shall I so arrest them as to bring up their thoughts and feelings from the low channels of worldly association, in which they flow as naturally, and almost as irresistibly downward, as do the mountain rills that sparkle, and ripple, and leap in their onward course toward the vales beneath? While I was studying some plan to arrest the attention of the good sister by my side, my eye caught a view of a celebrated animal by the road-side.

"Did you ever see a polecat, madam—a skunk? look there!" She instantly put her head out, where she could get a good view of the "Americana Mephitic." A boy was in pursuit with a stone in his hand, to "engage in a very unequal contest with his skunkship." My lady passenger laughed immoderately, and I heard no more of her regrets or complaining. From that on to the end of our journey, she was one of the most pleasant, cheerful ladies I had met in a month. "Well," thought I, "it would not do to introduce such animals as that into the pulpit, but we must have something that will surprise and wake up the people, or fail to arrest their attention."

LETTER II.

SURPRISES.

My Dear Brother,—Settle it in your mind that you will arrest the attention of your hearers. It is hardly possible to do that to a degree necessary to good effect, without exciting feeling—waking up the emotions of the soul. Commonplace statements, as I have shown, and modes which chime in with the anticipations of your hearers, however excellent in themselves, will not stir the heart's emotions. It is not my purpose to give you a formal essay on rhetoric or elocution, nor to speak here of all the various appliances of power which the orator may use in moving the masses. But, I wish, in this letter, to illustrate what may be termed the *lever* power of the orator—the power of sudden surprises. Many of my illustrations in this case are not such as I use in the pulpit, by any means, but such as I think, in familiar correspondence, will best illustrate my subject; and when you thus become well acquainted with the principle, you can apply it as occasion may require.

A sudden surprise will always excite feeling—emotion pleasant or sorrowful, varying in degree and kind according to the nature of the surprise itself. The sudden flutter of a bird, the bound of the hare, the cracking of a falling limb in the grove, the scream of a child in the wild-wood; any thing, however insignificant in itself, producing a sudden surprise, must, in the same degree, excite feeling and arrest attention.

The surprise power of sudden transitions of thought from the point anticipated by the hearer, to another point remote but opposite, is a lever by which the masses are often moved.

On one occasion, when the question of granting transfers to missionaries, who had left, or should leave, their work in California, was being discussed before the conference, a brother, in an animated speech, having spoken of the distance we had come to save souls on the shores of the Pacific, and the privations and difficulties to be endured, said: "We did not come to California, my brethren, to

'Lie on flowery beds of ease,'

and *eat chickens*." We were all expecting him, in his high declamatory style, to quote the rest of the verse:

"While others fought to win the prize,
And sailed through bloody seas."

But the sudden transition—dropping down from the grand conception of fields of carnage and seas of blood, to the chicken-eating propensities with which ministers are often charged, produced a surprise that upset the gravity of the whole conference, and carried the bishop with all the rest.

I mention this, not for any intrinsic value contained in the thing itself, but simply to illustrate my point. A lucifer match is a very little thing, but it contains the power which, **if applied to** the magazine, will blow up the ship.

Tupper illustrates the wonderful effects resulting, **sometimes,** from very insignificant occasions, thus:

> "A child touched a spring;
> The spring closed a valve;
> The laboring engine burst.
> A thousand lives were in that ship,
> Wrecked by an infant's finger."

Aboard the steamship George Law—afterward called the Central America, in the wreck of which so many lives were lost—in which I came from Aspinwall to New York on my return from California, was a lady passenger, who had for a traveling companion a small grayhound.

The dog occupied a place in her state-room, and was her almost constant attendant, in doors and out.

One day I saw one of the waiters leading the dog in from the deck to his state-room. Opening the state-room door, the dog seeming anxious to go in, he let him go. The dog made a sudden bound to his state-room door, but, by design, alighted just past the door on the outside, and ran for the deck as fast as he could go. Now, there is nothing remarkable in this, except the *dodge of the dog*, which produced a sudden surprise that tapped the fountains of emotion in the bosom of every witness, causing a roar of laughter.

John Philpot Curran, a celebrated Irish advocate, used to plead before a certain judge, who was constantly in the habit of anticipating the point which the advocate was making, and of cutting off the speech by announcing the point before the speaker could reach it. Curran became so annoyed with it, that he determined to retaliate on his lordship. So, one day, on a festal occasion, at which the judge and Curran were both invited guests, the latter was late, and the company, after waiting awhile for him, sat down to dinner without him. Curran soon after made his appearance, panting as though he was almost out of breath.

"Mr. Curran," cried the judge, "what upon earth is the matter with you?"

"Please your lordship," answered C., "I've just witnessed a tragedy that thrills me with horror."

"Pray tell us, what is it? what is it?"

"Well, your lordship," said Curran, "as I was passing the shambles, a few minutes ago, I saw the butcher come out with a long knife in his hand, and he seized a calf, and just as he drew his knife to stick it his little child ran along"— "And he stuck the child," cried the judge. "No, your lordship," answered Curran, "you are always anticipating the point, but you don't always hit it. It was the calf he stuck, sir." The house was brought down at the judge's expense.

A lady residing in Stamford, Connecticut, took several letters out of the post-office, on one occasion. The first one she broke was from her dear husband in California, in which he gave her a graphic description of rustic life in the mines, which so entertained her that she ran home and read it to mother and the family, before she thought of opening the others. After they had all enjoyed a hearty laugh over the California letter, she opened another, which contained an announcement to this effect: "Two nights ago your husband went out of the cabin. A few minutes after his companions were startled with the report of a pistol, and running out to see what was the matter, found your husband in the bushes near by shot dead." The surprise was so sudden and so awful, that the whole family fell as instantly as if they had been shot. The poor widow came very near dying from the effects of the shock.

A young widow, the daughter of a wealthy planter, was returning on a large Mississippi steamboat to her father's house. Her nurse was one evening standing at the stern of the boat, holding in her arms a bright-eyed baby girl, the only remaining relic of the young widow's late happy home. By a sudden jump the child sprang out of the nurse's arms into the terrible current that sweeps toward the falls, "and immediately disappeared." The shrieking of the mother arrested the attention of a gentleman, who, with a large New Foundland dog lying by his side, was reading his paper. Running abaft, and hearing the agonizing cry, "O my child! my child!" he anticipated the difficulty, and called for an apron of the child, and causing his dog to smell it, and pointing in the direction of the drowning child, commanded him to jump in and fetch it up. The dog sprang into the rushing waters, and soon disappeared. A boat was immediately sent on the search. It hardly got under way before the dog was seen rising and struggling far down the river with something in his mouth. His strength was failing fast, but soon the pursuing sailors shouted, "He's got it! He's got the child! It's alive! It's still alive!"

The sturdy tars soon got the dog and his precious freight into the boat, and brought them aboard. Snatching the child, and assuring herself that it was really alive, the young mother rushed forward, and sinking beside the dog, threw her arms about his neck, and shed over him a flood of grateful tears.

Caressing his shaggy head, she looked up to his owner and said, "O sir, I must have this dog! I am rich; take all I have—every thing, but give me the deliverer of my child from death!"

"I am very glad, madam," replied the gentleman, "that he has been of service to you, but nothing in the world could induce me to part with him."

In this simple story, which was published in the Christian Advocate and Journal some months ago, we have two surprises—one overwhelmingly horrible, and the other transportingly joyous, which swept every chord of that young mother's soul, and produced a corresponding effect on all the witnesses of the scene, to the exact extent of their sympathy with her; and will reproduce the same feelings in the hearts of all who read of the scene, in the precise degree that they enter into sympathy with the subjects of it.

Genuine wit is a species of this surprise power. Witty men soon learn the secret of their power, and are very apt to rely on that, to the neglect of more solid and useful studies.

It was said of a medical student in Philadelphia, that he was a great wit, and, though a poor student, was always ready with an answer. One day, when a professor came into the lecture-room to address the students, he good-humoredly propounded to Dr. Wit this question:

"Doctor, suppose a man was blown up in a steamboat explosion; what is the first thing you would do in such a case, sir?"

All eyes and ears were open to catch his reply, when he promptly said, "Well, Doctor, the *first* thing I would do in such a case as that, sir, would be to wait till the man would *come down*."

Such a man would pass pretty currently, whether he ever gave a scientific answer or not, and hence did not feel the same stimulus prompting him to dig for the truth which would ever prompt a man less ready. The devil and bad men have made such a monopoly of this surprise power, that its abuses constitute a large proportion of its history, and yet its abuse is not a valid argument against its use for purposes of good.

This surprise power is based on an essential law of humanity. Consult simple, undisguised human nature on this subject.

Begin, for example, with the children. You try in

vain to arrest and please them, unless you furnish them something that has snap, and surprise power in it. All their little plays and amusements, from the "peep bo," up to the sky-rocket, go to illustrate this fact. Go into the street on the night of our glorious independence day, and you'll see a boy entertaining a score of little boys and girls with a Roman candle. Round and round he whirls it, sending forth a shower of sparks and blue blazes. All look on with interest, but there is no burst of feeling, till *pop* goes the charge from the candle like a pistol shot, then they all shout. In a moment all are quiet again, looking at the sparks, waiting till pop goes another charge, and then all shout in joyous surprise. Of what interest would the Roman candle be to them if it had no sparks? and they would fail to hold attention but for the pop. John Chinaman seems to understand this law of humanity, and hence tries to meet its demands in America, by sending us ship-loads of firecrackers to do our popping for us. Some may consider this but a childish whim that ought not to be indulged, but I take it as an indication of an essential law of our being, which should be properly guarded and restrained, and judiciously applied to the great purposes for which it was designed. It is no *childish* whim, for the old folks are as fond of pops as the children, but they must be of heavier caliber adapted to mature years. We are so constituted, physically, intellectually, and spiritually, as to demand variety, with all its appropriate transitions.

There is no more utility in trying to ignore this

law, than of trying to ignore the laws of nutrition and growth.

I am not speaking of the law of carnal enmity, of which St. Paul speaks, when he says, "I find then a law that when I would do good, evil is present with me. For I delight in the law of God after the inward man; but I see another law in my members, warring against the law of my mind, and bringing me into captivity to the law of sin which is in my members." All sinners have experience in the practical workings of that law, but I am speaking of an essential law of the mental constitution. Some men affect to despise it, and are unwilling to avail themselves of its power.

A minister of the Gospel once kindly remonstrated against my efforts to simplify my preaching, adapting it to the capacity of even the most illiterate, in words they could understand, without waiting to go home to examine their dictionaries, and by simple illustrations of truth that would wake up their feelings.

"Brother T.," said he, "you should cultivate a pure classical style, maintain your dignity as a minister, and educate the people to think, and bring them up to your standard." I knew but little about it at that time, but even then perceived that, while his advice, in a qualified sense, was good, the dry, abstract style which he recommended and practiced, failed utterly to take hold of the people. I concluded that the literary education of the people belonged to the schools, rather than the pulpit, and as my message to them was very important, and as the "king's business demanded haste," I had better not wait till all could study the hard words in the dictionary, but by some means find an avenue at once to their heads and hearts, and let them know all about it. It is folly for a man to say, "I'll bring that river up over the top of this hill, or I'll keep trying till the day of my death." Would it not be better for him to consult the law of gravitation, use his water-level, and gently conduct the river round the hill to the point where he wants it?

You may just as well wage war against the law of gravitation, as against essential laws of the mental constitution. When you find those laws abused and misapplied, do n't try to ignore them, but try to correct the abuse, and turn them into the right channel.

Allow me again, my dear brother, to repeat, that there is an essential law of humanity, implanted within by Him who made us, which imperiously demands variety, with all the sudden transitions and contrasts which characterize the kingdoms of nature, providence, and grace.

Do you ask me to define that law, or tell you what it is? I can not undertake to do that. We simply know that such a law exists, by the uniformity and constancy of its demands in human experience. I think it originates in the soul's immortality, and its instinctive longings for fountains, and food, and walks, and flights, and rapturous joys, which are no where to be found in this world. The soul in its tenement of clay, is like the unfledged eagle brought up within the narrow limits of his cage. He has never had any liberty outside its walls. He knows but little of the great world around and above him, and yet he do n't feel at home in so small a sphere. He walks round in his cage, from side to side, seeking something to entertain him. He spreads his wings, and feels that it is a good thing to have wings, though he has never yet learned their use; but somehow they excite in him a desire to soar, he knows not wherefore, nor whither, for he has never had an opportunity of trying them by a single flight. He is restless, and wants to go somewhere, or do something that will break the dull monotony of prison life. His cage is often moved from place to place, but still he is in it, and can't know much beyond it. He gazes at the sun and thinks it a pretty thing to look at, but knows not that it is a beacon fire to guide his upward flight to regions far above this world of trouble, where he may bathe his plumage in its bright effulgence; mean time, he seeks pleasure in all the little surprises and excitements of every-day life, instinctively hoping all the time that some of them will break to him the problem of his own life, and bring in his long-sought joys.

The human soul is endowed with wonderful powers

of intellect and heart, and possesses a capacity for development which is as unlimited in its effectiveness as the eternity of its duration. The glorified soul, in its progressive development, will doubtless rise to degrees of intelligence, moral strength, and glory, which transcend all our anticipations. The eagle's ken surveys the sun, but his weary wings can only sweep the near shore of the vast ethereal sea which intervenes. "Eye hath not seen, nor ear heard, neither hath it entered into the heart of man the things which God hath prepared for them who love him;" but high, and grand, and glorious as those things may be, the children of God shall not only see them afar off, as my noble bird does the sun, but they shall penetrate their depths, scan their hights, and realize their rich fruition, for God hath already revealed the earnest of "these things unto us by his Spirit." I desire no better proof and illustration of the immeasurable capacity, value, and future dignity of the human soul, than the incarnation of the Son of God.

Could God have consented to a union with a nature incapable of honorable affinity, association, and dignified identity with himself? If man had been so groveling in his nature, except when chained down by sin, and so limited in his capacity as to make his union with Divinity, in the person of Jesus Christ, disgraceful to the Godhead, would the angels and all the family in heaven have consented to such a marriage union? What would they have said when the bans were published in his holy temple? Would not the last one of them have united with all the rest, in a protest against the marriage, and shown cause why, for the honor of the whole family in heaven, it should not take place?

The orang-outang is said, by naturalists, to be the next animal in the chain of being below man, only one link below us; and yet, if it were possible, and a man should, in the possibility of the case, enter into a matrimonial alliance with an orang-outang, dear me, humanity would be shocked, and such a man, as says Job, "would be chased out of the world"—kicked out of creation. And yet, incomprehensibly great as is the disparity between God and man, such is the dignity and improvability of man's nature, that God enters into a union with it, more intimate and indissoluble than any matrimonial alliance can be. "God was manifest in the flesh," took a brother body of mine, and a brother soul of mine, into an inseparable union with the Godhead. When the bans of this union were proclaimed in heaven there were no objections.

When the God-man appeared, the everlasting Father said, "Let all the angels of God worship him. And of the angels he saith, Who maketh his angels spirits, and his ministers a flame of fire." The angels not only fall, with glad consent, in humble adoration at his feet, but so exult in the privilege of being workers together with him in his mission of mercy, that at their appointment to the office of "ministering spirits, sent forth to minister for them who shall be heirs of salvation," their rapturous zeal is compared by Him who saw it to "flaming fire." When that flaming angel, who had the honor of being the express messenger to announce to a sinking world the coming of its great deliverer, received his orders, he descended with lightning speed, proclaiming, "Behold, I bring you good tidings of great joy, which shall be to all people; for unto you is born this day, in the city of David, a Savior, which is Christ the Lord." "And suddenly there was with him a multitude of the heavenly host, praising God, and saying, Glory to God in the highest, and on earth peace, good-will toward men."

After Jesus had "borne our griefs and carried our sorrows," for "he was wounded for our transgressions, bruised for our iniquities," and bore in his own body the dreadful chastisement necessary to procure our peace, we see him, in the person of his risen body, on the Mount of Olives, conversing with his apostles. The last words of a departing friend are very impressive. The last words of Jesus, before his ascension, fell from his lips on that occasion. What blessed words they are! "They asked him, saying, Lord, wilt thou at this time restore again the kingdom of Israel? And he said unto them, It is not for you to know the times or the seasons which the Father hath put in his own power." There is a limit to human knowledge—my brother, there are many things that we are not to know in this world; but the most important thing for us to know is here pledged: "But ye shall receive power after that the Holy Ghost is come upon you: and ye shall be witnesses unto me both in Jerusalem and in all Judea, and in Samaria, and unto the uttermost parts of the earth."

And when he had spoken these things, while they beheld, he was taken up; and a cloud received him out of their sight. He had drank the contents of the bitter cup. The struggle was passed. That human body and soul, our brother, indissolubly united with, and sustained by the Divinity, had stood the fiery ordeal, and had become "perfect through sufferings," and was now ready for a triumphal march into the eternal city. Our brother ascended to the scene of his grand coronation, on the mediatorial throne. He will there "prepare a place for us;" and says he, "If I prepare a place for you, I will come again and receive you unto myself, that where I am there ye may be also." The apostles saw him go up: "And while they looked steadfastly toward heaven as he went up, behold two men stood by them in white apparel; which also said, Ye men of Galilee, why stand ye gazing up into heaven? this same Jesus, which is taken up from you into heaven, shall so come in like manner as ye have seen him go into heaven."

St. John says, "Beloved, now are we the sons of God, and it doth not yet appear what we shall be, but we know that when he shall appear, we shall be like him; for we shall see him as he is." I have introduced these facts illustrating the dignity of human souls redeemed, simply to convey to your mind, my brother, a clearer idea of their wonderful **powers and capabilities**.

These **souls, in the** language of Eliphaz the Timanite, "dwell in houses of clay, whose foundation is in the dust, which are crushed before the moth." Like the caged eagle we have always been in our clay houses, and know not the extent of our own capacity nor the hights to which we may soar, when our earthly house, or tabernacle, shall have been dissolved, and our redeemed spirits uncaged shall wing their mystic flight to a "building of God," not a mere tent, "a house not made with hands, eternal in the heavens." We live in a beautiful world, and our earthly houses are admirably adapted to our pilgrimage life, and there is much to entertain us by the way; but after all, there is a quenchless longing of the soul for something beyond its imprisoned grasp. Souls enlightened by the Spirit, and united to God by faith in Jesus, know what their soul-satisfying portion is, and receive a foretaste of it, which thrills them with "joy unspeakable and full of glory," and leads them to sing,

> "O would he more of heaven bestow,
> And let the vessels break,
> And let our ransomed spirits go,
> To grasp the God we seek!"

"For," as says St. Paul, "in this tabernacle we do groan, being burdened; earnestly desiring to be clothed upon with our house which is in heaven."

I have often heard their songs of triumph, my brother, as they were breaking through their prison walls and preparing for their upward flight.

I saw the eagle's cage knocked over and broken. The frightened bird sprang out of the wreck, and spread his untried wings, and up he went. A circling sweep or two lifted him high above the hills, then upward darting beyond the region of storms, he soon passed the boundaries of earthly vision. There lay the broken cage in which he had tried for many years to find entertainment and happiness, but now the noble bird had flown.

Those who know not God are an inexplicable mystery to themselves—know not what their wings are for, but they want to fly, or do something that will satisfy the instinctive yearnings of their souls. Hence, their heaven-given powers are employed in all sorts of worldly schemes which promise them present or ultimate happiness. Some seek it in military glory; some in trying to hoard up the treasures of earth; others in worldly pomp and display; others still in the honor or profit of new discoveries in science or mechanics; a large majority try to fill the aching void within with the pleasures of to-day, on the epicurean motto, "Eat, drink, and be merry." All see the rainbow, occasionally, and believe the bag of gold may be found at the end of it, and all run to get it, but all are disappointed, for the simple reason that it is not there.

This universal pursuit of happiness is the stimulus,

which, like a mighty engine, keeps all animate creation in motion; and though our souls are caged up and incumbered by numberless disabilities, how wonderful are the achievements of the human mind in this world, furnishing grand illustrations of its mighty powers! Whether we know God and enjoy his pardoning mercy, or not, this mighty giant in chains—the soul—is always ready to start at a surprise rap at the door, and runs to receive a new hope or fear, or something that will afford variety, and break the monotony of prison-life.

If we look into God's books of nature, Providence, or inspired word, we find that he has ever recognized this law of our being, and adapted himself to its demands for variety, with all possible startling surprises of sudden transitions and contrasts.

LETTER III.

SURPRISE POWER—CONTINUED.

My Dear Brother,—Look into God's book of nature and see what surprise power breaks forth from every page.

In smoothing down the earth's surface, he did not make it all one grand, level prairie. What an astonishing variety of hill, dale, and mountain it presents!

In planting a forest, the Lord does not set out a field of oaks in straight lines, another of hickory, and another of walnut trees. He scatters them broadcast in endless variety of size, shape, kind, and position. How the traveler is surprised and entertained by the variety of landscape scenery, and no less surprised by the endless variety of sounds which strike his ears, from the chirp of the cricket up to the roar of the lion, and from the ripple of the rill to the thunder of the cataract!

The elements around him, and the heavens above him, all unite in producing surprises and entertainment for his restless, mighty soul.

In making a river, God did not spring it all up from one fountain, and convey it in gentle eddies across a continent through a straight canal. Trace, if you please, one of God's rivers. In pursuit of the bounding deer in his mountain home, weary and thirsty, you see, breaking from beneath the granite cliff, a sparkling little fountain. You drink, and lie down to listen to its rippling music and enjoy sweet rest.

Having refreshed yourself, you start, with joyous steps, to pursue the baby river. Now delighted with its meanderings, and its sudden bounds and falls; now another kindred stream comes leaping down the mountain, and mingling with its sparkling waters, on they go, with gathering strength, as other rills, rivulets, and creeks, break in from behind the ridges, where you least expected to see them.

Now the river moves in manhood's strength, but still keeps up all the startling variety of the baby fountain; now moving in gentle eddies in a straight line; now sweeping a curve; now dashing into a cataract, roaring and thundering, causing the earth to tremble under its heavy tread, and spouting up showers of spray, adorning the upper air with rainbow-tints.

Soon again you see it rolling on in quiet beauty among the meadows, inviting the anglers to its quiet shore, and the bathers into its cheerful bosom. Sometimes looking ahead you see the end of it. No visible outlet—completely blockaded by impassable mountains. But suddenly you see that it has leaped its barriers, perhaps cleft a mountain right in two to do it, but it's out and gone, singing in its wild career,

> Sink down, ye hills and mountains,
> Before my thousand fountains,
> In matchless union joined,
> We are to the ocean bound.

The perfection of the painter's art is found in a correct copy of the landscape, just as it is in nature, with all its variety of hills, dales, rills, rivers, lakes, and oceans, with all the lights and shades and coloring of their native drapery. On the perfection of the copy from nature, whatever the subject may be, depends the surprise power of the painting, whether on canvas or on mind by the skill of the orator.

God's book of providence reveals as great, and even greater varieties than his book of nature. Its surprise power is greatly increased, from the fact that we know so little of the laws of providence, and have so limited an opportunity of anticipating the sudden surprises that break upon us daily. The book which contains the most numerous and the most startling and interesting surprises in the world, is God's book of revealed truth—the holy Scriptures.

Read the first chapter of Genesis. The narration of every creative act is a startling surprise, and you will not find a chapter, from that to the last of Revelation, which does not contain more or less of surprise power abounding in stirring effect.

I will only select a few passages.

Take, for illustration, the trial of Abraham's faith. God called him, and he answered, "Behold, here I am. And he said, Take now thy son, thine only son, Isaac, whom thou lovest, and get thee into the land of Moriah, and offer him there for a burnt offering upon one of the mountains which I will tell thee of." How natural for him to say, "Surely, this is contrary to the laws of parental obligation; contrary to the laws of civil society and of justice; contrary to God's own promise, that my seed should be as the stars for multitude. What! kill the only living heir to the promise? Then, O, what would his mother do? How can I slay my son, my beloved son, mine only son, Isaac?"

That was a terrible surprise to the good man, but he furnished another equally great, in the prompt and steady action of his unwavering fidelity to God. He does not tell Sarah. He knows that her feelings would bring her into collision with his settled purpose to obey God. He had enough to do to resist the tide of his own sympathy, without opening the floodgates of a kindred tide, which would probably sweep him away from the anchorage ground of his faith.

"And Abraham rose up early in the morning and saddled his ass, and took two of his young men with him, and Isaac, his son, and clave the wood for the burnt offering, and rose up and went unto the place of which God had told him." Two nights were spent on the journey. What dreadful nights they must have been to the man of God! His confiding son lay on his bosom! He could hear the throbbings of his heart. "And O, shall this hand—a father's hand—drive the knife into that heart—my son's heart? I love my son, but I love God more. I will obey God, and let him take care of the consequences."

"Then, on the third day, Abraham lifted up his eyes and saw the place afar off." What an awful-looking place it was! but he staggered not. He did not want to encounter the opposing sympathies of the young men. "And Abraham said unto his young men, Abide ye here with the ass, and I and the lad will go yonder and worship and come again to you. And Abraham took the wood of the burnt offering and laid it upon Isaac, his son"—Jesus bore his own cross up that very same mountain—"and he took the fire in his hand, and a knife, and they went, both of them together. And Isaac spake unto Abraham, his father, and said:

"My father; and he said, Here am I, my son.

"And he said, Behold the fire and the wood: but where is the lamb for a burnt offering?"

What response could his agonized heart give to that question?

No time for the discussion of such a question. He could only refer the whole matter to God. "And Abraham said, My son, God will provide himself a lamb for a burnt offering." God did do it, "and gave his only-begotten Son." "So they went both of them together. And they came to the place which God had told him of: and Abraham built an altar there, and laid the wood in order"—then came the mortal tug—"and bound Isaac his son, and laid him on the altar on the wood. And Abraham stretched forth his hand, and took the knife to slay his son." The knife gleams in the sunlight, and in a second will pierce the heart of Sarah's only son.

Hark! the angel of the covenant—the pealing

notes of the voice divine, arrest the death-dealing stroke: "Abraham! Abraham!" and he dropped his hand and said, "Here am I."

And he said, "Lay not thine hand upon the lad, neither do thou any thing unto him: for now I know that thou fearest God, seeing thou hast not withheld thy son, thine only son, from me. And Abraham lifted up his eyes and looked, and behold, behind him, a ram caught in a thicket by his horns," the most interesting-looking ram he ever saw in his life. Did he not pitch into him with a will? "And he offered him up for a burnt-offering in the stead of his son."

There is, in my opinion, more surprise power in this narrative of a few lines, than you can find in any modern history or novel of five hundred pages. The authorship of Moses was as remarkable as his statesmanship. He gives the very language and expression of each party represented, and draws the whole picture to the life.

Take another example from the pen of the same writer—the history of Joseph. Read it, and mark its sudden transitions. To assist you, I will name and number its leading surprises.

1. The murderous plot of the nine wicked brothers, when they saw in the distance the weary lad approaching.

2. The successful interposition of Reuben in his behalf.

3. The surprise and anguish of poor Joseph when cast into the pit.

4. The company of Ishmaelites, and the sale of Joseph to them.

5. Reuben's disappointment in not finding him in the pit, when, with a brother's yearning heart, he came for his rescue. "And he rent his clothes, and returned unto his brethren and said, The child is not: and I, whither shall I go?"

6. The dreadful tidings, borne by the guilty brothers to the old patriarch, holding up to his view at the same time the bloody coat of his own dear Joseph, saying, "This have we found; know now whether it be thy son's coat or no. And he knew it, and said, It is my son's coat; an evil beast hath devoured him; Joseph is without doubt rent in pieces. And Jacob rent his clothes, and put sackcloth upon his loins, and mourned for his son many days. And all his sons and all his daughters rose up to comfort him; but he refused to be comforted, and he said, For I will go down into the grave unto my son mourning. Thus his father wept for him."

7. Joseph's chastity. Potiphar's wife, with "her much fair speech, and with the flattering of her lips, could not cause him to yield."

8. Her ingenious diabolic accusation to her husband.

9. Joseph's imprisonment.

10. His interpretation of the butler's dream—a sweet surprise to the poor fellow.

11. His interpretation of the baker's dream—a horrible surprise, rendered doubly horrible by its con-

trast with that of the butler, the pleasing termination of whose dream had inflated the poor baker's hopes, which now suddenly set in the darkness of despair.

12. Pharoah's extraordinary dream, and fruitless efforts to find an interpreter.

13. The wonderful story of the butler to the king about one of the convicts in jail who could interpret dreams. He had just thought of him after two years of ungrateful neglect.

14. Poor Joseph had about given up all hope of release, when the king's messenger rushed into the dungeon, saying, "Joseph, the king wants to see thee in court immediately." He shed off his dirty duds covered with vermin, washed and shaved himself, and in raiment nice and clean walked into the palace. And Pharaoh said unto Joseph, "I have dreamed a dream, and there is none that can interpret it: and I have heard say of thee, that thou canst understand a dream to interpret it." And Joseph answered Pharaoh, saying, "It is not in me: God shall give Pharaoh an answer of peace."

15. The interpretation.

16. His sudden promotion. "And Pharaoh said unto his servants, Can we find such a man as this is, a man in whom the Spirit of God is? And Pharaoh said unto Joseph, Forasmuch as God hath shewed thee all this, there is none so discreet and wise as thou art. Thou shalt be over my house, and according unto thy word shall my people be ruled: only on the throne will I be greater than thou. And Pharaoh

said unto Joseph, See, I have set thee over all the land of Egypt. And Pharaoh took off his ring from his hand, and put it upon Joseph's hand, and arrayed him in vestures of fine linen, and put a gold chain about his neck; and he made him to ride in the second chariot which he had, and they cried before him, Bow the knee: and he made him ruler over all the land of Egypt. And Pharaoh said unto Joseph, I am Pharaoh, and without thee shall no man lift up his hand or foot in all the land of Egypt. And he gave him to wife Asenath, the daughter of Potipherah, priest of On. And Joseph went out over all the land of Egypt." Was that not a *surprising* rise in the world?

17. The first interview of Jacob's ten famine-pinched sons with the governor of Egypt. "And Joseph was the governor over the land, and he it was that sold to all the people of the land; and Joseph's brethren came and bowed down themselves before him with their faces to the earth. And Joseph saw his brethren, and he knew them, but he made himself strange unto them, and spake roughly unto them; and he said unto them, Whence come ye? And they said, From the land of Canaan, to buy food. And Joseph knew his brethren, but they knew not him. And Joseph remembered the dreams which he dreamed of them"—and what an association of scenes, precedent and subsequent, crowded into his mind!—"and he said unto them, Ye are spies; to see the nakedness of the land ye are come

And they said unto him, Nay, my lord, but to buy food are thy servants come. We are all one man's sons: we are true men; thy servants are no spies. And he said unto them, Nay, but to see the nakedness of the land ye are come. And they said, Thy servants are twelve brethren, the sons of one man in the land of Canaan; and behold, the youngest is this day with our father, and one is not. And Joseph said unto them, That is it that I spake unto you, saying, Ye are spies. Hereby ye shall be proved. By the life of Pharaoh, ye shall not go forth hence, except your youngest brother come hither. Send one of you and let him fetch your brother, and ye shall be kept in prison, that your words may be proved, whether there be any truth in you; or else, by the life of Pharaoh, ye are spies. And he put them all together into ward three days"—gave them a small taste of what he had endured on account of their cruelty for years.

"And Joseph said unto them the third day, This do, and live, for I fear God. If ye be true men, let one of your brethren be bound in the house of your prison; go ye, carry corn for the famine of your houses. But bring your youngest brother unto me, so shall your words be verified, and ye shall not die. And they did so.

"And they said one to another, We are verily guilty concerning our brother, in that we saw the anguish of his soul, when he besought us and we would not hear; therefore is this distress come upon us. And Reuben answered them, saying, Spake I not unto you, saying, Do not sin against the child; and ye would not hear? therefore, behold, also his blood is required. And they knew not that Joseph understood them"—had no idea that the governor understood Hebrew—"for he spake unto them by an interpreter. And he turned himself about from them, and wept; and returned to them again, and communed with them, and took from them Simeon, and bound him before their eyes. Then Joseph commenced to fill their sacks with corn, and to restore every man's money into his sack, and to give them provision for the way; and thus did he unto them. And they laded their asses with the corn, and departed thence.

18. "And as one of them opened his sack, to give his ass provender in the inn, he espied his money; for, behold, it was in his sack's mouth. And he said unto his brethren, My money is restored; and lo, it is even in my sack; and their hearts failed them, and they were afraid, saying one to another, What is this that God hath done unto us?" How terrible are the accusations and forebodings of a guilty conscience!

19. They reported all these things to Jacob. "And it came to pass, as they emptied their sacks, that, behold, every man's bundle of money was in his sack; and when both they and their father saw the money, they were afraid. And Jacob, their father, said unto them, Me have ye bereaved of my chil-

dren; Joseph is not, and Simeon is not, and ye will take Benjamin away. All these things are against me.

"And Reuben said unto his father, Slay my two sons, if I bring him not to thee; deliver him into my hands, and I will bring him to thee again. And he said, My son shall not go down with you, for his brother is dead, and he is left alone; if mischief befall him by the way in which ye go, then shall ye bring down my gray hairs with sorrow to the grave.

"And the famine was sore in the land. And it came to pass, when they had eaten up the corn which they had brought out of Egypt, their father said unto them, Go again, buy us a little food. And Judah spake unto him, saying, The man did solemnly protest unto us, saying, Ye shall not see my face, except your brother be with you. If thou wilt send our brother with us, we will go down and buy thee food. But if thou wilt not send him, we will not go down; for the man said unto us, Ye shall not see my face, except your brother be with you. And Israel said, Wherefore dealt ye so ill with me, as to tell the man whether ye had yet a brother? And they said, The man asked us straitly of our state, and of our kindred, saying, Is your father yet alive? have ye another brother? and we told him according to the tenor of these words. Could we certainly know that he would say, Bring your brother down?

"And Judah said unto Israel, his father, Send the

lad with me, and we will arise and go, that we may live, and not die, both we and thou, and also our little ones. I will be surety for him, of my hand shalt thou require him; if I bring him not unto thee and set him before thee, then let me bear the blame forever. For except we had lingered, surely now we had returned this second time. And their father Israel said unto them, If it must be so now, do this; take of the best fruits in the land in your vessels, and carry down the man a present, a little balm, and a little honey, spices and myrrh, nuts and almonds. And take double money in your hand, and the money that was brought again in your sacks, carry it again in your hand; peradventure, it was an oversight. Take also your brother, and arise; go again unto the man. And God Almighty give you mercy before the man, that he may send away your other brother, and Benjamin. If I be bereaved of my children, I am bereaved.

"And the men took that present, and they took double money in their hands, and Benjamin, and rose up, and went down to Egypt and stood before Joseph. And when Joseph saw Benjamin with them, he said to the ruler of his house, Bring these men home, and slay, and make ready; for these men shall dine with me at noon. And the men did as Joseph bade, and the man brought the men into Joseph's house.

20. "And the men were afraid, because they were brought into Joseph's house, and they said, Because

of the money that was returned in our sacks at the first time, are we brought in; that he may seek occasion against us, and fall upon us, and take us for bondmen, and our asses. And they came near to the steward of Joseph's house, and they communed with him at the door of the house"—they wanted an intercessor between them and the governor— "and said, O, sir, we came indeed down at the first to buy food, and it came to pass, when we came to the inn, that we opened our sacks, and behold, every man's money was in the mouth of his sack, our money in full weight, and we have brought it again in our hand. And other money have we brought down in our hands to buy food; we can not tell who put our money in our sacks. And he said, Peace be to you, fear not; your God, and the God of your father, hath given you treasure in your sacks; I had your money. And he brought Simeon out unto them. And the man brought the men into Joseph's house, and gave them water, and they washed their feet; and he gave their asses provender. And they made ready the present against Joseph came at noon; for they heard that they should eat bread there. And when Joseph came home, they brought him the present which was in their hand into the house, and bowed themselves to him to the earth. And he asked them of their welfare, and said, Is your father well, the old man of whom ye spake? Is he yet alive? And they answered, Thy servant, our father, is in good health:

he is yet alive. And they bowed down their heads and made obeisance.

"And he lifted up his eyes, and saw his brother Benjamin, his mother's son, and said, Is this your younger brother, of whom ye spake unto me? And he said, God be gracious to thee, my son! And Joseph made haste; for his bowels did yearn upon his brother: and he sought where to weep; and he entered into his chamber and wept there. And he washed his face, and went out, and refrained himself, and said, Set on bread. And they set on for him by himself, and for them by themselves, and for the Egyptians, which did eat with him, by themselves. And they sat before him, the first-born according to his birthright, and the youngest according to his youth: and the men marveled one to another. And he took and sent messes unto them from before him: but Benjamin's mess was five times so much as any of theirs. And they drank and were merry with him. And he commanded the steward of his house, saying, Fill the men's sacks with food, as much as they can carry, and put every man's money in his sack's mouth. And put my cup, the silver cup, in the sack's mouth of the youngest, and his corn money. And he did according to the word that Joseph had spoken. And as soon as the morning was light, the men were sent away, they and their asses. And when they were gone out of the city, and not yet far off, Joseph said unto his steward, Up, follow after the men: and when thou doest overtake them, say unto them,

Wherefore have ye rewarded evil for good? Is not this in which my lord drinketh, and whereby indeed he divineth? ye have done evil in so doing. And he overtook them, and spake unto them these same words.

21. "And they said unto him, Wherefore saith my lord these words? God forbid that thy servants should do according to this thing. Behold, the money which we found in our sacks' mouths, we brought again unto thee out of the land of Canaan: how then should we steal out of thy lord's house silver or gold? With whomsoever of thy servants it may be found, both let him die, and we also will be my lord's bondmen. And he said, Now also let it be according unto your words: he with whom it is found shall be my servant, and ye shall be blameless. Then they speedily took down every man his sack to the ground, and opened every man his sack. And he searched, and began at the eldest, and left at the youngest: and the cup was found in Benjamin's sack.

22. "Then they rent their clothes, and laded every man his ass, and returned to the city. And Judah and his brethren came to Joseph's house; for he was yet there: and they fell before him on the ground. And Joseph said unto them, What deed is this ye have done? Wot ye not that such a man as I can certainly divine? And Judah said, What shall we say unto my lord? what shall we speak? or how shall we clear ourselves? God hath found out the iniquity of thy servants; behold, we are my lord's servants, both

we, and he also with whom the cup is found. And he said, God forbid that I should do so; but the man in whose hand the cup is found, he shall be my servant; and as for you, get you up in peace unto your father.

"Then Judah came near unto him, and said, O my lord, let thy servant, I pray thee, speak a word in my lord's ears, and let not thine anger burn against thy servant: for thou art even as Pharaoh. My lord asked his servants, saying, Have ye a father, or a brother? And we said unto my lord, We have a father, an old man, and a child of his old age, a little one; and his brother is dead, and he alone is left of his mother, and his father loveth him. And thou saidst unto thy servants, Bring him down unto me, that I may set mine eyes upon him. And we said unto my lord, The lad can not leave his father; for if he should leave his father, his father would die. And thou saidst unto thy servants, Except your youngest brother come down with you, ye shall see my face no more. And it came to pass when we came up unto thy servant, my father, we told him the words of my lord. And our father said, Go again, and buy us a little food. And we said, We can not go down: if our youngest brother be with us, then will we go down: for we may not see the man's face, except our youngest brother be with us. And thy servant, my father, said unto us, Ye know that my wife bare me two sons: and the one went out from me, and I said, Surely he is torn in pieces; and I saw him not since: and if ye take this also from me, and mischief befall him, ye shall bring down my gray hairs with sorrow to the grave. For thy servant became surety for the lad unto my father, saying, If I bring him not unto thee, then I shall bear the blame unto my father forever. Now therefore, I pray thee, let thy servant abide instead of the lad a bondman to my lord; and let the lad go up with his brethren. For how shall I go up to my father, and the lad be not with me? lest peradventure I see the evil that shall come on my father.

"Then Joseph could not refrain himself before all them that stood by him; and cried, Cause every man to go out from me. And there stood no man with him, while Joseph made himself known unto his brethren. And he wept aloud; and the Egyptians and the house of Pharaoh heard.

23. "And Joseph said unto his brethren, I am Joseph; doth my father yet live? And his brethren could not answer him; for they were troubled at his presence. And Joseph said unto his brethren, Come near to me, I pray you. And they came near. And he said, I am Joseph your brother, whom ye sold into Egypt. Now therefore, be not grieved, nor angry with yourselves, that ye sold me hither, for God did send me before you to preserve life. For these two years hath the famine been in the land: and yet there are five years, in the which there shall neither be caring nor harvest. And God sent me before you to preserve you a posterity in the earth, and to save your lives by a great deliverance. So now it was not you

that sent me hither, but God; and he hath made me a father to Pharaoh, and lord of all his house, and a ruler throughout all the land of Egypt. Haste ye and go up to my father, and say unto him, Thus saith thy son Joseph, God hath made me lord of all Egypt: come down unto me, tarry not; and thou shalt dwell in the land of Goshen, and thou shalt be near unto me, thou, and thy children, and thy children's children, and thy flocks, and thy herds, and all that thou hast: and there will I nourish thee; for yet there are five years of famine; lest thou, and thy household, and all that thou hast, come to poverty. And behold, your eyes see, and the eyes of my brother Benjamin, that it is my mouth that speaketh unto you. And ye shall tell my father all my glory in Egypt, and of all that ye have seen: and ye shall haste and bring down my father hither. And he fell upon his brother Benjamin's neck and wept; and Benjamin wept upon his neck. Moreover he kissed all his brethren, and wept upon them: and after that his brethren talked with him. And the fame thereof was heard in Pharaoh's house, saying, Joseph's brethren are come: and it pleased Pharaoh well, and his servants. And Pharaoh said unto Joseph, Say unto thy brethren, This do ye; lade your beasts and go, get you unto the land of Canaan; and take your father and your households, and come unto me: and I will give you the good of the land of Egypt, and ye shall eat the fat of the land. Now thou art commanded, this do ye, take your wagons out of the land of Egypt for your little ones, and for your wives, and bring your father and come. Also regard not your stuff; for the good of all the land of Egypt is yours. And the children of Israel did so: and Joseph gave them wagons, according to the commandment of Pharaoh, and gave them provisions for the way. To all of them he gave each man changes of raiment; but to Benjamin he gave three hundred pieces of silver, and five changes of raiment. And to his father he sent after this manner: ten asses laden with the good things of Egypt, and ten she asses laden with corn and bread and meat for his father by the way. And they went up out of Egypt, and came into the land of Canaan unto Jacob their father,

24. "And told him, saying, Joseph is yet alive, and he is governor over all the land of Egypt. And Jacob's heart fainted, for he believed them not. And they told him all the words of Joseph, which he had said unto them: and when he saw the wagons which Joseph had sent to carry him, the spirit of Jacob their father revived. And Israel said, It is enough; Joseph my son is yet alive: I will go and see him before I die. And Israel took his journey with all that he had, and came to Beersheba," the well of the oath, where his old grandfather used to offer sacrifices and worship God. Israel was very anxious to see his son, but would not go till he had consulted the God of his fathers "and offered sacrifices unto the God of his father Isaac.

"And God spake unto Israel in the visions of the

night, and said, Jacob, Jacob; and he said, Here am I. And he said, I am God, the God of thy father; fear not to go down into Egypt: for I will there make of thee a great nation. I will go down with thee into Egypt, and I will also surely bring thee up again: and Joseph shall put his hand upon thine eyes." God knew where Joseph was all the time, and could have told his servant Israel, but knew that it was best that he should not know, till the appropriate time should come. We here "know but in part." "And Jacob rose up from Beersheba: and the sons of Israel carried Jacob their father, and their little ones, and their wives, in the wagons which Pharaoh had sent to carry him. And they took their cattle, and their goods, which they had gotten in the land of Canaan, and came into Egypt, Jacob, and all his seed with him. And he sent Judah before him unto Joseph, to direct his face unto Goshen; and they came into the land of Goshen. And Joseph made ready his chariot, and went up to meet Israel his father, to Goshen, and presented himself unto him; and he fell on his neck, and wept on his neck a good while."

When father Gennella, from Switzerland, met his son Joseph from California, on the steamer, in New Orleans, after a separation of eighteen years, he fell on his son's neck, and wept three hours before he could speak a word. "And Israel said unto Joseph, Now let me die, since I have seen thy face, because thou art yet alive."

I have in this narrative marked twenty-four surprises, each suddenly opening a new channel for thought and feeling, into which the tide of the reader's sympathy flows as readily as the pent-up waters when the fountain is tapped.

My space will not allow me to multiply specimen illustrations from the Scriptures.

Every prophetic announcement, and every miracle, was in itself a grand surprise, the power of which, at this remote period, we can not very readily conceive. The first proclamation of every doctrine of the Bible, so directly antagonistic to the current notions of the world, produced a startling surprise. Every Scripture narrative comes down to us flashing with surprises. "Holy men of God spake as they were moved by the Holy Ghost;" and the divine oracles were written out to the life, in simplicity. They did not merely give an abstract statement of the truths they wished to communicate; but as far as possible, in all cases, introduced each character represented, and allowed them to act their part, and to tell what they had to say in their own language. No matter who is the speaker, God, angels, devils, or men, all are reported, where narration in detail is admissible, by a repetition of their own words.

"The Lord spake unto Moses, and told him to command the children of Israel to be holy, for the reason that God is holy"—No, sir; that was not the mode.

"The Lord spake unto Moses, saying, Speak unto all the congregation of the children of Israel, and say unto them, Ye shall be holy: for I the Lord, your God, am holy."

"Hear, O heavens, and give ear, O earth; for the Lord hath spoken;" and what did he say? He said he had nourished and brought up children, and they had rebelled against him, and that they were more inconsiderate and stubborn than an ox or an ass. No abstract report of the matter, my brother. He spake saying, "I have nourished and brought up children, and they have rebelled against me. The ox knoweth his owner, and the ass his master's crib, but Israel doth not know, my people doth not consider."

The prophet Daniel says: "And while I was speaking, and praying, and confessing my sin, and the sin of my people Israel, and presenting my supplication before the Lord my God, for the holy mountain of my God; yea, while I was speaking in prayer, even the man Gabriel whom I had seen in the vision at the beginning, being caused to fly swiftly, touched me about the time of the evening oblation. And he informed me, and talked with me, and said, O, Daniel, I am now come forth to give thee skill and understanding. At the beginning of thy supplications the commandment came forth, and I am come to show thee, for thou art greatly beloved; therefore, understand the matter and consider the vision. Seventy weeks are determined upon thy people and upon thy holy city, to finish the transgression and to make an end of sins, and to make reconciliation for iniquity, and to bring in everlasting righteousness, and to seal up the vision and prophecy, and to anoint the most holy." Daniel does not give us an abstract rehearsal of what the angel said, but lets us hear him speak in his own words, just as they first fell from angelic lips.

"Now there was a day when the sons of God came to present themselves before the Lord, and Satan came also among them. And the Lord said unto Satan, Whence comest thou?"

The sacred historian gives us Satan's reply, exactly in his own words: "Then Satan answered the Lord, and said, From going to and fro in the earth, and from walking up and down in it."

"And in the synagogue there was a man which had a spirit of an unclean devil," and cried to Jesus to let him alone—No. "And cried out with a loud voice, saying, Let us alone; what have we to do with thee, thou Jesus of Nazareth; art thou come to destroy us? I know thee, who thou art; the holy one of God. And Jesus rebuked him, saying, Hold thy peace and come out of him. And when the devil had thrown him in the midst he came out of him and hurt him not. And they were all amazed, and spake among themselves, saying, What a word is this! for with authority and power he commandeth the unclean spirits and they come out. And the fame of him went out into every place of the country round about." In this example you have the exact language of Jesus, of the devils, of the multitude, and of the writer, introducing the different characters, and describing the effect.

When the multitudes heard Peter's pentecostal sermon, "they were pricked in their hearts, and said unto Peter and the rest of the apostles, Men and brethren, what shall we do? Then Peter said unto them, Repent and be baptized, every one of you, in the name of Jesus Christ, for the remission of sins, and ye shall receive the gift of the Holy Ghost. For the promise is unto you and to your children, and to all that are afar off, even as many as the Lord our God shall call. And with many other words did he testify and exhort, saying, Save yourselves from this untoward generation."

In graphic description and dramatic effect, the Bible exceeds every other production as far as the sun, for brightness and power, exceeds the comets and meteors that flash athwart the sky. The delineatory productions of men are but imitations of the grand old model of Moses and the prophets. The devil stole the model and passed it over to his scribes, who were too ignorant, or too lazy, or too corrupt, to dig for truth, which might have been both interesting and profitable to mankind, and hence employed their God-given powers of intellect and heart in fictitious creations. The devil immediately forged a copy-right, running to the end of time, covering, not only the new productions of tragedies, comedies, operas, and novels, but the grand old model itself. Doctors of Divinity stood back aghast. Lucifer had stolen their thunder—the instrumental leverage-power by which the Bible teachers had moved the world, and had prostituted and applied it to the lowest, meanest, and most soul-destroying purposes, carrying the masses by mere fiction, known to be such, and nothing in itself; but the manner of telling it, the graphic power and dramatic effect which had been borrowed from the Bible and corrupted, gave to fiction and farce their power. Teachers of religion were driven from the highway of popular sympathy into the regions of abstract theology and metaphysics, and lost their hold on the great masses.

I presume to say to you, my brother, in confidence, that the devil is the greatest monopolist in the universe. The incorrigible old squatter drove down his stakes and laid claim to the globe—"all the kingdoms of the world and the glory of them." He had the audacious temerity to maintain his squatter sovereignty before Him who made the world, and to whom the "earth and the fullness thereof belongs," trying to ignore his creative rights, and told him to his face, that the only condition on which he could obtain power in the world, was to acknowledge the pretended claims of his diabolical highness, saying most patronizingly, "All these things will I give thee if thou wilt fall down and worship me." He has flattery and bribes to offer to political aspirants after power, to this day.

The devil monopolized all the best music, and so covered it with his diabolical copy-right that the Church was confined to a few dry old chants, and the Psalms of David without any tunes to them, till the

Wesleys repudiated his claims, ignored his copy-right, and, in the name of their Master, seized hold of all the good music they could find, and passed it over to their street-preachers and young converts, saying, "The devil has no right to all the good music." Since that, whenever we find a good piece of music, we take it into a revival of religion and have it converted, and then its cheering melody is heard along the "king's highway," from pilgrims as they journey to their home in heaven.

Sometimes we get a few pieces, which, like our stony-ground converts, become very unprofitable stock to us, and then we have to make the best we can of a bad bargain. But we do n't think of giving up the good fish, nor of giving up the business, because we occasionally find a frog in the net.

But the allied forces of hell have concentrated all their diabolic energies, especially to suppress the preaching of the Gospel, or to adulterate it, or at least to monopolize the peculiar instruments of its success—the Bible naturalness, simplicity, and graphic power with which it was preached with so great success. Satan gravely maintained that the preaching of the Gospel in the world was a violation of his rights, and that it must be stopped. To this end, he waged war against the saints, and slaughtered them by the sword of heathen kings, through a period of three hundred years, with relentless cruelty. The devil then began to distrust his policy; for though the earth was flooded with the blood of saints, their numbers and power were all the time increasing. Every new victim seemed to drop, from the curling flames through which he ascended to heaven, a mantle, which was seized by a score who immediately stood up in the place of their departed brethren, as candidates for the stake and a martyr's crown.

For a time there was a suspension of hostilities. The war counsels of hell, in secret conclave joined, were evidently devising some new stratagem—what it might be none could tell. A general amnesty was soon after proclaimed, and the devil marched up to the baptismal altar, witnessed a good *profession*, and joined the Church. He who " would rather reign in hell than serve in heaven," could not be an honorary member, or mere drone. He soon assumed to be bishop, and royal pope of the whole fraternity. Every thing under his wise supervision was remodeled. The old self-denying, cross-bearing modes were ignored; worldly honors and wealth were poured into the visible Church in full tide; splendid churches were built; old heathen temples were surmounted with the cross, and converted into cathedrals; the former simple "worship in spirit and in truth," was superseded by an endless circle of forms and ceremonies. The Bible was withheld from the people, and its divine teachings superseded by the traditions of the fathers and the mandates of the devil. Preaching was tolerated, but it must be in Latin, so as to awe the common people by its dark mysteries, and every body must submit to the new order of things, or be persecuted to the death. Thus the devil held uninterrupted sway in the Church for ages, none daring to call in question his piety or prerogatives, except a few bands of persecuted mountaineers, cross-bearers of the original type.

I will not, my brother, pretend to give you a history of Satan's religious professions and character, for you are well posted on this subject. I will simply add that, when the Bible was again restored to the people, and they recovered the pure doctrines of the Gospel, his next business was to conceal the simple, effective Bible modes of preaching it, and introduce a heavy system of abstract theology, and a still more abstract, dry system of homiletics. Though the various branches of the Church have recovered the Gospel in its purity, and have it preached by their living ministry, called of God, and laboring earnestly for the salvation of souls, still, however, the devil has laid his plans so ingeniously, and executed them so faithfully, that the power of the pulpit, mighty as it has been for two hundred years past, has been, and still is, sadly trammeled by dry forms and stiff modes, which do not take hold of the masses like the preaching of John the Baptist, of Jesus, or his apostles, and their early successors. A few leading spirits in different ages have, by the strength of Jesus, not only with thousands of their brethren, embraced the sound saving doctrines of the Gospel, but also, in spite of the devil and his time-honored modes, have seized and used the simple Bible-modes of preaching them. They thus became men of might, swaying the masses by the simplicity and power of Gospel eloquence. I will reserve their illustrious names and modes, till after I shall have illustrated to you the model preacher and his mode.

LETTER IV.

SURPRISES APPROPRIATE TO THE PULPIT.

My Dear Brother,—Having alluded to so great a variety of surprises, you naturally inquire, what kind of surprise power is appropriate to the pulpit? In trying to answer that question, I will first mention some varieties which I consider inappropriate.

1. All eccentric oddities in words or gestures not called for by the subject nor suited to the occasion.

I remember, when a boy, of hearing a preacher say, in connection with a great many singular contortions of his face and strange gestures, "You may call me a wild man, or a South American tiger, or an African lion, or what you please, but by the grace of God I am a Methodist preacher."

Another once arose and said to his audience, "I have got up here to display my ignorance before you all." He did all that he proposed to do.

An old brother told me, a few days since, that he once went to Vincennes to hear Lorenzo Dow preach on backsliding. Said he, "An immense concourse of people assembled in the woods, and waited some time for Dow's arrival. Finally he made his appearance, and at the time we all expected the sermon, he arose, climbed up a smooth sapling, and cried out, 'Hold on there, Dow, hold on.' Then he began to slide down, now and then stopping, and repeating, 'Hold on there, Dow, hold on.' He soon slid down to the ground, and put on his hat and left. That was all the sermon we got that day."

In my allusions to Lorenzo, I do n't mean to cast any reflections on his character or precious memory. When I was stationed in Georgetown, D. C., a number of years ago, I took "reformation John Adams," of New Hampshire, to see Lorenzo's grave, in a cemetery in the northern suburbs of Washington City. Adams wept over it and said, "Precious man of God, he was my spiritual father, and I have no doubt that I will meet him in heaven."

Many, I have no doubt, will in heaven record sweet memories of that eccentric servant of God; but we should not imitate his oddities.

2. All such as are of a doubtful moral propriety, or likely to have a demoralizing effect.

It is said of a celebrated American preacher, who knows well how to arrest attention, and hold it, and generally does so by appropriate means, that on a very warm summer day, when he arose in his pulpit to preach, his first sentence was, "It's d——d hot this morning." That was a sudden surprise, which arrested and astonished every hearer. After a moment's pause, he proceeded, saying, "I heard that shocking expression fall from the lips of a man as I entered the church a minute ago." He then preached a withering sermon against the sin of profane swearing. He accomplished, by that surprise, all that he designed, but at too great a cost. The startling announcement, coming from such a source, fixed so deep an impression on the mind of every hearer, especially of the young, that his whole sermon could not eradicate it, nor neutralize its poisonous effect. It rang, I doubt not, in the ears of every boy who heard it for a week, and he involuntarily repeated it to himself a thousand times, and perhaps quoted it to others, and apologized, by "Mr. —— said it." The effect, upon the whole, must have been bad, decidedly bad.

At a camp meeting I attended last fall in Ohio, the brother who was appointed to preach Sunday, P. M., arose in the stand at the hour for preaching, and said, "I seldom ever tell an anecdote, but for the purpose of getting your attention, I'll relate one. I can not vouch for its truth, but I give it to you as I got it." (Never tell a congregation, my brother, that you wish to arrest their attention, or that you will relate an anecdote. You can do all that much more easily, and effectually, without a previous advertisement of your design.) He then occupied about fifteen minutes in relating an old Egyptian legend, the hero of which, in company with his brother, was a robber of the king's treasury. The king set a trap of some kind, in which his brother was caught. Then to escape detection through his unfortunate brother, he cut off his head, and took it away with him, leaving the body so mutilated that it could not be identified. By various wonderful deeds of rapine and murder—which the preacher described—he became so notorious, that the king offered his daughter to any man who would detect and arrest him. The murderer was attracted by the fair reward, sought the acquaintance of the king's daughter, and having ingratiated himself into her favor, gave himself up to her, as the murderer for whose apprehension she was to be the reward. He thus succeeded in getting her for his wife, and was promoted to high official position by the king. He appended no moral, but told it simply to arrest attention. It did arrest attention, but at quite too great a cost, for it honored and rewarded the deepest, darkest deeds of infamy, and had a very bad moral effect.

I was shocked and grieved, and especially surprised, that a man of his experience and ability should resort to such means of arresting attention; for he is much more than an ordinary preacher, and could have arrested attention by the power of truth and appropriate illustration.

3. I would set the contraband seal on whatever is silly or irrelevant.

An old brother, while preaching at a camp meeting on one occasion, finding that his hearers were listless and sleepy, stopped in the midst of his discourse, and, after a pause of sufficient length to cause them all to look up, pointing upward, he said, "The fork of that tree would make a good pack-saddle." He thus arrested their attention, and then proceeded with his sermon. I think that was better than to let them go to sleep, but it was irrelevant, and hence inappropriate. He should have arrested attention, but he should have done it by a surprise that would have carried their thoughts and feelings to the subject of discourse, and not from it.

A brother, still living, was, on one occasion, preaching on the subject of hell. When he was about reaching the climax of his descriptions of the infernal regions, language seemed to fail under the weight of some wonderful forthcoming thought, when, after a little pause, he pulled a match out of his pocket, and, striking it, held it up, saying, "Do you see that? See its blue blazes and curling smoke; and, O, what a smell! and yet this is a very small matter compared with the dreadful hell to which sinners are hastening." That was a silly trifling with the subject and the occasion.

4. All stratagemical performances involving deception.

A brother, who is a man of considerable power, was preaching one night to a large audience, but failed to arrest their attention. In the midst of his sermon three young men came into church, to whom he addressed himself as they were entering, saying: "If I had known that you were coming in with that dagger to arrest these men, I could have had the whole matter amicably adjusted, and avoided all this trouble." The people were so startled that many sprang to their feet, and he had to assure them that there was no danger, and that he had only adopted that plan to wake them up, before he could get them quiet. He succeeded in arresting attention, but "paid too dear for the whistle." It was an uncertain sound of the trumpet. His hearers felt that he had been trifling with them, and the reaction was very unfavorable.

It is said that, at one time, when Lorenzo Dow preached under a large spruce pine, in South Carolina, he announced another appointment for preaching in the same place, on that day twelve months. The year passed, and as Lorenzo was entering the neighborhood the evening preceding his appointment, he overtook a colored boy who was blowing a long tin horn, and could, as I have often heard them, send forth a blast with rise, and swell, and cadence, which waked the echoes of the distant hills.

Overtaking the blower, Dow said to him: "What's your name, sir?"

"My name Gabriel, sir," replied the brother in ebony.

"Well, Gabriel, have you been to Church Hill?"

"Yes, massa, I'se been dar many time."

"Do you remember a big spruce pine-tree on that hill?"

"O yes, massa, I knows dat pine."

"Did you know that Lorenzo Dow had an appointment to preach under that tree to-morrow?"

"O yes, massa, every body knows dat."

"Well, Gabriel, I am Lorenzo Dow, and if you'll take your horn and go, to-morrow morning, and climb up into that pine-tree and hide yourself among the branches before the people begin to gather, and wait there till I call your name, and then blow such a blast with your horn as I heard you blow a minute ago, I'll give you a dollar. Will you do it, Gabriel?"

"Yes, massa, I takes dat dollar."

Gabriel, like Zaccheus, was hid away in the tree-top in due time. An immense concourse of persons, of all sizes and colors, assembled at the appointed hour, and Dow preached on the judgment of the last day. By his power of description he wrought the multitude up to the opening of the scenes of the resurrection and grand assize, at the call of the trumpet peals which were to wake the sleeping nations. Then, said he, "Suppose, my dying friends, that this should be the hour. Suppose you should hear, at this moment, the sound of Gabriel's trumpet." Sure enough, at that moment the trump of Gabriel sounded. The women shrieked, and many fainted; the men sprang up and stood aghast; some ran; others fell and cried for mercy; and all felt, for a time, that the judgment was set, and the books were opened. Dow stood and watched the driving storm till the fright abated, and some one discovered the colored angel who had caused the alarm, quietly perched on a limb of the old spruce, and wanted to get him down to whip him, and then resumed his theme, saying: "I forbid all persons from touching that boy up there. If a colored boy, with a tin horn, can frighten you almost out of your wits, what will ye do when you shall hear the trumpet

APPROPRIATE SURPRISES. 81

thunder of the archangel? How will ye be able to stand in the great day of the wrath of God?" He made a very effective application. That was better than a long, dry sermon, conveying no impression, except that the tidings of Gospel mercy were of no moment at all, and sinners in no danger, or in danger so trifling as not to wake up the souls of either the preacher or his hearers. The deception involved in the latter case is quite as great, and much more fatal than the temporary deception of Dow's stratagem. But still, while that may have been admissible for Lorenzo Dow, such a thing, with all kindred stratagems, is not necessary to effective Gospel preaching, and should not be resorted to.

5. Extravagant flights of fancy, and chimerical surprises.

A modern preacher of considerable power and great celebrity, among other fanciful pictures drawn, on one occasion, for the entertainment of his audience, represented an "angel running on a rainbow with a basket of stars in each hand."

Another, speaking of a conveyance to the better world, said, "I will jump astride a streak of lightning, put spurs to it, and dash off to glory." Such fancies may arrest attention, but represent no reality in this world or the next, illustrate no truth, convey no definite instruction, and are hence inappropriate.

A young preacher in Indiana, I was informed, was preaching to a congregation, two-thirds of which were Campbellites, and said in his discourse, "The

Campbellite Church is the devil's drag net, which he is dragging through this world, raking up all the tadpoles in creation. The next morning after the resurrection, he'll have a grand fry out of you all." Many of his audience, as might have been expected, took offense, and some of them threatened to whip him. He heard of their threats, and, the next time he preached, told them that they need not suppose they could frighten him; said he, "I would not be afraid if I should meet your daddy, the devil, with a head as big as this world, and hell fire flashing out of both eyes." Such things display some ingenuity, but are foolish and offensive, and can produce no good effect.

One of the greatest preachers of the west, whose memory is still as a sweet perfume to thousands who have caught inspiration from his lips, and expect to meet him in heaven, was preaching one night to a large audience, but failed for some time to arrest their attention. He knew the importance of doing that thing, and could not consent to waste his time and strength. Just as some of his hearers were settling down for a snooze, he paused till he got them to look to see if he was still there, and then exclaimed, "God have mercy on your pot-metal souls." Turning to the venerable man behind, he said, "Brother Havens, what kind of souls have you got here? I can't do any thing with them. I'll sit down, and let you try them. Get up here, brother Havens, and sluice hell and damnation upon them by the hogshead."

Brother Havens refused to get up, and the preacher turned again to his startled audience, and preached a sermon which swept down the sinners like men slain on the field of battle, till the preacher's voice was drowned by their wailings of distress and cries for mercy. His figure of "sluicing hell and damnation on the people," was of the chimerical order; but extreme cases require extreme measures, and such a master as he was is the best judge as to what the occasion demands; and there were so much thunder and lightning in his surprises, that they proved themselves to be just the thing in that case necessary to extraordinary effect for good. It would not, however, be safe for you or me to try to imitate him, and yet we may gather a valuable lesson from him.

6. All attempts at soaring above our capacity—what Mr. Wesley calls "grasping at the stars and sticking in the mud."

An Irish orator once said, in his sermon, "Could I place one foot upon the sea, and the other upon the Georgiumsidus, dip my tongue into the livid lightnings, and throw my voice into the bellowing thunder, I would wake the world with the command, Repent, turn to God and seek salvation."

'T is said that a friend of mine, thinking that very sublime, once tried in the pulpit to take the same flight, saying, "Could I place one foot on the sea, and the other on—ahem—on the Georgiumsidus—ahem, ahem—I'd howl round this little world." He choked on the big word, forgot the rest, and down he came a howling.

A young man, whose aspirations for celebrity as a preacher were only equaled by his want of all the essential elements except confidence, and who was finally discontinued from the work, was once discoursing on the expansive character of the human mind, and said, "Yes, my friends, the mind of man is so expansive that it can soar from star to star, and from satchelite to satchelite, and from seraphene to seraphene, and from cherrybeam to cherrybeam, and from thence to the center of the doom of heaven." We have but few young men, I think, who would undertake such a flight as that. One such would finish the reputation of any young preacher as effectually as Mr. Thurston was finished by his last balloon ascension.

7. There is a great deal of what is known as "flowery preaching"—pretty sayings, and fanciful figures, which represent no specific truths, and illustrate nothing but the want of ideas. They seem to be used simply as the ornamental work of the performance. Such things, however, can not appropriately come under the head of surprises; for though they may tickle the ear, they are quite too light and ethereal to wake up the soul, having about the same effect on the conscience of a sinner as bird shot on the hide of a rhinoceros. Nearly akin to this, I will add, there is a highly-rhetorical style of preaching which arrests attention and excites admiration, but is too elaborate

and abstract to impress the memory, and produce much lasting good.

The appropriate surprise power of any production, of the pulpit or the pen, is contained essentially in the truth itself, and not simply in the narration of it. Every thing, as I have said before, that God has revealed to us in his great magazine of truth—his revelations in nature, in his providence, and in his inspired word—is full of surprises. If "we meditate on all his works, and talk of his doings" correctly, and truthfully transmit the impression of them to the minds of our auditors, we will thus convey the surprises just as we receive them. But if we run God's simple truths through a metaphysical mill, and grind them down, and then recast them by the model of a great deal of the abstract divinity of these days, we will mar and caricature all God's beautiful forms of truth, and render the truth itself pointless and powerless.

In my opinion, many misguided friends of religion thus murder the virgin of Truth, tear the flesh off her bones, and then dress up her skeleton according to their own ideas of ministerial dignity, and then bring her out for exhibition in splendid widely-expanded silk and satin. Some gaze with admiration, some cry, "Great is Diana of the Ephesians," and some go up and draw aside her vail, and find, alas! that she is dead—a pack of bones exceedingly dry.

But to the question. The appropriate surprise

power of the pulpit, my brother, you will find, *first*, in the essential truth of God, which you wish to communicate to the people; and, *second*, in the facts and illustrations you may employ to assist you in arresting attention, and in conveying the truth to the heads and hearts of your hearers. Gospel truth, with its essential surprises, was much more effective in arresting attention on its first announcement, than it can ordinarily be, after its frequent repetition to the same persons. The simple announcement of new doctrines, so directly opposite to the popular standards of the times, had a startling effect. In this regard, the early teachers of Christianity had a great advantage over the modern. Take for example a few specimens of the Savior's sermon on the mount.

The scribes and Pharisees claimed to be the most pious people under the sun, but Jesus publicly denounced them as hypocrites, saying, "For I say unto you, that except your righteousness shall exceed the righteousness of the scribes and Pharisees, ye shall in no case enter into the kingdom of heaven."

The D. D.'s of those days confined the application of the moral law to the outward life, and even in that regard sanctioned so many invasions of its authority, as to render it nugatory, making the word of God of none effect by their traditions.

They taught, saying, "Thou shalt not kill." Jesus taught, as summed up in the language of the beloved disciple, "Whosoever hateth his brother is a murderer."

APPROPRIATE SURPRISES. 87

They applied the law to the overt act, saying, "Thou shalt not commit adultery."

Jesus taught, "That whosoever looketh on a woman to lust after her, hath committed adultery with her already in his heart."

They said, "Whosoever shall put away his wife, let him give her a writing of divorcement." Even Josephus, the celebrated Jewish historian, in his life, tells us, with the utmost coolness and indifference, "About this time, I put away my wife, who had borne me three children, not being pleased with her manners."

Hear the great Teacher on that subject: "But I say unto you, That whosoever shall put away his wife, saving for the cause of fornication, causeth her to commit adultery; and whosoever shall marry her that is divorced, committeth adultery."

They sanctioned a great variety of profane swearing, and taught that, unless they swore by the Lord directly, they might with impunity, without incurring any obligation or guilt, swear by heaven, by the earth, by the temple, by the gold of the temple, etc.

But Jesus commands, "Swear not at all; neither by heaven, for it is God's throne; nor by the earth, for it is his footstool; neither by Jerusalem, for it is the city of the great king; neither shalt thou swear by thy head, because thou canst not make one hair white or black. But let your communication be, yea, yea; nay, nay; for whatsoever is more than these cometh of evil."

They perverted the law of equal justice: "An eye for an eye, and a tooth for a tooth;" designed to regulate the decisions of the magistrate, to a divine authorization of all sorts of personal retaliation and revenge.

"But I say unto you," proclaimed the great Teacher, "That ye resist not evil, but whosoever shall smite thee on thy right cheek, turn to him the other also. And if a man sue thee at law, and take away thy coat, let him have thy cloak also. And whosoever shall compel thee to go a mile, go with him twain: give to him that asketh thee, and from him that would borrow of thee turn not thou away."

They taught that they were bound to love their friends, and members of their own Church, and hate every body else with a perfect hatred, contemptuously calling them dogs.

Jesus knocks the underpinning from that refuge of lies also, saying, "But I say unto you, Love your enemies, bless them that curse you, do good to them that hate you, and pray for them which despitefully use you, and persecute you; that ye may be the children of your Father which is in heaven; for he maketh his sun to rise on the evil and on the good, and sendeth rain on the just and on the unjust. For if ye love them which love you, what reward have ye? Do not even the publicans the same? And if ye salute your brethren only, what do ye more than others? Do not even the publicans so? Be ye therefore perfect, even as your Father, which is in heaven is perfect." From the heart-searching application of the law, the Savior next proceeds in his discourse, to the outward manifestation of the inward life—to works of mercy and works of piety. Every announcement was startlingly antagonistic to all the popular notions of the day. When to the teachings of Jesus were added the wonderful tidings of his resurrection and ascension, the descent of the Holy Ghost, the full development of Gospel truth and Gospel appliances, and their astonishing success in saving souls, the preaching of the Gospel became the greatest attraction of the age; startling, convincing, and reforming the people by the hundred thousand.

So, after the truth had been hid from the nations during the dreary night of the dark ages, the simple theses of Luther went like thunderbolts to the consciences of the people. Millions of souls responded and rallied to the standard of the reformer.

How the pure doctrines of the Gospel, brought up from the rubbish and filth of ages, by Wesley and his coadjutors in the great reformation of the eighteenth century, and preached in original simplicity, struck the world with *surprise*, and sent forth its living waters for the healing of the nations!

But, notwithstanding the surprise power contained in Gospel truth itself, and especially on its first announcement, the Savior and his apostles show always the difficulty and essential necessity of arresting attention, by the various means they employed to wake up their hearers. They employed surprise notes of attention—"Hearken!" "Behold! behold!" "Verily, verily I say unto you." They employed, also, partly for the same purpose, an endless variety of startling facts, and literal figures from real life. If these collateral modes just named were necessary to arrest attention when Gospel truth was so fresh and startling in itself, how much more necessary are they now that the truths of the Gospel are so familiar to the minds of the masses!

I do n't mean to say, my brother, that the living Gospel of Jesus has lost any of its inherent freshness or power, but the words, the doctrinal formulas of the Gospel, and especially the abstract recasting of them, have become familiar to the minds of the people, and the repetition of them fails to arrest attention.

The *words* of the Bible were written under the inspiration of the Holy Spirit, and are, hence, always invaluable and true; still they are but the shell, and not the kernel; the shadow, and not the substance; the unerring delineation of the vital thing, but not the thing itself; the body, but not the soul.

A great deal of the scholastic divinity of modern days has but a very small sprinkling of even the shells of Gospel truth, but little of the shadow, and much less of the substance, pointing out to a poor blind sinner the way to heaven about as clearly as Don Quixotte's windmills.

A great many preachers who "hold fast the form of sound words," and preach the pure doctrines of the Gospel—and it has often been so with myself—nevertheless fail to preach "in demonstration of the spirit and of power." It is, however, a truth, which I suppose all admit, that the novelty of Gospel preaching, when first proclaimed, gave to the primitive preachers a great advantage not enjoyed by their modern brothers, in the matter of arresting attention. We have, to be sure, some compensative advantage over our ancient brothers, in the cumulative evidence of the truth and power of the Gospel furnished in the history of its conquests in the world.

But the advantage they had over us in arresting attention by the novelty of Gospel truth, we should supply by the use of those collateral modes before mentioned—fresh, thrilling facts and figures drawn from the material world, the daily manifestations of Providence, the developments of humanity in all its forms and phases, as delineated in the Scriptures, and revealed in every-day life within us and all around us, and from the movements of the present, living, mighty God of the Gospel marching at the head of the armies of Israel in the world.

I will now repeat what I said before. The appropriate surprise power of the pulpit is contained, *first*, in the truth of the Gospel itself; and, *second*, in the facts and illustrations you may employ to assist you in arresting attention, and in conveying the truth to the understanding and hearts of your hearers. I have much to say in regard to the illustrations which I consider appropriate to the pulpit; but as I have already drawn out this letter to an undue extent, I will give you my thoughts on this latter division of this subject, after I shall have introduced to you the *Model Preacher*, and his modes.

LETTER V.

THE MODEL PREACHER.

My Dear Brother,—You desire to know whom I select as my model. Some of my friends have been trying to anticipate me by guessing, and have nominated a number of celebrated men—such as Whitefield, Spurgeon, Henry Ward Beecher, J. P. Durbin, Bishop Simpson, and others.

There are many model preachers these days, workmen great and good, who need not be ashamed, and who are not ashamed to defend the right, and would stand for God 'mid fire, flood, and death, if put to the test.

I need not name the many who are regarded as models by various parties of different tastes. I will, however, insert a poetic description of a model preacher, composed by Sanford P. Cox, Esq., of Lafayette, Ia. Brother Cox is by profession a lawyer, and not a poet, and yet there are many bearing the name with much less poetic genius than he possesses. By the way, I am told he is about to publish a volume of his original poems, which I hope will justly entitle him to worthy rank among American poets.

The occasion suggesting the following poem was a sermon preached by Rev. Richard Hargrave, at a camp meeting held near Shawnee Prairie, Ia., upward of twenty years ago:

THE EVANGELIST.

Awhile he stood, absorb'd in tho't profound;
Deep and momentous was the awful theme
That struggled in his philanthropic breast,
Where all the finer attributes of soul
In harmony most sweet, commingling grew:
And Faith and Hope, deep-rooted and serene,
Beam'd from his countenance and steadfast eye
As round he gazed, solemnly and meek,
As angels gaze, when kneeling at the throne.

Then from his lips, attun'd to strains divine,
And themes most worthy of the deep research
Of him who deals the sacred lore of heaven,
Flow'd in sweet numbers, and convincing power,
Each paragraph of truth—empyrean truth,
Strong with the potent eloquence of heaven:
For 't was from thence the oracle came down—
A transcript of the Eternal's righteous will,
Who, in his goodness vast, vouchsaf'd to man
Wisdom sufficient, if improved, to gain
A knowledge suitable, and just, of Him
Who spoke from Chaos' dark dominions,
Of blackness vast, and void immensity,
Innumerous worlds, illuminated spheres,
And shining orbs, and blazing satellites;
And o'er them all proclaimed his righteous laws,
That should each govern, in its grand career,
Circling through heaven; and unto those
High-favored beings, with his goodness crown'd,
That should inhabit and admire these spheres,
As he had right to do.

Man's primal purity first loud he rung
In witching melody, as if the lyre

Of some bright seraph, hovering round this sphere,
Had wak'd Doxologies, or lent a strain
To thrill this ball with cadence heavenly sweet.
He spoke of Eden's sunny bowers, and trees
Crowned with celestial fruits, whose leaves
Of heavenly emerald were wont to drink
Ambrosial sweetness, teeming from on high,
And glittering mildly as the new-made sun
Rode up the eastern sky in car of gold,
To flood creation with his broad, bright smile,
As God had bade, to intimate to man
His approbation of the sinless world,
As yet unmarred, and undefiled by man;
And spoke of streams that glided gently through
Elysian groves, and flower-embroider'd plains,
Where no fell herb, of poisonous juice, distill'd
Unwholesome odors 'midst the gentler flowers;
Nor thorn, nor thistle grew.

Then of the Fall—rebellious act of man,
That call'd its dark grim colleague, Death,
From his dread lair, to plant aloft
His sable colors, inscribed " Mortality,"
O'er blooming wreaths, where erst, and lately flow'd
In light divine, and balmy winds of heaven,
The flag of endless life and innocence.

Then of Redemption spoke, with lips of fire,
And ardor, kindling high, and holy awe,
As he portrayed, in diction apt, and heavenly phrase,
The pathos deep, of an offended God,
Who, to maintain the honor of his throne,
And broken laws, and rescue man from death—
Eternal death, did, in his condescension vast,
And mercy infinite, throw round himself—
The eternal great I Am, the menial garb
Which sin-stain'd mortals wear, and thus abas'd,
Came bending from the skies—

From his own court of majesty supreme,
Where angel choirs celestial anthems swell,
And from their golden harps, which never fail,
Pour through the empyrean ceaseless strains of love·
And offered his own sacred person on the cross;
Proffering back immortality to man.

God hung upon a cross!
While angels mourned, if grief can enter heaven,
And earth, convulsed and trembling on its poles,
Rock'd to and fro in throes of burning shame;
While Phœbus, blushing to behold the scene,
Shut in his radiance, folded all his beams,
And beckon'd to the clouds to come and aid,
By weeping freely o'er expiring God!
On, in **confusion**, rush'd **the** weeping clouds,
Led on their path by fitful streams of light,
That 'scap'd from heaven's inconstant flambeau's glare;
That rous'd from far, and every bourne of heaven,
The potent thunders of the universe,
Which, wildly raving through each hollow vault,
Wak'd every sphere, however distant far,
That God had made, and bade them come and mourn:
Till every planet, orb, and distant world,
Responsive wail'd, **and in** their **track stood** still,
Transfix'd in woe, and quivering **to behold**
Jehovah bruis'd, and bleeding **for this world.**

Nor need I now, in labor'd strains, rehearse
His melting story of the rising God,
Who, ere three days had settled nature's mien,
Rose in their aid, triumphant from the tomb,
And cast a smile of bright salvation round,
That pierced the tomb of many a sleeping saint,
Who shouting rose, put on immortal life,
And with the Lamb, triumphing, entered heaven;
Leaving behind a record of his will,
Which the meek preacher wav'd, and sternly said,
This is God's Law—Man's Polar Star to Heaven.

That is the description of *a* model preacher, but not of *the* model preacher. Who then is the model?

Jesus was a great preacher. He understood his business, and furnished a model for all his embassadors to work by, to the end of the world.

In presenting a point or proposition, or in defining and enforcing a duty, his plan was first to state the subject clearly, in the fewest and simplest words possible—then illustrate—then apply. When argument was necessary, it was of the same pointed, practical character of his illustrations.

For example, when preaching on the subject of prayer, he said, "Men ought always to pray, and not to faint." He spent no time in telling them what the old dead Greeks and Romans had said on the subject a thousand years before, nor in proving what was self-evident to all his hearers. He took it for granted that they understood what he meant, when he said men ought always to pray and not to faint, and hence proceeds at once to illustrate an essential characteristic of prayer—namely, importunity—"saying, There was in a city a judge, which feared not God, neither regarded man." (We have a few more left of the same sort.) The ears of every old man and little boy in the congregation were open to hear about that judge.

"And there was a widow in that city, and she came unto him, saying, Avenge me of mine adversary." Every heart was now in sympathy with the poor widow, and burning to know the result of her suit against the extortionary wretch who, probably, on an overcharge for room rent, or otherwise, was about to take away her bed and turn her out of doors. The judge, at first, refused to entertain the case, but she continued to cry, "Avenge me of mine adversary. And he would not for awhile: but afterward he said within himself, Though I fear not God nor regard man; yet, because this widow troubleth me, I will avenge her, lest by her continual coming she weary me." This he said within himself, but Jesus heard him say it. "And the Lord said, Hear what the unjust judge saith." All eyes, and ears, and hearts were open. They heard it all, and felt it, too.

Having driven a nail in a sure place, he proceeds at once to clinch it with his application, saying, "And shall not God avenge his own elect, which cry day and night unto him, though he bear long with them? I tell you he will avenge them speedily."

Observe the naturalness of his touching appeal to their filial hopes: "*I tell you* that he will avenge them speedily."

He then, without any formality, proceeds to illustrate another essential characteristic of prayer—namely, *humility*—adapting that part of his discourse to certain persons in the congregation, "which trusted in themselves that they were righteous, and despised others:" saying, "Two men went up in the temple to pray; the one a Pharisee and the other a publican"—definite in his locality and personality, every hearer could, in his mind, see the temple, and see the two men walking up. "The Pharisee stood and prayed thus with himself, God, I thank thee that I am not as other men are, extortioners, unjust, adulterers, or even as this publican. I fast twice in the week, I give tithes of all that I possess." The long-faced fellow presented no petition at all. He was good enough, and only wanted to tell the Lord how extraordinarily pious he was.

"The publican, standing afar off, would not lift up so much as his eyes unto heaven, but smote upon his breast, saying, God be merciful to me a sinner. I tell you, this man went down to his house justified, rather than the other."

Then comes his application, as in the other case. He does not wait to bring it up in separate propositions at the close of his sermon, but strikes every time while the iron is hot. "For every one that exalteth himself"—like that Pharisee—"shall be abased; and he that humbleth himself"—like that poor publican—"shall be exalted."

On another occasion, when Jesus was preaching on the same subject, he especially illustrated the importance of importunity. "And he said unto them, Which of you shall have a friend, and shall go unto him at midnight, and say unto him, Friend, lend me three loaves: for a friend of mine in his journey is come to me, and I have nothing to set before him. And he from within shall answer and say, Trouble me not: the door is now shut, and my children are with me in bed; I can not rise and give thee. I say unto you, Though he will not rise and give him, because he is his friend, yet because of his importunity he will rise and give him as many as he needeth.

"And I say unto you, Ask, and it shall be given you; seek, and ye shall find; knock, and it shall be opened unto you. For every one that asketh, receiveth; and he that seeketh, findeth; and to him that knocketh, it shall be opened." If the door of mercy is not opened at once, let him continue to knock like the man who wanted to borrow the three loaves. "It shall be opened"—God hath said it. The preacher, by that life-picture, arrested the attention of all his hearers, and then added another which tapped the fountains of every heart.

"If a son shall ask bread of any of you that is a father, will he give him a stone; or if he ask a fish, will he, for a fish, give him a serpent; or if he shall ask an egg, will he offer him a scorpion?" Can the father be found, who, having listened to the cry of his starving child—"O father, give me a piece of bread, please give me a piece of bread"—will not only refuse bread, but frighten the poor child to death by throwing a snake on it?

How comforting the application of the Master, in these words, "If ye, then, being evil, know how to give good gifts unto your children, how much more shall your heavenly Father give the Holy Spirit"—all good gifts in one—"to them that ask him?"

I have given these as specimens of the naturalness, simplicity, and point of the Savior's preaching. According to the stiff standard of sermonizing that many adopt, we would take the great Teacher's sermon on prayer, and strip from it all the simple drapery with which the Master clothed it, abstract the truth, and draw it out into a sermonical arrangement, with as many heads and horns as some of those monstrous animals which Daniel saw in vision, and have it as dry as Gideon's dewless fleece, so abstract and ethereal, at least, that most of it would evaporate above the sleepy heads of our listless hearers, and hardly one drop of it fall down into their hearts.

Now, my dear brother, I wish you to understand, distinctly, that I am not opposed to systematic study, nor to systematic preaching. There is a natural and a logical order of truth, and you may state the points, and number them too, when necessary to clearness and efficiency.

Sermonizing is but a means to that end, and not the end itself. It is but the scaffolding, and not the building. If the end of preaching may, in any instance, be more directly attained without formal sermonizing, do not lose your time, nor incumber your message with needless formality; if necessary, let the necessity determine the extent of its use. But the practice of sacrificing nearly every thing necessary to the success of Gospel preaching for the mere idea of being a systematic sermonizer is a humbug, nay, a sin against the souls of perishing men and women. I opened a book of sermons, a few days since, and the first one I glanced at contained forty-two divisions, all numbered. What time has such a preacher left for the illustration and application of truth? The great Teacher's model for Gospel preaching embraces five essential characteristics:

I. CLEARNESS.—Clearness of perception, and hence clearness of statement, illustration, and application.

II. EARNESTNESS.—Earnestness of thought and feeling, burdening and thrilling the soul of the preacher.

III. NATURALNESS.—Naturalness of delivery, embracing gesture, tones of voice, every thing pertaining to the act of proclaiming the tidings of mercy to the souls of the people.

IV. LITERALNESS.—Literal facts demonstrating the truth and power of the Gospel, and literal figures from real life, illustrating the great principles of the Gospel.

V. APPROPRIATENESS.—A wise selection and adaptation of truth to the varied condition of the hearers.

I will take up these characteristics or essential elements of power in the order in which I have stated them, and, to some extent, illustrate them separately, and then bring them out in their harmonious, symmetrical combination, as the model of Jesus, for efficient Gospel preaching, and then, by a careful test, show its conformity to the examples furnished by Christ and his apostles.

LETTER VI.

CLEARNESS.

My Dear Brother,—I wish to illustrate the characteristics of the Master's model in the order in which I have stated them, beginning with *clearness*—a clear perception and understanding of the subject of discourse, and clear conceptions of the points you wish to make, and of the arguments and illustrations you may wish to employ. You will then be able to state your points clearly—often in axiomatic form—and, through the whole discourse, show a facility and an appropriateness of illustration which must arrest attention, convey instruction, carry conviction to the conscience, and produce good effect.

If you discourse on any scientific question, your success will depend, essentially, first, on your clear understanding of the subject, or that particular phase of it on which you wish to speak. You can then present every part of your discourse with transparent definiteness.

So, also, in speaking on political economy, temperance, or any other subject.

To preach the Gospel with clearness, you must, in addition to a clear, theoretical knowledge of the questions, or doctrines, you wish to advocate, have the illumination of the Holy Spirit. The Holy

Ghost has been sent into the world for this very purpose—to enlighten and purify the embassadors of Christ, and accompany their message with clearness and effect to the hearts of their hearers.

In one of those comforting farewell sermons of Jesus, he said to his disconsolate little flock, "Let not your heart be troubled; ye believe in God, believe also in me. In my Father's house are many mansions. If it were not so, I would have told you. I go to prepare a place for you. And if I go and prepare a place for you, I will come again and receive you unto myself; that where I am, there ye may be also." "If ye love me, keep my commandments. And I will pray the Father, and he shall give you another Comforter, that he may abide with you forever"—not a few years, as I have done, and then go away—but "that he may abide with you forever: even the Spirit of truth, whom the world can not receive, because it seeth him not, neither knoweth him; but ye know him; for he dwelleth with you, and shall be in you." "These things have I spoken unto you, being yet present with you. But the Comforter, which is the Holy Ghost, whom the Father will send in my name, he shall teach you all things, and bring all things to your remembrance, whatsoever I have said unto you." "But now I go my way to him that sent me, and none of ye asketh me, Whither goest thou? But because I have said these things unto you, sorrow hath filled your heart. Nevertheless I tell you the truth: It is expedient for you that I go away; for if

I go not away, the Comforter will not come unto you; but if I depart, I will send him unto you. And when he is come, he will reprove the world of sin, and of righteousness, and of judgment: of sin, because they believe not on me; of righteousness, because I go to my Father, and ye see me no more; of judgment, because the prince of this world is judged. I have yet many things to say unto you, but ye cannot bear them now. Howbeit, when he, the Spirit of truth, is come, he will guide you into all truth; for he shall not speak of himself, but whatsoever he shall hear, that shall he speak; and he will show you things to come. He shall glorify me; for he shall receive of mine and shall show it unto you."

There are many mysteries, my brother, which this divine Teacher, the Holy Spirit, will never unlock to us in this world, as declared in the last words that fell from the lips of our ascending Lord. Out on the Mount of Olives, "When they were come together, they asked of him, saying, Lord, wilt thou at this time restore again the kingdom of Israel? And he said unto them, It is not for you to know the times or the seasons, which the Father hath put in his own power. But ye shall receive power, after that the Holy Ghost is come upon you: and ye shall be witnesses unto me, both in Jerusalem, and in all Judea, and in Samaria, and unto the uttermost part of the earth." However numerous and dark the mysteries that surround us in this world, the unerring Teacher, sent from God, is present to instruct us in every thing necessary to our great work of bearing the tidings of the Gospel to the "uttermost part of the earth."

In reading a book, have you not, my brother, often said to yourself, "O, I wish I had the author here to tell me the precise thoughts he meant to convey by this passage?" When reading the book of God, just remember that the Author is present, and waiting to give you all the instruction you need—to tell you, as far as necessary, the precise meaning he designed to convey when he first indited the words, "and guide you into all truth."

I am afraid we rely too much on the expositions and opinions of men; rummage through a whole theological library to find the meaning of some passage of Scripture, when right by our side stands the original Author, waiting to explain it, and apply its truth to our hearts; but we do n't even ask his advice, or if we do, we go right off to something else, and do n't wait to hear what he has to say on the subject.

I think I have a due appreciation of our standard theological works and commentaries. They are invaluable as helps to the study of the Scriptures, but were never designed to supersede the daily teachings of the Spirit. Learn all you can from books and from living men, for God will not supply by the Spirit what we may acquire by the natural force of thought and application; but when you want light on any vital, practical question, go into your closet and say, "O my Father in heaven, thou hast promised to give the Holy Spirit to them that ask thee. I beseech thee, for the sake of Jesus, to give me now thy Holy Spirit, to impart light and purity, that I may fully understand and clearly present thy message this day to dying sinners. O my Jesus, though thou hast ascended to thy throne, and I can not look upon thy face, as did thy disciples on the mount, and hear from thy lips the things which thou hast sent me to proclaim; yet I thank thee that thou hast sent the Comforter. O divine Comforter, coequal and coeternal with God the Father, and God the Son, and equally interested in the redemption of the world, I humbly beseech thee to 'open my understanding, that I may understand the Scriptures,' and know definitely what thou dost mean by the words of the message I am to bear to-day to my dying brothers and sisters. I have consulted thy servants, Dr. Clarke and Mr. Watson, and sought to know this, but still my mind is dark. I will wait at thy feet for the light of truth, and depend wholly on thy presence and unction, when I stand before the people to give it saving effect." For a clear understanding of the Scriptures, my brother, especially in relation to all things experimental and practical, rely mainly on the word itself, carefully examining all its collateral revealings on the same subject, and upon the unction of the Holy Spirit.

The neglect of this Divine unction will account, mainly, for the want of point and clearness so manifest in much of the preaching of these days I have a sad experience of my own on this subject, and do not speak censoriously, but with all due respect to the feelings of my brethren in the ministry, and a just appreciation of their sincerity and usefulness.

How many sermons do we hear that are made up of ambiguous words, general, abstract terms; some quotations from the poets, which mean nothing in that connection; some pretty little poetic figures, which represent no definite ideas; some good Scripture quotations, repeated as commonplace phrase to fill up and cover over the dry bones of the sermonical skeleton. The whole performance is passed through as a school-boy would repeat an old speech he had learned, but could not understand.

But where is the point, the clearness, the unction, the saving effect of such a sermon?

In other cases when the forms of truth are exactly in accordance with the word, and every point is made to represent a definite idea, the minds of preacher and hearers seem to take hold only of the shadow, and not the substance.

There are many preachers who search the Scriptures daily, and make a thorough study of theology, as a theory, and become very clear and expert in "the letter," and yet seem to know but little of "the power."

Such theology is something like the *abstract* science of astronomy. The teacher gives out his lessons, which the pupils learn so well as to answer every question with ease and confidence. The science in the book is brought fully to view in all its symmetrical proportions. In the public examination the people are astonished at the expertness of the young astronomers. They can answer every question in the catechism, and repeat a whole gospel from memory. But take them out under the starry heavens, and ask them to point out the planets, and they run to their books, and point to their representatives on the map. Ask them at noonday to point out the great center of the solar system, and they open their books, and point to a large white spot on the map, which they call the sun. What! is the sun and the planets, with other suns and systems of the visible universe, all contained in a 12mo. volume? Just as certainly as that the Bible, which is the inspired word of God, contains the real "Sun of righteousness," with all the grand laws and luminaries of which it treats.

The little book on astronomy is simply to teach us about the heavens above us; so the Bible furnishes the inspired lessons which are to mark out to our view the spiritual heavens; not as a mere science which we may study or not with impunity, but to define the way, and, by the appliances of Gospel grace, prepare us for a flight far beyond the suns and systems of the material universe, up to the palace of God, the home of redeemed and glorified souls.

Many good men, truly called of God to preach, confine themselves mainly to an abstract Gospel, which does but little execution among sinners, and as little to edify the Church.

On the other hand, it is possible for an unconverted man to preach many of the dogmas of religion with clearness and effect. But a man must be converted, called of God to the work of the ministry, obtain a clear understanding, not of the letter simply, but of the spirit and power of the word, and act under the unction of the Holy Ghost, as before shown, before he can be "approved of God, a workman that needeth not to be ashamed, rightly dividing the word of truth."

The necessity of all this preparation is clearly seen in the light of St. Paul's exhibit of the various branches of the great work to which the different orders of ministers are called. Speaking of the gifts of Christ to the Church, he says: "And he gave some apostles, and some prophets, and some evangelists, and some pastors and teachers." For what purpose? "For the perfecting of the saints." Ah! what could an unconverted man, or a superficial, abstract theorist, do in such a work as that? "For the work of the ministry"—the ministry of reconciliation to sinners. "For the edifying of the body of Christ;" building up the Church collectively. "Till we all come;" the preachers certainly, but not them only, but *all* the members of "the body of Christ." "Till we all come in the unity of the faith, and of the knowledge of the Son of God, unto a perfect man, unto the measure of the stature of the fullness of

Christ: that we henceforth be no more children, tossed to and fro, and carried about with every wind of doctrine, by the sleight of men, and cunning craftiness, whereby they lie in wait to deceive; but speaking the truth in love, may grow up into him in all things, which is the head, even Christ: from whom the whole body, fitly joined together and compacted by that which every joint supplieth, according to the effectual working in the measure of every part, maketh increase of the body unto the edifying of itself in love."

> "'T is not a cause of small import,
> The pastor's care demands;
> But what might fill an angel's heart,
> And filled the Savior's hands."

For the purpose of qualifying the embassadors of Christ fully for this great work, they are generally, if not invariably, led up in the order of providence, like their Master, "into the wilderness, to be tempted of the devil." They thus obtain a practical knowledge of all the modes of diabolic warfare, and a thorough training in varied Christian experience, so as to perceive clearly the condition of every variety of case coming up in their ministry, and be enabled to make a judicious application of Gospel remedies.

You should, my brother, so study the character of the sinner, as delineated in the Bible and developed in real life, as to be able to pursue him through all the dark labyrinths of sinful thought and action—track him to his den, and there pierce him through with the sword of the Spirit: "For the word of God is quick and powerful, and sharper than any two-edged sword, piercing even to the dividing asunder of the soul and spirit, and of the joints and marrow, and is a discerner of the thoughts and intents of the heart." It seems to me that a skillful swordsman, with such an instrument as that in his hand, ought to do execution every time. When you drive that sword into the conscience of the sinner, do you expect to hear his shriek of anguish then, or at some future period? When the wounded sinner comes to you crying, "Sir, what must I do to be saved?" unless in the clear light of experience you understand his case, and the remedy, what could you do? You would be like a preacher James Caughey tells about.

The preacher said to Caughey, "Why is it that your preaching is attended with such stirring effects, and I, preaching the same Gospel, see no fruit of my labor?"

Caughey handed him one of his written sermons, saying, "Read that to your people next Sunday, and see what the effect will be."

The preacher read it to his congregation, and they wept; and as he came down from the pulpit a poor weeping penitent met him, saying, "O, sir, what shall I do?"

"My dear friend," replied the preacher, "have I hurt your feelings? I ask your pardon, sir; I did not mean to hurt your feelings."

What was St Paul's advice to the Philippian jailer?

Did he say, "You have been a very bad man, sir, and now you must reform and lead a new life. Here is a copy of the holy Scriptures for you to read and study. You must also pray in secret, and set up your family altar, and pray for your neglected children, attend the public means of grace, and let your private life and your conduct toward the prisoners be such as to show to the world the genuineness of your repentance?" That is just the kind of advice many modern teachers would give to such a case. Did St. Paul give such advice? Not a word of it. He understood his business. He clearly perceived that the poor jailer was pierced with the sword of the Spirit, and was willing then to submit to any terms of mercy. Submission to the will of God is the end or object of repentance. If the sinner, by the power of the awakening Spirit, can reach that point by five minutes' repentance, he is ready just then to receive mercy, as much so as if he had repented five years. The apostle, seeing that the trembling sinner had reached that important point, would not trouble his head with questions and doctrines which would delay the onward action of his penitent heart, or divert his mind from the essential point already reached. Why turn his feet right away from the gate of mercy, "to go about" in the dreary paths of formality "to establish his own righteousness," instead of at once submitting himself to the righteousness of God—to God's righteous method of saving the sinner by faith, without works? It is not appropriate to talk to a criminal at the bar, under sentence of death, about his duties as a citizen of the commonwealth. The first thing, sir, is to have, if possible, the death sentence revoked and the poor culprit restored to citizenship, and then your advice about the relations and duties of life will be apposite to the case.

St. Paul knew that the poor jailer's heart was corrupt, and that "a corrupt tree would necessarily bring forth corrupt fruit." He knew that no works of righteousness which he could ever perform would better his condition a single iota. But he saw his willingness at once to submit to the will of God—to give up every thing opposed to his will—all sin—sins of the life and of the heart, and acquiesce heartily in all God's decisions concerning him, and hence directed him at once to the great Physician who alone could cure him, but who, in compassion, having anticipated the peril of the jailer's soul, had already entered the dungeon, and was waiting to save him. "Say not in thy heart, Who shall ascend into heaven? that is, to bring Christ down from above; or, Who shall descend into the deep? that is, to bring Christ up again from the dead." Doing and delaying are now out of the question. But what saith it—what saith the Gospel? The word is nigh thee—the word of life—the living Jesus, whom we preach, and in whom we believe, is nigh thee now. Dost thou not feel his awakening power in "thy heart," and express it by crying and praying with "thy mouth?" Yes, my penitent brother, and he loves you more than your mother ever did or ever can. A mother's love would save you if she had the power; but, alas! poor mother has no power to save. Jesus loves you with more than maternal tenderness; even to the pouring out of his heart's blood for the ransom of your soul; and is able to save to the uttermost all who come unto God by him. Can you not intrust your soul and body in the care of such a friend as that? Do you not now give your heart to him? Do you not now confide in his mercy—his saving merit? "Believe in the Lord Jesus Christ, and thou shalt be saved, and thy house." He did believe, and his family also, and were saved; and the whole of them were baptized and received into the Church in that hour.

Then followed their good works, as the legitimate fruit of their faith. He washed the wounds of the persecuted preachers, "and set meat before them, and rejoiced, believing in God with all his house."

I give this as a specimen of the *clearness* with which the way of salvation is marked out to a penitent sinner, according to the Gospel mode.

Many modern D. D.'s would put such a case as that of the ungodly jailer under treatment for months before they would consider his salvation practicable or possible. Under the clear teaching of Jesus the way was made so plain that the worst sinner in the nation, who would submit himself, had to cry for mercy but once to obtain healing power for body and soul.

For example: "There came a leper to him,

beseeching him, and kneeling down to him, and saying unto him, If thou wilt, thou canst make me clean." Did Jesus tell him to go away and use certain curative remedies, and reform, and come again? No, sir. "And Jesus, moved with compassion, put forth his hand and touched him, and saith unto him, I will; be thou clean. And as soon as he had spoken, immediately the leprosy departed from him, and he was cleansed."

LETTER VII.

CLEARNESS—CONTINUED.

My Dear Brother,—The Church may be compared to a great hospital for the treatment of sin-sick souls, and a nursery for the development and training of the babes in Christ. It contains cases of every variety, from the soul covered with the leprosy of sin up to the soul purified in the blood of Jesus, and from the babe in Christ up to the "perfect man." You will require, my brother, a clear, experimental acquaintance with God and his Gospel to enable you to take charge of such an institution as this, and make a judicious application of Gospel remedies, "give to each" an appropriate "portion in due season," and superintend all its departments of labor.

What would you think of the superintending physician of a hospital who should daily send in a box of pills, to be given indiscriminately to all his patients, and distribute his dietetics in the same way? You would think that quite as appropriate, I presume, as for a minister, unacquainted with the power of Gospel remedies and the condition and wants of his patients and partially-developed Christians, to think of healing and "feeding the Church of God" by serving out to them, one day in seven, a dish of dry, stale abstractions.

A good physician, sir, will thoroughly test the nature and power of his remedies, and before he applies them, you will see him daily passing round among his patients, saying to each one, "Let me feel your pulse—put out your tongue." By a careful examination of their symptoms, he is prepared to judge what kind of remedy is required to meet the wants of each case.

A man might have the eloquence of an angel, and yet, unless he makes himself well acquainted with his people, he will accomplish but little good. The success of any remedy depends on its application. That requires not only an acquaintance with the remedy, but also with the case to which you apply it.

Learn all you can from books, my brother, but keep yourself well posted in the daily developments of humanity around you, in the Church and out of it. Learn to scan and to delineate character; ascertain the soul's symptoms and wants, and give to each an appropriate "portion in due season."

For example, when you find a soul groaning to be "cleansed from all the filthiness of flesh and spirit, and desiring to perfect holiness in the fear of the Lord," don't read to such a one a dry, dogmatical essay on the subject, nor say to that struggling soul, "Don't be discouraged, my sister; you have again renewed your covenant with God. He will carry on the good work he has commenced in your heart. Watch and pray much, read the Scriptures, attend the means of grace, and live near to God."

Such advice to such a case appears so plausible, and contains so much that is good in itself, and, withal, is so common, that it requires very clear spiritual discernment to detect the fatal error to which it often leads.

That fatal old error which St. Paul so clearly exposed, eighteen hundred years ago, is, in my opinion, the most common practical error in the Church today.

Says he, "Brethren, my heart's desire and prayer to God for Israel is, that they might be saved. For I bear them record, that they have a zeal of God, but not according to knowledge. For they, being ignorant of God's righteousness, and going about to establish their own righteousness, have not submitted themselves unto the righteousness of God." This going about to establish their own righteousness instead of submitting themselves to God's terms of salvation by faith in Jesus, is not only common among penitent sinners, but among all partially-developed Christians.

I will illustrate this by a part of the experience of a friend of mine. Brother W. was a zealous exhorter in the Church; a young man of unblemished outward deportment, and striving for high attainments in religious experience. But, said he, "though I prayed daily, 'Create in me a clean heart, O God, and renew a right spirit within me;' and though I had many seasons of refreshing from the presence of the Lord, I was, nevertheless, painfully convinced of a sad want of conformity in my heart to the will of

Christ. I knew that I had the leaven of saving grace in my soul, for I had been clearly converted, and had not backslidden for a day; but I found so much of the unsanctified meal of 'carnal affections and lusts' surrounding it, that I was often greatly distressed about my state.

"At every sacramental meeting, especially, I was in the habit of entering into a careful examination of my heart, and of renewing my covenant with God. On those solemn occasions I would weep, confess, and pray, saying, 'O Lord, thou knowest that I desire to love thee, but how cold and heartless have been my efforts to serve thee! I have done so little for him who gave his life for me. O Lord, I am sorry for these, my misdoings, and would repent before thee in dust and ashes; but, O Lord, I will do better. I will pray more earnestly in secret, and fast more frequently. I will study the Scriptures more diligently, visit the sick more, be more liberal in distributing to the necessity of saints, and live near to God.' I felt some comfort in having renewed my covenant. I had a beautiful plan laid out in my mind for holy living, and looked forward to the fulfillment of my vows, as the period when I would be brought into the sweetest union with God. But one fortnight proved to me that, while I kept up the form according to the terms of my covenant, I had made no perceptible progress in the essential thing—inward, vital union with God. I mourned over my barrenness of soul, and reproached myself for having failed to keep my vows.

Perplexed and confounded, I said, 'What shall I do? I have renewed my covenant so frequently, and failed to fulfill the spirit of it every time. I have broken my vows so often, I am afraid to vow again, and afraid not to vow—that would be giving it up. I can't give up the struggle—I must try and save my soul by the grace of God.' I finally made known my case to my minister, who said, 'I wish all my members were as good as you are. Those inward struggles you speak of are the result of strong temptation from Satan. You are on the right track, brother; go on, and the Lord will bless you. You'll come out all right, I warrant you.' I took courage, and tried it again with greater earnestness—renewed my covenant, and went through the same routine of outward duties, with the same unsatisfactory result. I worked hard enough, but it was like a horse in a treadmill—I made no real progress till I learned the more excellent way of full salvation by faith, without works, and yet a faith working by love, purifying my heart, and manifesting itself in appropriate good works."

Brother W.'s case is by no means a rare one. There are thousands of sincere servants of the Lord, who have a zeal for God, but not according to knowledge—having a small development of saving faith, but trammeled and baffled in its exercise by a mixture of self-dependence. Why is it that so many, after the struggle of years, still remain in bondage? Not, to be sure, the bondage of guilt and unpardoned sin, for I am not speaking of lifeless, inconsistent souls, who are trying to coast along between religion and the world; trying to maintain a peace with God, the world, the flesh, and the devil. I have been describing such as have religion, and have grown in grace to a degree which keeps their consciences awake, and they are groaning for full redemption in the blood of Jesus, but still keep marching round in the wilderness, now by the Red Sea, then up by the thundering mountain, and over by the borders of Moab. God hath not forsaken them, for they see the pillar of cloud daily, and have the guiding light of the pillar of fire amid their darkness; but still they do not march over and possess the promised land of perfect love. What is the difficulty in such a case? I can tell you, my brother, as I have told you before, when we used to talk on this subject in California, what was the difficulty in my case, for four years after I obtained the pardoning mercy of God, and I believe that to be the difficulty with thousands of such as I have described.

Just at that point of humiliation, confession, and the renewal of the covenant described in the experience of brother W., I have bent hundreds of times.

Right there at the mercy-seat where I wept and vowed stood Jesus, bending in sympathy over me, waiting to impart purity to my heart. It was his presence, through his blessed Spirit working in me, to will and to do his good pleasure, that waked up the struggle in my soul, but at the point of my submission to the will of God, where I should have *believed*—lifted, by faith, the flood-gate of my heart to let the tide of purifying love flow in, I substituted a *pious vow* for believing. With a renewed covenant in my mouth, I left the sacramental altar as weak as when I approached it, and left Jesus standing there with the blessing he held out for my acceptance still in his hand—the very grace I needed to enable me to do better, and without which all my promised works of righteousness were utterly worthless.

When I bowed there at the feet of Jesus I ignored all my past works as filthy rags, not current in the spiritual kingdom at all; but what next did I do? Why, in my renewed covenant, I solemnly promised the Lord some more of the same sort, or, as I hoped, an improved article; but one week's effort proved to me that they were of the same sort exactly. When I again approached the mercy-seat I ignored the last productions of the same sort, in their turn, and again promised to do better.

O, how glad I was when the Lord in mercy revealed to me that most plausible but deceptive error which had made my way so hard, and had so long trammeled my faith and involved my soul in a labyrinth of difficulty! It was by no means a theoretical error—for I repudiated the idea of salvation by works—but a most subtile, practical error, which for years escaped detection.

I then saw that I had been something like a man, who, wishing to irrigate his meadow, and feeling the importance of cutting ditches to convey the water to every part, spends all his time working in the ditches. There he toils and sweats, working hard enough, to be sure, to secure a great harvest of hay. The heat and drought of summer almost wilt him, and his grass dies. Poor fellow! What's the matter? Why, to be sure, with all his nice ditches and good works, he has omitted to lift the flood-gate and turn on the water. That was the essential thing. The ditches were necessary, but of what avail were they without the water? I saw that I had worked hard enough, but had failed to lift the flood-gate by present believing, and make a connection between my thirsty heart and the purifying fountain. Then I approached the mercy-seat, and said, "O Lord, I have been very unfaithful, and have long struggled to make my case better, but can not. I have no confidence in the flesh. I know that such is my utter helplessness, and such is the power of the influences of evil that surround and oppose me, that I will never be any better than I have been, nor do any better than I have done, unless my heart is made better. Unless the tree be good, the fruit can not be good; unless the fountain be clean, the stream must remain impure. How is the motive fountain of my heart to be purified? 'Not by works of righteousness which I have done,' or may hope to do, 'but through thy mercy, by the washing of regeneration, and renewing of the Holy Ghost, shed on me abundantly through Jesus Christ my Savior.'

"If by the *renewing* of the Holy Ghost, through

the all-cleansing blood of Jesus alone, why not now? I am as good as I ever will be till thou dost apply the blood, and cleanse me from all filthiness of the flesh and spirit, and thus make me better. My vows and pledges, looking to future fulfillment, are of no avail; but the blood of Jesus is sufficient, it covers the case. I am my Lord's, and he is mine. I 'rejoice in Christ Jesus, and have no confidence in the flesh'—in nothing that I have done, or hope to do. I am not 'sufficient of myself to think any thing,' or do any good, 'as of myself, but my sufficiency is of God.' 'I am crucified with Christ; nevertheless, I live; yet not I, but Christ liveth in me; and the life which I now live in the flesh, I live by the faith of the Son of God, who loved me, and gave himself for me.'

"The purity I have so long desired I find, not imparted separately from Christ, but 'in Christ Jesus, who of God is made unto me wisdom, and righteousness, and sanctification, and redemption'—Christ in the fullness of his saving mercy received in my confidence and heart's affections—'Christ in me the hope of glory.'

> 'Every moment, Lord, I need
> The merit of thy death.'

But, glory be to my present indwelling Savior!

> 'Every moment, Lord, I have
> The merit of thy death.'

"I have nothing to expect from myself, or my own works, past or future, but sin; not that I have any sympathy with sin—no, I hate it more than I hate death—but I know its deceitful power, and my own utter impotency; but 'I can do all things through Christ who strengtheneth me.'" Thus, my brother, you see I not only renounced all inbred sin and the love of it, but was stripped of all self-dependence, past and future. I threw all the "filthy rags" of my future righteousness into the same pile with my past works, and gave them up forever. Thus stripped of every dependence on the arm of flesh, I threw my helpless soul and body on the present all-cleansing virtue of the atonement. Thus receiving Jesus in the fullness of his saving power into my heart, and living "by faith in the Son of God," I found but little difficulty in doing the will of God in regard to outward works.

If we have the inward life of the Spirit, there will always be an appropriate outward manifestation of "the fruits of the Spirit," in word and deed. The end contemplated, and vainly sought by vows, and pledges, and renewed covenants, is thus effectively secured by faith. "The just shall live by faith."

Nearly fourteen years of my eventful life have passed since I learned the happy art of living by faith. I then entered into the bonds of a new covenant with God, not a covenant of vows and pledges, looking to a future fulfillment of good works on my part, but a covenant securing a present crucifixion of wrong desires and vain hopes of self-dependence—a present complete consecration of my all to God—a present believing in a present purifying Savior—a present experience of that for which the apostle Paul so earnestly prays, on behalf of the Hebrew Christians to whom his epistle was addressed, saying, "Now the God of peace, that brought again from the dead our Lord Jesus, that great Shepherd of the sheep, through the blood of the everlasting covenant, make you perfect in every good work, to do his will, working in you that which is well-pleasing in his sight, through Jesus Christ; to whom be glory forever and ever. Amen."

I believe it to be essential, my brother, to *clearness* in a Gospel preacher, and hence the duty of every embassador of Christ, to enter into the light described by St. John as the privilege of all Christians, when he says, "God is light, and in him is no darkness at all. If we say we have fellowship with him, and walk in darkness, we lie, and do not the truth: but if we walk in the light, as he is in the light, we have fellowship one with another, and the blood of Jesus Christ his Son cleanseth us from all sin."

I do not say that a minister should not preach on a subject—say, for example, the subject of perfect love—unless by the light of the Spirit, in his personal experience, it is entirely clear to his own mind; for that is an important means of enlarging and clearing his views on the subject, and of edifying others less thoroughly instructed, and in the act of imparting the light he has, the Holy Spirit may reveal to him the things of God with greater clearness than he could possibly obtain while remaining silent on the subject.

Perfection of knowledge in this life is out of the question. The wisest will know but in part. We may never be able to preach the Gospel with that clearness which characterized the preaching of Jesus and his apostles. Still, our efficiency as Gospel ministers will be in proportion, every thing else being equal, to the degree of clearness with which we perceive and present the truth.

LETTER VIII.

EARNESTNESS.

My Dear Brother,—The *second* characteristic of the model which I propose next to illustrate, you may remember, is *earnestness*, which is, in part, the result of clearness, and is an essential element of power embraced in the Savior's model for Gospel preaching—earnestness of soul, wrought up by a realizing belief in the truth of God's word—a faith which "is the evidence of things not seen," and by a clear perception, through the unction of the Holy Spirit, of the momentous realities thus revealed—heaven and hell, with their inhabitants; earth with its candidates for both the upper and lower regions; the essential and conditional causes on which hangs the destiny of the millions of his kind, and the important part he, as an embassador of Christ, should act in the drama of life, in saving souls from death, and swelling the number of the blood-washed host.

As a minister of the Gospel, my brother, your earnest zeal should embrace all that is contained in the word *philanthropy*, applied not only to the bodies of men, but especially to their souls. Your heart should be filled and thrilled with the undying love of Jesus. "For ye know the grace of our Lord Jesus Christ; that, though he was rich, yet for your sakes he became poor, that ye, through his poverty, might be rich." 2 Cor. viii, 9. "Let this mind be in you, which was also in Christ Jesus: who, being in the form of God, thought it not robbery to be equal." He could not err in his thoughts on the subject, and hence was equal with God. "But made himself of no reputation, and took upon him the form of a servant, and was made in the likeness of men. And being found in fashion as a man, he humbled himself, and became obedient unto death, even the death of the cross." The earnest love of Jesus, which we are commanded to imitate, led him not only to give up all his riches and become poor for our sakes, but to assume our nature and endure the death penalty in his own body, to save us from death. When brought fully into sympathy with Jesus in his yearnings for the salvation of the whole world, your earnest love will not be circumscribed by any boundary lines of family, sect, state, or nation. You will feel spiritually for the souls of the perishing very much as did a company of persons literally a couple of years since, for a man in peril of life near Niagara Falls.

In the neighborhood of the Suspension Bridge the people were startled by the dreadful cry, "Man in Niagara! man in Niagara!" They ran from every direction as the news spread, and crowding the bridge and the adjacent cliffs, they eagerly inquired, "Where is he? where is he?" "Poor fellow, he's gone." Presently one cried, "See, see, yonder he is, hanging on a rock!" pointing to a low, water-washed rock, about sixty yards below the bridge, on the American side. The same rock was pointed out to me when I was there last summer. Now the question was, "Can we save him? can we save him?"

They immediately prepared a rope ladder, hoping to be able to let it down within his grasp from the top of the overhanging cliffs, which towered about three hundred feet above the drowning man.

In suspending and dropping the ladder it got tangled, and hung on some bushes which grew out of the crevices of the rocks. It was a very doubtful experiment, and the whole crowd, now numbering several hundred, gazed in almost breathless suspense.

Now the question was, "Who will go down and clear the ropes, and try and save that man?" The attempt was so hazardous that every one felt that it was staking life for life.

But a stout, generous-hearted German butcher promptly responded, "I'll go down." He quickly descended to the bushes, and hung some time among the limbs clearing the ladder, but presently it dropped all clear. Down he went to the sweeping, boiling, thundering torrents beneath, oscillating and circling from point to point, till finally he set foot on the rock beside the drowning man. Holding on by one hand to the ladder, he with the other took hold of the poor fellow, and assuring him with words of comfort, prevailed on him to try to take hold and ascend the ladder. He could not carry him up. He had brought the ladder to him, and could only help him to get hold of it, and encourage him to climb for life.

The fear was that he was too much exhausted to climb, and to tie a rope round him, and haul him up, would only be to drag his life out against the projecting rocks and snags. But he took hold, and, after ascending perhaps one hundred feet, hung to rest.

The whole company above trembled in an agony of suspense, involuntarily crying, "Hold on, hold on," but expecting every moment that his feeble grasp would relax, and he drop down into the sweeping currents, to rise no more.

But after a moment's rest, he ascended another hundred feet and paused again. Now the multitudes of sympathizing hearts beat more hopefully—the noble butcher meantime steadying the ladder below. A moment's pause, and up with fast-departing strength he climbed, till within reach of some strong arms above, which seized and drew him up.

The multitudes laughed, and cried, and shouted, and in their eager joy carried him round on their shoulders, repeating their shouts long and loud.

What distinguished man was he, to be sure, whose peril could elicit sympathy so profound and so universal, and whose rescue caused such an overwhelming burst of gladness and joy? Bless your heart, my brother, the question had never been mooted, nor, as I suppose, had it entered the head of one person present whether the man was a foreigner or a native-born citizen, Whig, Republican, Democrat, Know-Nothing, Catholic, or Protestant. No such question thought of. He was a *man*, a *living man* in jeopardy. That was enough.

Thus, my brother, should we and every one who loves the Savior, feel toward every soul whom God has made, since each one is so dear that "Jesus Christ by the grace of God hath tasted death for every man."

Millions of our beloved race have fallen in the Niagara of sinful life. They are daily borne down by the fearful rapids, ingulfed in the thundering cataract, and lost forever. If you will but look, you will see many of them away beneath the cliffs, hanging on to the slippery rocks which rise above the surface of the rolling tide, and among them are our dear friends and kindred. Can we not save them? Are there no means of rescue?

Thank the Lord, we have a Gospel ladder sure and steadfast, prepared by sovereign Mercy to our hand. The patriarch Jacob saw the upper end of it, and informs us that "the top of it reached to heaven, and the angels ascending and descending on it." You may be sure its upper fastenings are secure, or they would have found it out. The apostle Paul saw the lower end of it, and assures us that it is long enough to reach down to the "chief of sinners"—the very worst—to reach even to the rapids of the cataract of death and the gates of perdition.

A coercive rescue is out of the question, and God wants earnest souls who will, like my generous Dutchman, go down on this ladder, and persuade their dying brothers to "lay hold on the hope set before them."

Where are the men who will hazard their lives in this work?

Alarm cries and thundering anathemas alone are not sufficient; smooth talk and fair pretenses are of no avail.

Go down, my brother, in the name of Jesus. When you reach the fearful rock from which hundreds have slid, and were "drowned in perdition," hold on with one hand to the Gospel ladder—for "he that standeth should take heed lest he fall"—and with the other take hold of thy perishing brother. Show him his danger and tell him how to escape. You will often find such in despair, saying, "O, I can't rise. My heart is so hard, I'm afraid there's no deliverance for me. If I climb part of the way up and fall back, it will be much worse for me than if I had not started. I can't, I can't."

Say to that despairing soul, "O yes, you can, for the Lord will help you. I was lower down than you—away down in the rapids—'my feet were taking hold on hell,' but the Lord helped me, and I was delivered from the power of darkness, and translated into the kingdom of God's dear Son."

I say to such, "My brother, when I was sinking down, and thought all hope was gone, a poor collier came down to me, and talked so sweetly about the saving power and presence of Jesus, I was encouraged to lay hold on the hope set before me.

"It was very hard at first, but I gained a little, and tried more earnestly. Holding on, and climbing for life, I cried to Jesus for help. 'I waited patiently for the Lord, and he inclined his ear unto me and heard my cry. He brought me up also out of a horrible pit, out of the miry clay, and set my feet upon a rock and established my goings. And he hath put a new song into my mouth, even praise unto our God.'"

How anxiously I have watched the ascending progress of penitent souls, and when they reach the rock of ages multitudes of sympathizing ones embrace them and shout for joy. Angels catch the strain and bear the news to their celestial home, and then the countless host of the redeemed repeat the shout, giving glory to God. "For there is joy in the presence of the angels of God over one sinner that repenteth."

The burning fires of holy *patriotism* should ever fill the heart of God's embassador, and bear him on the track of mercy and reconciliation by a kind of divine steam power.

The patriot's creed is short and strong—"My country—my country's honor, the prowess of her arms, the glory of her institutions, the sacred memory of her heroes—my country and my people—the liberties of my people.

"My country's in the right, and the right I'll maintain—my life is the wager—'Victory or death.'"

The philosophy of true patriotism is found in the fact that the patriot's life had been previously consecrated by him to his cause—laid on the altar of his country.

The illustrious signers of the Declaration of American Independence solemnly pledged to their country's cause, not only their property, their word and sacred honor, but their *lives*. Life is the price and insurance policy of true patriotism—all short of this is spurious.

This is beautifully illustrated by the patriotism of Arnold Winkelried, so familiar to every school-boy, as set forth by that immortal bard, James Montgomery.

"At the battle of Lampach, A. D. 1315, between the Swiss and Austrians, the latter having obtained possession of a narrow pass in the mountains, formed a serried phalanx with presented spears. Till this was broken the Swiss could not hope to make a successful attack. At last, Arnold Winkelried, leaving the Swiss ranks, rushed upon the Austrian spears, and receiving in his body as many points as possible, made a breach in the line, which resulted in the complete rout of the Austrian army."

"'Make way for Liberty!' he cried;
Made way for Liberty, and died!
In arms the Austrian phalanx stood,
A living wall, a human wood!
A wall, where every conscious stone
Seemed to its kindred thousand grown;
A rampart all assaults to bear,
Till time to dust their frames should wear

A wood like that enchanted grove
In which, with fiends, Rinaldo strove,
Where every silent tree possessed
A spirit prisoned in its breast,
Which the first stroke of coming strife
Would startle into hideous life:
So dense, so still the Austrians stood
A living wall, a human wood!
Impregnable their front appears,
All horrent with projected spears,
Whose polished points before them shine—
From flank to flank a brilliant line—
Bright as the breakers' splendors run
Along the billows to the sun.
Opposed to these, a hovering band,
Contending for their native land;
Peasants, whose new-found strength had broke
From manly necks the ignoble yoke,
And forged their fetters into swords,
On equal terms to fight their lords;
And what insurgent rage had gained,
In many a mortal fray, maintained.
Marshaled once more at freedom's call,
They came to conquer or to fall,
Where he who conquered, he who fell,
Was deemed a dead or living Tell!
And now the work of life and death
Hung on the passing of a breath.
The fire of conflict burned within;
The battle trembled to begin:
Yet, while the Austrians held their ground,
Point for attack was no where found.
Where'er the impatient Switzers gazed,
The unbroken line of lances blazed.
That line 't were suicide to meet,
And perish at their tyrant's feet.
How could they rest within their graves,
And leave their homes the homes of slaves?

Would they not feel their children tread
With clanking chains above their head?
It must not be: this day, this hour,
Annihilates the oppressor's power.
All Switzerland is in the field;
She will not fly, she can not yield.
Few were the numbers she could boast,
But every freeman was a host,
And felt as though himself were he
On whose sole arm hung victory.
It did depend on one, indeed;
Behold him! Arnold Winkelried!
There sounds not to the trump of fame
The echo of a nobler name.
Unmarked he stood amid the throng,
In rumination, deep and long,
Till you might see, with sudden grace,
The very thought come o'er his face;
And by the motion of his form
Anticipate the bursting storm;
And by the uplifting of his brow
Tell where the bolt would strike, and how.
But 't was no sooner thought than done;
The field was in a moment won.
'Make way for Liberty!' he cried;
Then ran with arms extended wide,
As if his dearest friend to clasp;
Ten spears he swept within his grasp:
'Make way for Liberty!' he cried:
Their keen points went from side to side;
He bowed among them like a tree,
And thus made way for Liberty.
Swift to the breach his comrades fly:
'Make way for Liberty!' they cry,
And through the Austrian phalanx dart,
As rushed the spears through Arnold's heart
While, instantaneous as his fall,
Rout ruin, panic, scattered all:

> An earthquake could not overthrow
> A city with a surer blow.
> Thus Switzerland again was free—
> Thus death made way for Liberty."

The Captain of our salvation, whose love for the justice and glory of the kingdom of God was equaled only by his love for the enslaved human race, laid down his life to redeem us from the curse of the law, and to emancipate us from the slavery of sin and Satan to the liberty of the sons of God.

He was a patriot and philanthropist of heaven's own type. It was "for the joy that was set before him"—the joy of redeeming the world—that "he endured the cross." "He gave himself a ransom for all."

> "Down from the shining seats above,
> With joyful haste he fled,"

made bare his own bosom to receive the steel that must have sent the whole race quivering to hell without remedy, and there in the bosom of the immaculate Son of Mary the sword of Justice bathed itself in the blood of the Son of God, till a sacrifice was made which was as full an equivalent for all the ends of the righteous government of God, as the execution of the whole penalty upon the guilty.

> "Here the whole Deity is known,
> Nor dare a creature guess
> Which of the glories brightest shone,
> The justice or the grace."

St. John thus defines the spirit of Gospel patriotism: "Hereby perceive we the love of God, because he laid down his life for us: and we ought to lay down our lives for the brethren." 1 John iii, 16.

That was the true spirit of the martyrs, which is but a participation of the self-sacrificing spirit of Jesus, which every believer in him should possess.

The Church needs martyr spirits now as much as she did when she first ran up her colors eighteen hundred years ago. She then enlisted soldiers of the cross with that distinct understanding.

St. Paul, urging the Church at Rome to a holy life, argues that as they were baptized and received into the Church as martyrs, they surely ought to live holy while life was prolonged. "Know ye not that so many of us as were baptized into Jesus Christ were baptized into his death?" When they stood at the baptismal altar, their very confession marked them at once as victims of persecution and death, and in their baptismal vows they not only renounced all sin, but presented their "bodies a living sacrifice" on the altar of God, to live or die for their crucified but risen and exalted Savior. As St. Paul declares also in his epistle to the Corinthians, "They were baptized for the dead," to fill up the ranks of fallen martyrs, and fall in their turn, should the glory of God, in the spread of the Gospel, demand it, and thus they "stood in jeopardy every hour." 1 Cor. xv, 30.

The patriot lays his life on the altar of his country before he engages in the mortal struggle; so every

Christian should lay his life on the altar of the Gospel which sanctified the martyrs.

Whether the patriot's life is actually taken or not, does not affect the genuineness of his patriotism, nor does that alternative affect the spiritual patriotism of the Christian. Though St. John died a natural death, he was doubtless as justly entitled to a martyr's crown as St. Peter or Paul, or any others who poured out their heart's blood on the altar of human redemption.

Nathan Coffin, a patriot of the American Revolution, when a prisoner of war on board a British ship, and tempted by the highest offers to enter their service, replied, "Hang me to the yard-arm of your ship if you will, but do not ask me to become a traitor to my country." The incident came through Mr. Coffin's grandson, C. H. Marshall, Esq., of New York, who recently gave a thousand dollars toward the purchase of Mt. Vernon.

The history of the Revolution is full of illustrious examples of patriotism, and such always command the admiration of the world; but while national patriotism bears a premium, at all times, in any market, Gospel patriotism is "on change" in the world, and in the Church militant, at a large discount. In the Church triumphant it is always at par.

The name of Arnold the traitor is an infamous byword among the nations, intimately associated with that of Judas, the betrayer of his Lord. But, in these days, men in high places and low places, on the walls of Zion, and down behind the walls, betray the Church, deny their Master, "crucify the Son of God afresh, and put him to an open shame," with impunity, so far as their respectability in life is concerned.

Having served in the Indian wars of the northwest, you know more about the rigid discipline of a soldier's life than I do, but from history I learn that desertion has always been regarded as about the most disgraceful act of which a soldier can be guilty.

I read some months ago of two deserters in the U. S. Army, in southern California. The esteem in which they were held in the army was exhibited in the following manner: Their heads were shaved; the letter T was branded on them with a hot iron brand; a small bundle of provisions was put on the end of a stick, which was placed across the shoulder of each, and then, before the points of drawn bayonets, they were marched beyond the encampment, accompanied by the doleful notes of the "rogue's march," discoursed by the drummers and fifers of the army. They were thus "drummed out of the camp," and dismissed.

How widely that differs from the "anathema maranatha" which the apostles pronounced on deserters from the army of Jesus, I can not tell. I can't say that I admire the treatment of the two deserters above referred to, but would certainly rather risk the "rogue's march" than the "anathema maranatha."

I don't mention these things to indicate what ought to be inflicted on our modern deserters from the army of Jesus, but simply to illustrate the low ebb to which Gospel patriotism has fallen. How have our colors been trailed in the dust, and the prowess of our arms dishonored!

And yet soldiers of Jesus have the greatest stimulus to patriotism of any other soldiers under the sun. The usual stimulants to patriotism are, first, the righteousness of its cause. Hence the leaders in mortal combat always try to impress their soldiers that the cause for which they fight is honorable, just, and glorious.

The most desperate fighters have always been those who make it a matter of conscience, and those who believe that God or the gods approve their conduct, and will give success to their arms.

You have heard of the old Quaker friend, who, passing through a wood near Gen. Washington's camp, on the eve of an engagement with the enemy, found the old General behind a tree on his knees.

He hastened home and said to his wife, "The army of Washington will have victory to-day!"

"How does thee know that?" inquired the good matron. He replied,

"As I came through the wood I saw Washington on his knees."

Washington not only had a God with whom to plead on behalf of his country, but a cause he was not ashamed to plead before him.

So Joshua turned the tide of battle against the Amalekites, and swept them from the field, because he had right on his side, and because, on an adjacent hill, Moses, the man of God, was kneeling, and stretching up his hands in earnest prayer to the great Arbiter of battles.

I suppose that no cause of carnal warfare has arisen which may be legitimately set down as entirely right, although the right may sometimes largely preponderate on one side or the other, nor can the final results of such wars be known in advance.

But the cause of God and salvation, for which soldiers of the cross contend, is wholly right—was always right, honorable, and glorious; and however long and apparently doubtful the contest may be, the Lord's side will ultimately gain the victory.

The little stone which Daniel saw will roll on, smiting and destroying every opposing force, till "it shall become a great mountain, and fill the whole earth." Our cause is not only a righteous one, but He who bowed on the mount so frequently, while sojourning among men, is still praying for the success of the arms of Israel. "He ever liveth to make intercession for us."

Again: add to the conscious right of the soldier's cause the evils to be averted or thrown off, and the advantages to be gained.

"Soldier, what is your object in bearing arms?" "To break the oppressor's yoke, and secure the liberties of my people!" It was the combined power of these two motives that roused the noble daring of Winkelried.

'T was this spirit, my brother, that fired the patriotic hearts of our old grandfather and his noble compeers in their deadly struggle for American independence. These two mighty motive forces led the patriots of the Revolution to mortal combat, nerving their muscles to drive the steel with deadly effect, and their hearts to receive it, and pour out their blood on the altar of liberty.

It was this that stirred the great soul of Jonathan to battle with the Philistine host. The utter degradation and bondage of Israel at that time are clearly set forth in a single paragraph by the sacred historian. "Now there was no smith found throughout all the land of Israel; for the Philistines said, Lest the Hebrews make them swords or spears: but all the Israelites went down to the Philistines to sharpen every man his share, and his coulter, and his ax, and his mattock. So it came to pass in the day of battle, that there was neither sword nor spear found in the hand of any of the people that were with Saul and Jonathan: but with Saul and with Jonathan his son was there found." Their enemies had taken from them all their swords, and all their smiths, so that they could manufacture no more.

But Jonathan surprised and took the old Philistine garrison in Gibeah, and the tocsin of war was at once sounded throughout Philistia: "And the Philistines gathered themselves together to fight with Israel, thirty thousand chariots, and six thousand horsemen, and people as the sand which is on the sea-shore in multitude: and they came up, and pitched in Michmash, eastward from Beth-aven.

"When the men of Israel saw that they were in a strait, (for the people were distressed,) then the people did hide themselves in caves, and in thickets, and in rocks, and in high places, and in pits. And some of the Hebrews went over Jordan to the land of Gad and Gilead." There was a general stampede of the soldiers and civilians all together, so that Saul had left to oppose this innumerable host, standing army, volunteers and all, six hundred poor fellows, "who followed him trembling," and but two swords in the army.

Jonathan and his armor-bearer withdrew from the little trembling band to prepare for battle. I have no doubt that Jonathan found a secret place among the rocks, where he bowed before God under the burden of his country's woes and prayed, by the greatness and goodness of their patriarchal fathers and the prowess of their arms, by the prosperity and liberty of past years, by the penitential grief of his people for the sins which had brought on them such calamities, by the honor of God as the Lord of Israel's hosts, by the absolute slavery of his people and the overthrow of the altars of God, by the present impending storm of war, especially by the promises of God that though his people might sin, yet upon repentance he would be gracious and deliver them from their enemies. Jonathan importuned till, by the righteousness of his cause, and the belief that

God was on his side, he conceived the daring design of attacking the Philistine host alone, lay himself with his faithful armor-bearer on the altar of his country, and conquer or die.

"And Jonathan said to the young man that bare his armor, Come let us go over unto the garrison of these uncircumcised: it may be that the Lord will work for us: for there is no restraint to the Lord to save by many or by few. And his armor-bearer said unto him, Do all that is in thy heart: turn thee: behold I am with thee according to thy heart." Earnest, noble, godly patriots were these. Their faith and courage were owned of God—the hosts trembled, the earth quaked, panic and dreadful slaughter ensued, the field was swept, and the yoke of bondage broken.

Saul, meantime, was puddering round the ark of God, and consulting a priest to know what he had better do.

The Church has always been burdened with these formal, poking souls, who are always behind the times, expecting God to do his business by their stereotyped modes; and when, through some *earnest* Jonathan, he gives to the Church a great victory, then they come in to share the spoils, and mar the work by their unreasonable dictation and burdens, and Jonathan must be slain if he does not conform to the letter.

Why may we not have the patriotism of Jonathan infused into all the captains and soldiers of the militant Church? We have an infinitely more glorious altar on which to offer our lives, greater evils to avert, greater achievements to gain—victory and reward immutably certain.

The history of the militant Church furnishes illustrious examples of that earnestness which the importance of the work demands; but why can we not have them multiplied? Look at Moses "in the breach." Look at Aaron running out into the congregation to meet and arrest the fatal plague, or fall with his people. The plague was staid, and there stood the man of God on the line between the living and the dead. Look at the God-man drinking the poison-cup of death to secure for us "the cup of salvation." "We have an altar," which was sanctified and honored by the offering up of the body of Christ upon it. It was the early martyr's glory to die on that altar. St. Paul hailed the opportunity with gladness, saying, "I am now ready to be offered, and the time of my departure is at hand. I have fought a good fight, I have finished my course, I have kept the faith: henceforth there is laid up for me a crown of righteousness, which the Lord, the righteous Judge, shall give me at that day: and not to me only, but to all them also that love his appearing."

How this glorious reward contrasts with that of the poor soldier who falls in mortal combat! He gets a hole shot through his body, the burial of an ass, his name spelled wrong in the papers, a small pension for his poor family, and, in too many cases, alas! gets his poor soul into perdition.

Saving souls, my brother, is the greatest business in this world, and I doubt if God has for us a more glorious work in heaven. Think of the priceless value of a soul. Think of the horrors of hell, of the joys of heaven, the ministration of express angels, who bear our war dispatches daily to headquarters, and to all the family in heaven. Think of the Captain of our salvation at the head of the army in every engagement, looking to see us do our duty. Should we not be in earnest, my brother? The great Teacher was sociable, affable, kind, very affectionate to the little children, but always in *earnest*.

LETTER IX.

NATURALNESS.

My Dear Brother,—The *third* characteristic of the great Teacher's model which I desire now, by the help of the Holy Spirit, to illustrate, is *naturalness*, which is an element of power quite as essential to success as clearness or earnestness—naturalness in opposition to affectation; in opposition to monotonous sameness, and to a stiff, formal style.

The thoughts of the mind, the emotions of the soul, the intonations of the voice, are all characterized by the same variety that marks all God's works in the kingdoms of nature, providence, and grace.

There is such harmony in nature, such an adaptation of nature in all its variety to the demands and tastes of the human mind, that every object in nature is to us a matter of interest; even the gnarled oak is an object of interest. We watch its growth, and see how it struggles to recover itself from the injuries it received when but a sapling or a sprig.

The song of birds, the murmur of the stream, the roar of the water-fall, the varieties of the landscape, the welcome sunlight of early morn, every thing in nature so addresses itself to the eye, the ear, the head, the heart, as to arrest attention, excite feeling, and impart instruction.

NATURALNESS.

The natural, easy attitudes of the human form, the natural expressions of the human face, the spontaneous, unrestrained manifestations of the thoughts of the mind, and the soul's emotions, all come under this rule, but should exceed, in interest and attractiveness, every other department of nature, as far as its superiority rises higher than any other variety or form of nature.

If a man has an interesting story to tell, has it clear in his mind, has his own heart's emotions stirred with it, and will tell it naturally—that is, let the spontaneous intonations of his voice express the variety of his own thoughts and feelings on the subject—I'll warrant you he will arrest attention, impart not only his thoughts, but his emotions, waking, stirring, and interesting his hearers.

Another man just his opposite, as far as possible, in every thing, size, gesture, tone of voice, manner of thought and expression, yet, if he is a man of equal force, and has a story to tell of equal interest, and will conform to the same rule of naturalness, he will arrest attention, and make as marked an impression as the other.

But if they depart from this rule, and try to imitate each other, or any body else, each will make a fool of himself; exciting in the minds of their hearers disappointment and sorrow, or contempt, according to their disposition toward them. A preacher, for example, who tries to imitate the style of Bishop Simpson, or any other distinguished orator, descends from the dignity of an original, attractive man, as God has made him, to the grade of a four-footed animal, if not one of the long-eared tribe, one at least not more respectable and less useful—namely, an *ape*. If the imitation be voluntary, it is contemptible; if involuntary, it is pitiable; in either case fatal to effectiveness for good.

Many causes contribute to an unnatural, monotonous, stiff style, some of which I will mention:

1. A want of a just appreciation of our own naturalness, as an essential element of power in public or private discourse.

2. A want of clearness as to the matter of discourse, or suitable language in which to express it, which leads to confusion and embarrassment.

3. A want of emotion on the part of the speaker, either because he has nothing worth communicating, or is so indifferent in regard to it that it fails to wake his own emotions, and must, therefore, fail to awake the emotions of his hearers.

4. The adoption and imitation of an absurd, fallacious standard of oratory, embracing, as its leading excellences, beautifully-rounded periods and a highly-wrought, ornate style, in tones of lofty declamation, such as some may imagine that Cicero or Demosthenes may have employed. The test of true oratory is found in the hearts of the hearers, and not in their ears alone.

Persuasive speaking, that imparts light to the understanding, conviction to the conscience, emotion to the heart, enabling the speaker to cause the thoughts and feelings of his audience to flow freely into the various channels of interesting reflection which his subject may open before them—that is eloquence, whether the speaker be man, woman, or child.

5. A servile fear of violating some favorite standard in the minds of critical hearers, which restrains the spontaneous expressions of the speaker's thoughts and feelings, and results in stiffness and embarrassment.

6. Nearly allied to this is a want of confidence and self-possession on the part of the speaker, arising from constitutional or habitual bashfulness, or ignorance of his own power, or ignorance of his subject of discourse, or fear to encounter the prejudices or criticisms of his hearers, or conscious inability to carry the stronger intellects of his audience. Self-conceit—an overestimate of one's power—what is vulgarly known as the "big head"—is fatal. Solomon says "there is more hope of a fool than of him."

7. The usual modes of declamation practiced in our schools and colleges have a great deal to do in creating the stiff, straight-jacketed, formal declamation of the times—most unnatural and inefficient.

8. Many good ministers, in the manifestation of their earnestness, "run off in the gears," and spoil their naturalness. They shoot up like a balloon about an octave above their ordinary tones, and swing, and sweat, and harp there on one key, dropping per-

haps a tone at the close of each sentence. The audience loses sight of the subject through their excited fears that the man will "burst a boiler," and expire. Finally, with a shattered, squeaky voice, he takes his seat, and the fears of the audience give place to their rising hopes that their dear preacher, having again run the gauntlet, has escaped without any serious injury to himself.

If any man wishes to test the unnaturalness of such a performance, just let him go into the parlor of one of his intelligent parishioners, and repeat the same thing there in his domestic circle. Before he is half through, his parishioner will beg him: "O, sir, if you please, that will do! that will do! I understand it all; do, O do quit!"

I speak of this matter in all seriousness, my brother, for it is a very serious matter, involving the destiny of deathless souls, but I speak advisedly from what I have felt, seen, and heard on the subject, for I have had a sad experience in this matter. This style, however, is greatly superior to a prosy, phlegmatic style, deficient both in sense and sound, for the former often embraces, in a good degree, the two first essential elements of power of which I have spoken, and hence is frequently very effective.

If, however, their naturalness was equal to their clearness and earnestness, the good effect would be doubly great.

I sincerely sympathize with my dear brethren, who from long habit find themselves unable to break the cords of a strait-jacket, the trammels of which they have long felt and deplored.

We can not fully appreciate or know that perfection of naturalness exhibited in the great Teacher's intonations and action, and yet the fact that the popular masses, the most illiterate as well as the most learned, were so carried away by his eloquence, even the little boys and girls could understand him, and shouted "hosanna" under his preaching, and the fact that his social qualities were so remarkable, causing him to mix freely with all classes, embracing the children—all these, together with the transparent simplicity and naturalness of his discourses recorded in the New Testament, go to prove clearly that perfect naturalness was a prominent characteristic of his ministrations. It is still an essential element of power in any kind of speaking, in the pulpit or out of it.

I do not mean to say, my brother, that we should not correct any natural awkwardness or defects in nervous, muscular, and vocal action, nor that we should not improve them.

Our muscles, nerves, and vocal powers, in reference to style of delivery, are as susceptible of education and require it as much as any other function of the physical and mental constitution; but the true idea of education in regard to any or all of these, does not consist in stuffing and stereotyping them, according to some fixed standard, but in their development, in all their native simplicity and originality of strength and variety.

By naturalness of delivery, adapted to the pulpit or the platform, I do not mean a colloquial style alone. It embraces that, but much more.

The human voice possesses wonderful compass and variety of tone, adapted to the expression of all the variety of the heart's emotions. Every variation of thought and of feeling, from the ripple of the rill up to the thunder of the cataract, has its appropriate tone, varying from the soft whisper of secret confidence and the sweet call of the fond mother, "Come here, my little Johnny, come to ma," up to the scream of sudden horror, the shriek of wild despair, the trumpet command, and the thunder of defiance.

If the speaker possess the emotions in his own heart, let him give them out in their appropriate tones to the life. If he does not possess them, he need not try to impart them.

I remember one night, nearly ten years ago, in San Francisco, when water was worth a shilling per pail, having previous permission, I went to a neighbor's well for a bucket of water. I pumped away for a minute, but no water came. I went at it again with more earnestness of effort to make it come, when I heard the good lady of the house, who did not know that she was talking to her minister, exclaim in a most authoritative tone, "Let that pump alone! The water is all out of the well, and you'll spoil the pump." If there is no water in the well, no emotion in the soul, you had better let the pump alone till the water rises.

A man can not speak with naturalness unless he has something to say, and feels it in his own heart. A man getting up simply to say something, is not likely to speak with interest or advantage to his hearers or himself.

Do not think, my brother, of trying to interest an audience with any thing that you could not tell with interest to one man. That is a very good rule of testing your preaching matter, which has been practical in my experience for years.

Any dry arrangement that would be a bore to one man, will be no better when preached to a thousand, and a style that would not please and entertain one man, will be but little better suited to the mass. But for the fact that custom has so long sanctioned the stiff, unnatural style so common, the people would not endure it. Yet that is one principal reason why we so often preach to empty seats.

Let the subject-matter of your discourse, together with your arguments, illustrations, and points of application, be clear in your own mind. Let your heart be burdened and thrilled with its importance; claim the promised presence of Jesus; arise before your audience with the conscious fact in your heart, "I am an embassador of Christ, sent to treat with dying, eternity-bound souls: upon the effect of my message to-day hangs probably the destiny of more than one of my hearers. O Jesus, hast thou not sent me? Am I not 'teaching them to observe all things whatsoever thou hast commanded?' Thou wilt be with me according to thy promise. Holy Spirit, thou wilt attend thine own truth. I can not sound the depths of the heart. I can not turn the tide of depravity in the sinner's heart. Thou alone canst do the work. I will by thy grace do the best I can, and leave myself, my cause, and my people in thy hands."

Having thus, my brother, invoked divine aid, then talk to the mass as you would talk to one man; speak with sufficient volume of voice and distinctness to be heard by all. You instinctively know the elevation of voice necessary to reach every ear in your audience. When speaking to a man at your side you know how loud to speak; so when speaking to a man across the street you by instinct know the volume of voice necessary to reach him, and you speak to him as naturally as to the man by your side.

The ease and clearness with which you can be heard depend as much upon the distinctness and emphasis of your pronunciation as upon the volume of your voice. Each syllable should be pronounced distinctly; not in a slow, measured, stiff style, but with the ease and naturalness of familiar conversation. Your emphasis, especially, should be clear and distinct. You can not make every word in a sentence emphatic, much less all the words in a discourse.

In emphasizing all, you destroy the entire effect of emphasis—you have a picture all light or all shade, that is no picture at all. Emphasis pertains especially to words and syllables.

Each word representing a new or an additional idea

in the sentence is, upon its introduction into the discourse, an emphatic word. The same word repeated in the same connection is not emphatic. If you repeat it in connection with a qualifying word, designed to add force to the thought, then the emphasis will be on the qualifying word—adjective or adverb, as the case may be.

In listening to children and half-tamed savages, you will find that they, so far from emphasizing little connectives and unimportant words, frequently leave them out altogether, giving simply the emphatic words.

Words and syllables not emphatic should only receive stress of voice sufficient to make them heard, and should be pronounced more rapidly than the emphatic ones. You make a word or syllable emphatic, not only by the force of voice you give it, but by the tone you give to its pronunciation, with a short pause both before and after it. These suggestions apply alike both to speaking and reading.

I have but little to say in regard to gestures, only do not make too many, and try to correct any awkward habits of gesture into which you may have fallen. Gestures should not be employed to cover over your poverty of thought and want of emotion, but should follow as the result of burning thoughts and emotions struggling for utterance, not only by the voice, but by the light and shade of the countenance, the flashing of the eye, the attitudes of the body, and action of the limbs.

In giving your own thoughts and feelings consult your native instincts, and give them to the life, in all simplicity and naturalness.

In representing the thoughts and emotions of others, try to bring yourself fully into sympathy, both in thought and emotion, with the originals you wish to represent, and give them, as far as practicable, in their own words, and in tones and gestures to the life, such as we would naturally conceive the originals would employ. To do this successfully a man must be thoroughly acquainted with his subject.

Any common school-boy can commit an old speech and repeat it from memory, according to the ordinary standard of declamation, but to conform to the law of naturalness to which I refer, a man must be "master of his art." I don't mean that a man must be perfect in it before he can attain to great usefulness by it; and yet his success, every thing else being equal, will be in proportion to his conformity to this law. I am not sure that we have had a perfect master in it since the days of Jesus, though a great many are perfect beyond the detection of ordinary hearers. So far as I am concerned, though I think I have a clear ideal of it, yet, as it regards my own progress in it, I feel something like Sir Isaac Newton felt in regard to his scientific attainments, when he said, "I am like a child gathering up pebbles along the shore, while the great ocean of truth, unexplored, is spread out before me."

A minister said to me, not long since, "There is no

such thing as naturalness. We are all imitative beings. Our first acts of volition are acts of imitation, and we go on from that time in the same way. If there is such a thing, where shall we find a standard by which we may know what is natural and what is not?"

I admit that, masked and trained by the rules of etiquette, as much as humanity is, it would be very difficult to find much naturalness in "polite society."

A minister, by invitation, went to dine with a gentleman who lived in a mansion, and had every thing about him in great style.

Soon after the preacher was seated, he incidentally heard the lady of the house, whom he had not yet seen, talking to her husband in another room, and saying, "I'll teach you how to bring a strange preacher here without giving me due notice! You know better than that. I've not prepared a dinner for strangers to-day, and there's no time now to prepare it, and I wouldn't do it if there was. I'm ashamed of you for such conduct, and I want you never to be guilty of the like again."

The curtain lecture, which was distressingly natural, closed, and soon after the same lady, splendidly attired, was introduced to the preacher, saying, as she bowed gracefully, "I am delighted to see you, sir. I have heard my dear husband speak of you so often, that I felt that I was acquainted with you before, and now it is with unfeigned pleasure that we welcome you as our guest."

To find a standard of naturalness by which to unlearn the stiff, unnatural modes we have acquired by habitual imitation, we have to go back to our starting-point in life, and take lessons from the children, and from the undisguised and unrestrained manifestations of thought and feeling as furnished in the ordinary walks of life.

Look and listen at the naturalness of the little boys and girls in action, intonation, emphasis, every thing. Hear one relate the story of an exciting scene which he has just witnessed; he will scarcely misapply a tone. He will put the emphasis, in most cases, just where it ought to be. When he comes to a very emphatic point he will pause, according to the rule before indicated, as if to select a word strong enough, and to "gather a head" of breath and emotional power to express it, then pause again, and proceed with his narrative in a softer tone till he comes to another emphatic point. His ideas may be very erroneous, but his conceptions of what he wants to say are clear, and his earnest little soul is filled with the subject. He has clearness, earnestness, and naturalness; he is an orator.

I took a little girl of four summers on my knee, a few days ago, and having so commended myself to her good feelings, that she felt quite at home in my company, I said to her, "I had a sweet little girl once, and called her Oceana, because the Lord gave her to us away out on the ocean. She was a very pretty little girl. The Lord loved her, and took her up to heaven to live with Jesus."

"Did you tell her she might go?" inquired little Alla.

She afterward frequently said to me, "I'm going to live with Jesus too, when I die, and I'll see your little girl up there, won't I?"

At the tea-table she again introduced the subject, saying, "Your little girl went up to heaven to live with Jesus, did n't she?"

"Yes, Alla, she went to live with Jesus," I replied.

"Yes," continued she, "Mr. Jesus come out to the fence when he saw her coming, and stood and looked till your little girl got up close, and said, 'Come in, my little girl, come in.'"

When my little Charlie, four years old, was nearly dead with the small-pox, he would frequently wake me during the night to pray for him, saying, "Pa, pa, won't you tell the Lord to please to make me well?"

I would then tell the Lord to pity my dear boy and make him well.

"I'm glad that Jesus died for sinners, an't you pa?"

Wearied with watching—for I nursed him day and night for nearly a month, and was sick with varioloid at the same time, myself—I would soon fall asleep again, but the sleepless little sufferer would soon wake me up, saying, "Pa, pa, won't you tell me how to pray to the Lord to make me well?"

"Yes, my dear boy, the Lord loves you, and he is listening, and I'll tell you what to say to him."

He then repeated after me a little prayer adapted to his case.

Then said he, "Pa, if the Lord loves me, why don't he make me well?"

"I think, my dear boy, he will make you well. If he don't, he will take you up to live with the angels, and with your little brothers, and your little sister Oce, where you'll never get sick any more. But I think he will make you well."

"Well, pa, when do you think he will make me well?"

"In about two weeks."

"How long is two weeks?"

Then I counted the days in the week and explained.

"O," said the little fellow, "I do wish He would make haste."

"During the prevalence of yellow fever in New Orleans last summer, a gentleman was walking out Spruce-street, in that city, and saw a little boy lying on the grass with a raging fever. He shook him and said, 'What are you doing here, my boy?'

"'I'm waiting for God to come and take me,' replied he. 'What do you mean?' inquired the gentleman.

"'God took away my father and mother, and my little brother; and mother told me to look to God, and he would take care of me. I have been lying out here all night and all day, looking up in the sky for God to come and take me. He has not come, but he will come, for mother said so, and mother never told a lie. He will come, won't he?'

"The man, now moved to a flood of tears, said,

'Yes, my son, God has sent me to take you, and I'll be a father to you.'

"'You were a long time on the way, but I know'd that mother would n't tell a lie, and God has sent you.'"

I give these incidents, my brother, to convey to you an idea of the simplicity of matter, and not the manner of little children; that you will find out by observation.

You will learn among the children, and in the unrestrained walks of life, in doors and out, and among the suffering in hospitals and prisons, what the simplicity of nature is, and by diligent study and practice, you will be able to shake off the trammels which imitative habits have fastened upon you; and by attention to your own instincts, and the dictates of common-sense, you will not only get back into harmony with nature in this regard, but may so educate your nerves, muscles, and vocal powers as to employ them naturally and effectively.

When this habit of naturalness is formed, its spontaneous manifestation will be such as to require but little attention, except to the subject of discourse.

A minister once said to me, "I am afraid to adopt the natural style lest my preaching should be considered *common talk*, unsuited to the dignity of the pulpit."

One said to me not long since, "The Gospel is a very solemn thing, and should be preached in a very solemn and dignified manner."

"A stiff, affected, unnatural style," I replied, "is inconsistent with the dignified solemnity and honest simplicity of the Gospel."

Dignity and solemnity, my brother, do not consist in big words, highly-wrought, neatly-rounded sentences, and measured cadence.

When brother and sister K., of San Francisco, learned that their little boy, an only child of five years, was missing, they inquired, "Where was he last seen?"

Sister K. said, "He went out at the back door but a few minutes ago. O, I'm afraid he has fallen into the bay!"

Away they went inquiring of the neighbors, "Did you see our little boy?"

No tidings to comfort the anguished hearts of the fond parents.

They were seen all that day searching along the wharves, wringing their hands in despair, the mother repeating in tones that caused the sturdy sailors to weep, "O, my dear child! my dear little boy is gone! O that I could see him once more! Even if he is drowned, it would be such a comfort to see him! O, to think of my dear little boy being eaten up by the sharks! O, if I could only see him and kiss his marble brow, and bury him where I could visit his grave, plant sweet flowers on it, and water them with my tears! O, my child, my dear little boy!"

Late that evening some boatmen picked up the body of the drowned boy in the bay, and returned it to his mother. The next day I laid his little body in its last resting-place in Yerba Buena cemetery. That whole scene involved great solemnity, but no big words nor stately display.

Henry Helmcamp, an honest shoemaker, living in Terre Haute, Indiana, while at work a few weeks since, was startled by the roll of the well windlass, which was immediately followed by the shrieks of his wife, "O! O! Lizzie's in the well! O, Henry! Henry!" and fainted.

The half-frantic father ran to the well and called, "Lizzie, Lizzie, my dear child, are you yet alive?"

The well was sixty feet deep, containing ten feet of water.

He listened and heard her struggling in the water, and immediately seizing the well-rope, descended as fast as the laws of gravitation would carry him.

He said to me afterward, "As I went down, I felt the well-rope burning and tearing the flesh off my hands, and felt as though I must let go and fall, but the thought immediately struck me, 'You'll fall on your child and kill her,' so I held on."

Strange as it may appear, Lizzie, who was nine years old, was but little hurt. He tied her in the bucket, and she was drawn up. He then tied a rope round his own body, and his neighbors drew him up. The palms of his hands were burnt and torn off to the bone.

"O dear, Mr. Helmcamp," said his friends, "your hands are ruined!"

"Never mind my hands," replied he. "Thank God, I saved my child." There was solemnity and dignity too, but no big words nor pompous display, such as many would consider appropriate to the pulpit.

This same brother H., when connected with a fire company in Philadelphia, ran on one occasion to a great fire, and learned that in the third story of a building in flames, there was a child whose parents were absent at some public meeting in another part of the city. The second story floor had already fallen.

He hastily ascended a ladder to the third story window, and rushing in through smoke and flame, snatched from its bed the baby girl. Just as he got out on the ladder with the child in his arms, the walls fell in, but at the moment of the general crash, the noble vigilants below drew the ladder up and held it in a perpendicular line, while the rescuer deliberately descended to the ground with the babe unhurt.

The mother, who knew nothing of all this, soon after returned, and seeing the flaming ruins of her house, screamed in wildest frenzy, "O my babe!" and fell apparently dead.

When she recovered her child was placed in her arms. She pressed it to her bosom, laughing, crying, and shouting, in a rapture of gladness. This scene was solemn and sublime, producing a variety of effect, stirring the soul's profoundest emotions, but no affected display of words.

Read the solemn, simple, sublime, touching story

of the Shunamite, 2 Kings, chapter iv; also the Savior's account of the Prodigal Son.

A few weeks since I spent a night at Fort Wayne College. Brother Robinson, the President, his good lady, and myself, having returned from Church, were conversing in the parlor, when a messenger came in and handed the President a telegraphic dispatch.

"Where is it from?" inquired brother R.

"From Lafayette, sir. It contains very sad news," replied the messenger.

The President held it a moment before opening, evidently bracing himself to receive the shock of some dread lightning-bolt hurled along the wires, and about to enter his heart.

To assist him, I quoted, "He shall not be afraid of evil tidings." "The Judge of all the earth will do right."

Then breaking it open he read, "Your father is low"—"O, it's my dear father." Reading again, he said to his wife, "O no, my dear, it's your father; all the same to me."

The solemn words of the dispatch were, "Your father-in-law is dead; come quick."

How dreadful the shock that struck the good sister's heart!

Soon two of her sisters came in, and each looked at the little lightning-bolt which had felled the strong man and his companion, and exclaimed, "O! O! O! father is dead! He wrote but a few days ago that he was so well, and now he is dead!"

Before morning the three bereaved sisters and a brother were on their way to the Tippecanoe battle-ground to bury their father. Great was their sudden grief, but they sorrow not as those who have no hope.

Our good brother, John Poisel, had just got comfortably settled in the parsonage of the Eighteenth-Street Methodist Episcopal Church, New York, last year, and was waiting the arrival of his son Edwin from Baltimore. Edwin had just finished his college course, and was to be on to see his parents at a set time. His mother had prepared his room, and now they were expecting him every moment.

Hearing the bell ring, the father ran down stairs, saying, "Edwin, is that you?"

But opening the door, a messenger handed him a telegraphic dispatch, saying, "Your son Edwin is drowned; his body has been recovered and awaits your order."

Poor brother, just in the midst of sunshine and hope, how the lightning struck him! The only comfort of those bereaved hearts as they meekly bowed beneath the awful stroke, was that their dear boy was a devoted Christian, and had gone from the dark waters to a bright home beyond the tide.

I read an account in the Christian Advocate and Journal, a few days since, of a poor old lady in Philadelphia, who in her destitution had to beg in the streets to avoid starvation. As she stood on the corner of Chestnut and Fourth streets asking alms, a good-looking sailor looked at her and pulled out a handful of gold and silver, saying, "There, good mother, take that. You may as well have it as the land-sharks. The last cruise I had out of New York found me with four thousand dollars on hand; but as the neighbors told me my mother was dead, I got on a spree with the money, and spent it all inside of a week, and then I shipped again."

"O good sir, you are too kind to an old body like me! For your sake I will take it. O, you remind me of my poor son George White, who was lost at sea."

"George White! why, that's my name, and you are my mother!"

He embraced and kissed his mother as the tears ran down his bronzed cheeks. She was overcome, like Jacob, when he heard that Joseph was yet alive, with emotions of joy. Those who witnessed the scene could but weep. "The dead was alive; the lost was found."

He immediately called for a carriage and drove off with his mother to comfortable quarters.

The following, taken from the Western Christian Advocate, is solemn, sublime, and horrible, but requires no display of long adjectives and rhetorical flourishes to convey the impression to the life:

"A terrible accident occurred to the express train going east from Chicago to Toledo, on the Southern Michigan railroad, at midnight, June 28th, by which some sixty persons were killed. As the train, when between South Bend and Mishawaka, was passing over an embankment spanning a ravine, at the base of which is a culvert, the embankment suddenly gave way, and the whole train was precipitated into the ravine, which was filled with a perfect torrent of water.

"The engine was literally buried in the opposite side of the ravine in quicksand and mud, and the tender, baggage and express car, and two second-class cars were shattered almost into kindling-wood, and piled on top of the engine. The two first-class passenger cars followed, and were torn to pieces and carried down the stream, while the sleeping car, although making the leap with the rest, was less injured.

"The stream is naturally but a rivulet, but was swollen by the extraordinary rains of the previous afternoon and evening. Flood-wood probably checked the culvert, converting the embankment into a dam, and the great weight of water, with the concussion of the crossing train, caused the sad calamity.

"About one hundred and fifty persons were on the train; of these, sixty have been taken from the ruins dead, and fifty or sixty more wounded, or escaped unhurt; the rest not heard from, as many of the dead were drowned in the ravine.

"It is feared that others not heard from have lost their lives in the same manner.

"Mr. Bliss, the President of the road, and Mr. Hiram Sibley, one of the Directors, were in the sleeping car, and escaped uninjured. The engineer and fireman, both named Chulp, of Laporte, were killed;

Hartwell, of Toledo, expressman, and Babbington, baggage-master, were also killed, in the baggage car. C. W. Smith, Road-Master, was killed.

"Some of the incidents connected with the accident are harrowing. It was midnight, and the lightning from a storm near at hand was all the light the passengers had as to their condition.

"One woman who was on the train with her husband and five children, ran wildly about all night seeking her family, but without success till morning, when she found them all dead. She then went to a farm-house a few yards off, where, after sitting some minutes, the wretched wife and mother expired.

"Mr. Rice says, that a gentleman with his wife and two children were on the train on a pleasure trip to the east. But in the accident the parties became separated. The husband found one of his young ones dead in the morning; next he found his wife dead, but with her arms closely embracing the other child, who was saved."

The solemn marches, sublime charges, and horrible slaughter of the recent battle of Solferino, where about four hundred thousand men met in mortal combat, and left about forty thousand dead on the field, are all reported in simplicity. The facts are the things that strike, not a gorgeous display of words. The most sublime scene of prophetic vision is set forth by St. John in the following plain, natural words: "And I saw a great white throne, and him that sat on it, from whose face the earth and heaven fied away; and there was found no place for them. And I saw the dead, small and great, stand before God; and the books were opened: and another book was opened, which is the book of life; and the dead were judged out of those things which were written in the books, according to their works. And the sea gave up the dead which were in it; and death and hell delivered up the dead which were in them; and they were judged every man according to their works. And death and hell were cast into the lake of fire. This is the second death. And whosoever was not found written in the book of life was cast into the lake of fire." This whole scene is in another place set forth in fourteen monosyllables, and one little word of two syllables—"The great day of his wrath is come, and who shall be able to stand?" The most dreadful saying in the book of God is contained in five monosyllables—"The wrath of the Lamb." The mercy and merit of the Lamb furnish the only ground of my hope here and hereafter—"For there is none other Name under heaven given among men, whereby we must be saved." O "the wrath of the Lamb!" Who can endure it?

You see, my brother, from the simple specimens just presented, that solemnity, moral grandeur, and stirring effect, do not consist in a display of "magnificent words," but in the truth, with all its native simplicity and variety, just as we find it in nature, or providence, or in the Bible; and the truth, to produce its appropriate effect, must be communicated in all its simplicity and variety, in a style correspondingly simple and natural. A mere display of sublime words, solemn forms, and ministerial dignity, is, whatever the design may be, a burlesque on the solemn grandeur and dignified simplicity of Gospel truth, and the natural Gospel mode of proclaiming it.

LETTER X.

LITERALNESS.

My Dear Brother,—The fourth leading characteristic of the Savior's model for preaching, which I now wish to illustrate, is *literalness*—literal facts demonstrating the truth and power of the Gospel, and literal figures illustrating the great spiritual principles of the Gospel—facts of past history, facts of present experience and observation, and facts of prophetic vision yet to be developed in the roll of future ages—literal facts in opposition to abstract terms and metaphysics.

I do not pretend to say that abstract generalizing and metaphysics are not appropriate in their place, but that they find no place in the preaching of Jesus; and if admitted to the pulpit at all, it should be simply for the sake of arranging and classifying real definite facts. If we can give our facts tangibility, locality, and circumstantiality, all the better for stirring effect.

You observe that I employ the term "literalness" here in its application to all spiritual as well as material realities—real specific facts, in opposition to all abstract terms, general statements and imaginings, which represent no real definite thing in this world or the next; in opposition, also, to such a use of the legitimate forms of real definite truth, as renders them general and indefinite in their application.

When I shall have brought out in their symmetrical combination the essential elements of power defining the Savior's model for preaching, I will then, while comparing my model with "the pattern given in the mount," more fully illustrate this part of my subject.

For the present, I will speak of the literal figures of illustration appropriate to the pulpit. Literal illustration should be employed in the pulpit,

1. For the purpose of arresting attention. I have before shown that the surprise power necessary to arrest attention is contained, first, in the truth itself; and, secondly, in the figures and facts we employ to simplify and convey Gospel truth to the conscience.

If the truth itself will so strike the intellect and heart of the hearer as to arrest attention sufficiently, then, in that case, no collateral means are necessary.

If the alarm-cry, "Fire! fire! fire!" will wake up the people and stimulate them to save themselves or their property, then you have only to cry, "Fire! fire!" and ring the alarm-bell; but if by the frequency of such alarms they lose their stirring effect, you will then have to knock at the doors of those in danger, and wake them up by some startling unanticipated means.

If the Savior and his apostles, when Gospel truth was most fresh and exciting in itself, found it necessary to employ surprise notes—Ho! Hearken!

Behold, behold! Verily, verily!—and also an endless variety of literal figures, to arrest attention, how much more necessary now!

We practically demonstrate the necessity of arresting attention to the ordinary interests of life, before delivering an important message or command, or on the eve of any movement requiring attention.

A general, at the head of his regiment, giving command, first cries, "Attention! attention!" The sub-officers repeat it along the lines, "Attention! attention, company!"

How often at public gatherings, for raising a house, or other work requiring concert of muscular force, have you heard the cry, "O, yes! O, yes! all hands here!"

On ship-board you hear the cry, "All hands on deck! All hands ahoy!"

On the departure of every steamboat or rail-car, your attention is arrested by the bell ringing, the steam-whistle, and the final cry, "All aboard!" If all this is necessary in regard to the objects of sense about us, how much more necessary in presenting the invisible realities of the spiritual life!

In proclaiming the messages and commands of God, and in rallying the sacramental host to storm the citadel of sin, for the rescue of souls, shall we not cry, "Attention?"

In building the temple of God, shall we not cry, "O, yes! O, yes!" or by some means secure concert of action?

In manning the good ship Zion, shall we not cry, "All hands on deck!" and thrill them as Lord Nelson did his soldiers, on the eve of battle, when he cried, "England expects every man to do his duty?"

When the life-boat of Mercy or the car of Salvation is on the eve of departure, affording to many their last opportunity of a passage to heaven, shall we not ring the bell, blow the steam-whistle, and cry, "All aboard!" "Cry aloud, and spare not; lift up the voice like a trumpet, and show the people their sins" and their remedy?

2. A second object of literal illustration is to simplify the truth, and make it the medium of conveying the truth to the heads and hearts of the hearers. The spiritual reality should be brought vividly to light by some striking feature of resemblance to it contained in the literal figure. The particular point of resemblance in the figure designed to convey the truth, is to be determined by the subject of discourse; and the figure can not be legitimately applied beyond that.

For example: the Savior is called "the lion of the tribe of Judah." The prophet does not mean to say that he is a ferocious animal, with a long mane. The subject of discourse—his power and courage—determines the extent to which the figure may be applied.

Again: he is compared to a lamb—not a diminutive, woolly animal, but an immaculate sacrifice, offered for the sins of the world.

As the object is to simplify and illustrate truth, and

not to mystify it, we should only employ such figures as will legitimately secure that end.

3. A third object is, by familiarity with the figure, to fix the truth in the memory.

A very intelligent gentleman in Baltimore city, speaking of the effect upon his memory of two sermons he had heard from different ministers the day before, said, "I heard Bishop ——— preach a splendid sermon yesterday. I don't think I ever heard a more masterly piece of composition in my life. I was delighted, both with the matter of his discourse and the manner of his delivery, but after I got home I could not remember a single paragraph of it. I tried to bring it up, but it had nearly all passed away like a dream.

"Last night I went to Charles-Street Methodist Episcopal Church to hear ——— preach, and although I went with some prejudices against him, before I knew it he had me laughing and crying, and his sharp points and simple illustrations made such an impression on my mind that I never can forget them as long as I live."

While I can not remember a mere statementary sermon, however sound, a single day, the simple illustrations of truth which I heard when a little boy are as fresh in my mind as the scenes of yesterday.

It is very difficult to remember the statement of an abstract principle or proposition till you can get out of church, but if that principle be fixed in your memory by a familiar fact or incident, the illustration becomes, as it were, a stake to which you may tie the floating principle and hold it forever.

Who that heard the preaching of Jesus could ever forget his simple life-pictures and incidents!

4. Nearly allied to the last-named object of literal illustration is the fourth, and last one I shall here mention. Every literal object thus employed becomes a standing monitor, repeating its sacred lessons every time it comes in sight or hearing of the auditor.

The great Teacher's illustrations were so numerous and varied that his hearers could scarcely ever look at an object in nature, above, beneath, around, that did not have something to say about God and salvation. The birds, from the sparrow up to the eagle; animals of all varieties, wild and domestic; the fields and the wild woods; the rills, rivers, and seas; vegetation, from the tender blade of corn to the lofty cedars of Lebanon; human life in all its relations, in all its activities and pursuits, in all its forms and phases; the elements around us; the heavens with their starry host above us—all these varieties of nature, animate and inanimate, he endowed with a voice to rehearse his lessons of Gospel truth; and thus they become ministers of mercy to dying men down to the end of the world.

By thus associating Gospel truth with all the striking, familiar objects of sense, the constant recurrence of these objects, instead of diverting the mind and heart from God, as is too often the case, will all remind us of our duty, and contribute to draw us nearer to him.

In selecting matter of illustration appropriate to the pulpit, my brother, employ such only as is so exciting in itself as to arrest attention, and so apposite as to carry the truth right to the heads and hearts of your hearers.

You wish to convey the water of life from the Gospel reservoir to the thirsty souls of your auditors, but you should remember, as I have before shown, that they are all preoccupied—the "earthern vessels" of their hearts are tightly corked. It will avail nothing to pour the water over them, unless the corks are drawn. You want an illustration so exciting as to answer the purpose of a corkscrew to extract the cork and open the heart, and so apposite as to answer the purpose of a funnel, through which to pour the living water into the famishing soul.

I make my own feelings the test as to the exciting character of an illustration, and my common-sense, guided by the light of the Holy Spirit, the test of its appositeness. Whatever wakes me up, stirs my emotions, makes me laugh or cry, I set down as a thing of power. I am hard to move, and when any thing excites my soul's emotions, I conclude that it will move almost any person.

I would not think of trying to move an audience with any thing that would not, on its first introduction to me, excite my own heart's emotions; but finding such a thing in human experience, or any where in the wide world, I stick it down in my memory, or memoranda, to be kept as so much stock in trade for future use.

Formerly, when I met with such incidents, I said to myself, "Can I make any use of these for good?" and unless I could at once see wherein I could employ them to illustrate some truth, I let them slip. But riper experience taught me a better lesson. I then noted the stirring facts and incidents as they came within my observation or experience, without reference to their particular use.

When I am preparing a sermon, and want matter for illustration, I run over my stock, as a ship-builder culls over his timber. In filling his lumber-yard, he did not stop to determine, in advance, the precise use he would make of each piece of timber. He laid in a great variety of choice selections, large and small, crooked and straight, and when at work building his ship, the demand indicates the supply necessary each day as he progresses, and he picks it out of his general stock as he needs it.

I do not keep a diary—that is likely to contain too much commonplace repetition, too much chaff for the amount of wheat—nor do I keep a regular journal; but I always have in my pocket a memoranda book, and note in it only such things as strike me, and are likely to be useful for the illustration of Gospel truth. A great many of them I have never had occasion to use, but still treasure them up as available matter for future use if necessary.

The degree of excitement which you wish to produce by an illustration should be graduated by the character of the subject to be illustrated. The background of a picture may be so clearly drawn, and so highly colored, as to weaken or destroy the effect of the principal figure. So the exciting character of a mere incident may be such as to carry the feelings of the hearer away from the subject, instead of carrying them to it.

A minister of fine descriptive power was, on one occasion, preaching about heaven; and, to show the absurdity of Emanuel Swedenborg's ideas on the subject, drew a graphic picture of the Swedenborgian heaven, with its beautiful fields, fine horses, cows, and pretty women; and, in the midst of his glowing description, a good old sister, carried away with the scene, went into raptures and shouted, "Glory, glory, glory."

A friend of mine, who witnessed it, told me the preacher was so disconcerted that he paused, seeming hardly to know what next to do, till the presiding elder in the stand behind him cried out to the shouter, "Hold on there, sister, you are shouting over the wrong heaven."

Many of the figures of Scripture are very strong and striking, but the Holy Spirit would certainly never employ one too strong for a truthful representation of the subject. While, by your facts and incidents, you aim to excite only the *degree* necessary to illustrate and apply your subject, you should be careful, also, to excite the *kind* of feeling best adapted to wake up your hearers and bring them to the Savior. Use nothing in the pulpit that a Christian man, of good common-sense, can not, upon sober reflection, approve, but be sure, by some means, to stir the hearts of your hearers.

If you can not make them weep directly, make them laugh, and then make them cry. The distance between a laugh and a cry is very short, and the transition very easy. Smiles and tears, in many cases, go in company as harmoniously and as legitimately as sunshine and showers in spring-time.

You can gain access to some hearts only through their risible gateway, and if you refuse to enter through that, you will have to stay outside. First melt your metal, then mold it.

You should never excite risible feelings by any light, trifling, or inapposite thing; but if, by the startling appositeness of your illustrations, or the exciting effect of joyous, religious emotion, your hearers should smile, be it so.

If you find their risible steam rising so high as to be likely to run them off the track, put on the brakes, and fetch them up trembling and weeping. Do n't allow any to "switch off" into indifference. Keep up the steam, and while you can keep them on the track, there is but little danger of getting on too much.

Every minister of the Gospel should not only impart instruction to the intellect of his hearers, but so melt down the emotions as to enable him to leave the impression of the broad seal of truth on their hearts, and stimulate them to action.

I would leave it with the judgment of each minister and the leading of the Holy Spirit, to determine what means he may most successfully employ to that end.

Many affect to despise emotion, and advocate mere intellectual preaching, in opposition to the emotional.

The intellect is the engine, the emotions the steam; both are alike necessary to locomotion. What we most need in this enlightened age is momentum, to stimulate the people to action, proportionate to their knowledge.

Wake up the emotions, therefore, my brother, whether they manifest themselves at first in smiles or tears—wake them up by the grace of Jesus, and so direct them as to propel the soul toward the cross.

A great many pious persons associate long faces and sadness of countenance so intimately with the sanctuary, and every thing that pertains to religious worship, that they can not bear to see a smile in church, and would not excite one for any consideration.

But smiles belong as legitimately to our nature as tears. A smile or a laugh is the soul's spontaneous expression of joyous emotion—tears or weeping its expression of sorrow. A mixture of joy and sorrow, or the alternate transition from one to the other, manifest themselves accordingly, like the mixed or alternate sunshine and showers of May. This is the law, unless restrained by the force of education.

Some laugh to express the deepest sorrow, and some weep to express the profoundest joy, but these are the exceptions and not the rule.

The idea of suppressing these heaven-ordained manifestations of the soul's emotions by the awful sacredness of the sanctuary, is, in my opinion, a great mistake, soul-chilling, and, in many cases, soul-killing, in its effects.

Old Mr. B., of Indiana, was very skeptical—did not believe in the divinity of Christ—but he became attached to a certain preacher, and had him establish a preaching appointment at his house. By and by the old gentleman became so distressed that he could not rest, and by careful investigation and prayer, became clearly convinced of the divinity of Jesus, and thought he was in a very fair way to find the Savior, in the pardon of his sins.

The next Sabbath after the removal of his doubts, while listening to his favorite preacher, the truth fell upon his ear so sweetly that he involuntarily smiled.

The preacher saw his smile and said: "After all that I can do to try to save your soul, you just laugh in my face."

Mr. B. was so surprised and mortified by such a public rebuke, that he gave up seeking religion. The enemy took advantage of his weakness, ran him off the track, and he remains a poor sinner to this day, and fears he never will get so good a start as he had that day when the truth was gladdening his heart.

A good old doctor of divinity went, not long since, to hear a live preacher who always wakes up the people, and leads many souls to Christ. The doctor, determined to maintain his standard of ministerial dignity, would neither laugh nor cry, not he. He listened for a time with his face in his hands, looking like he was asleep. By and by he ventured to raise his dignified head and cast his eyes over the audience, but before he knew it he caught the prevailing sympathy, and both laughed and cried; for which, as I was informed, he became so displeased with himself, that he would not go to hear that preacher again.

The doctor was a very good man and a good friend of the said preacher; but such were his ideas of the solemn decorum befitting the house of the Lord, that he could hardly forgive himself for giving way to his feelings, and would not again risk his ministerial dignity under the preaching of that man.

A minister who had led the van of God's elect to many a battle, in which hundreds of souls were rescued from the power of the prince of darkness, preached on one occasion to a very large audience with good effect; but because some of the auditors smiled occasionally during the sermon, one of the Church members accosted the preacher, as he was passing down the aisle, thus, "I'll never go to hear you preach again, sir. You make the people laugh, and I can't stand such a thing in the house of God.

I hope you will never preach here any more;" and on he went abusing the strange minister in the presence of the dispersing multitude, in a loud, angry tone, till some of his brethren commanded him to be quiet.

Smiles and tears are both alike liable to misuse and abuse. Many persons waste their tears over a novel or a farce, just as many laugh at things trifling and silly. Many, too, on occasions worthy these spontaneous expressions of the soul, laugh or cry to excess.

Levity in the house of God is execrable, but the risible emotions excited by the appositeness of a happy illustration of truth, and serving to swell the sails that bear the soul heavenward, or that arise from religious joy in the soul, are just as appropriate in divine worship as tears. This last is an assertion so questionable with many persons, that I will stop a moment to examine "the law and the testimony" on the subject.

When God renewed his covenant with Abraham, and instituted the seal of circumcision, "God said unto Abraham, As for Sarai thy wife, thou shalt not call her name Sarai, but Sarah shall her name be. And I will bless her, and give thee a son also of her: yea, I will bless her, and she shall be a mother of nations; kings of people shall be of her. Then Abraham fell upon his face, and laughed." The old patriarch was so glad, he fell upon his face before God, just in the midst of their conversation, and laughed outright; and God did not reprove him for laughing, but went on with the announcement of the promises of the covenant. (Gen. xvii, 17.)

"And Sarah said, God hath made me to laugh, so that all who hear will laugh with me." Gen. xxi, 6.

Bildad the Shuhite, in his address to Job, says, "Behold, God will not cast away a perfect man, neither will he help the evil-doers: till he fill thy mouth with laughing, and thy lips with rejoicing." Job viii, 21.

The royal Psalmist, in magnifying the mercy of God in saving him from the intriguing malice of a "mighty man," by the destruction of his enemy, says, "The righteous also shall see, and fear, and shall laugh at him." Psalm lii, 6.

When God's ancient people held a grand celebration to commemorate their deliverance from Babylonish captivity, they together sang, "When the Lord turned again the captivity of Zion, we were like them that dream. Then was our mouth filled with laughter, and our tongue with singing." Psalm cxxvi, 1.

The Savior, in one of his sermons, said, "Blessed be ye poor: for yours is the kingdom of God. Blessed are ye that hunger now: for ye shall be filled. Blessed are ye that weep now: for ye shall *laugh*. Blessed are ye when men shall hate you, and when they shall separate you from their company, and shall reproach you, and cast out your name as evil, for the Son of man's sake. Rejoice ye in that day, and leap for joy; for behold your reward is great in heaven;

for in like manner did their fathers unto the prophets." Luke vi, 20–23.

The great Teacher, while thus informing his little band of martyrs what they might expect to suffer for his sake, assures them that in the midst of all, and over all, they shall "rejoice, and laugh, and leap for joy."

Many of the scenes connected with the ministry and miracles of Jesus occasioned, I have no doubt, both smiles and tears.

Who, that knows any thing about the sudden transition of the mind from sorrow to joy and gladness, can doubt that the bereaved sisters both laughed and wept, when their brother Lazarus was raised from the dead, and restored to their fond embrace?

At the close of one of the great Teacher's sermons in the temple, "The scribes and Pharisees brought unto him a woman taken in adultery; and when they had set her in the midst, they say unto him, Master, this woman was taken in adultery, in the very act. Now Moses in the law commanded us, that such should be stoned; but what sayest thou? This they said, tempting him, that they might have to accuse him.

"But Jesus"—pondering some weighty subject—"stooped down, and with his finger wrote on the ground, as though he heard them not." The guilty woman was doubtless wringing her hands in anguish and despair, in anticipation of the death penalty, and weeping in penitential sorrow.

"So when they continued asking him, he lifted up himself, and said unto them, He that is without sin among you, let him first cast a stone at her. And he again stooped down and wrote on the ground.

"And they which heard it, being convicted by their own conscience"—looked at each other, and the old fellows who led the prosecution broke for the door, and the younger ones followed, all glad of the opportunity, while Jesus had his eyes turned the other way.

"They went out one by one, beginning at the eldest, even unto the last: and Jesus was left alone, and the woman standing in the midst."

If I had witnessed that scene, my brother, you know I would have laughed to see how completely those long-faced fellows were taken aback and routed.

Then to see with what tenderness the Master spoke the poor penitent's sins forgiven, and sent her away in peace, at the moment when she supposed she would have been executed, saying to her, "Go, and sin no more," I should certainly have wept, and thanked God for a Gospel that could reach the chief of sinners.

I may simply add, on the subject of literalness, that the learned authors and teachers of science have all waked up to the importance of the literal illustration of their theories.

Take up any modern work you please, treating of any branch of science whatever, and you will find that the principles of the science are illustrated by literal facts and figures.

The same is true of the most popular scientific lectures.

A great deal of the teaching of these days is done by the use of the black-board, on the same principle.

Many speak of intellectual and logical preaching, *versus* literalness of illustration in presenting Gospel truth, as though intellectual research and the application of logic were confined to abstract reasonings and metaphysics.

Examine any modern work on logic itself, and you will see that the principles of the science are all brought out by means of literal facts and figures. A volume of proof and illustration of this subject could be produced. The children of this world, in this matter, are wiser than the children of light.

LETTER XI.

APPROPRIATENESS.

My Dear Brother,—The *fifth* essential characteristic of the great Teacher's model is his perfect adaptation of truth to the condition of the subject—the exact appropriateness of his discourses as to doctrine, spirit, and mode of application, to the occasion and peculiar wants of his hearers.

This might very properly be set down among the characteristics of the Savior's preaching as Number I, instead of Number V; but as you may see its importance more clearly in the light of the four already given, I place this last.

Appropriateness—a just adaptation of means to ends—is one of God's immutable laws. Our success in any undertaking pertaining to this world or the next, depends on our conformity to this law, and is usually in the exact proportion of our approximation to it.

The wholesomeness of any medicine depends on its application.

The efficiency of any piece of machinery depends on the appropriate application of the necessary forces.

It is not alone sufficient that we preach sound doctrine. From the Gospel treasury we should "bring forth things new and old," exactly suited to the occasion, and make such an application of them as will be most likely to secure the end we seek—the salvation of souls. Many a sound doctrinal sermon has fallen without good effect on account of its utter want of adaptation to the hearers, either as it regards the matter or the mode of its application, or both.

The adaptation of the Savior's discourses was perfect, because, looking right into the souls of his hearers, scanning every thought and emotion, he knew precisely what kind of an application to make.

Most of the themes of his recorded discourses seem to have been suggested by the secret workings and wants, or some special manifestation of the souls of his hearers on the occasion. A few cases may serve to illustrate this point.

"There were present at that season some that told him of the Galileans, whose blood Pilate had mingled with their sacrifices. And Jesus answering said unto them, Suppose ye that these Galileans were sinners above all the Galileans because they suffered such things? I tell you, Nay: but except ye repent, ye shall likewise perish"—and proceeded to preach a searching sermon on repentance.

"Then said one unto him, Lord, are there few that be saved? And he said unto them, Strive to enter in at the strait gate: for many, I say unto you, will seek to enter in, and shall not be able;" and then preached on the fearful consequences of failing to enter through the strait gate into the kingdom of grace.

"One of his disciples said unto him, Lord, teach us to pray as John also taught his disciples." He at once gave them a specimen prayer, and preached to them on the subject, illustrating and applying the truth in the most clear, tender, touching, encouraging manner.

Again: "The scribes and Pharisees began to urge him vehemently, and to provoke him to speak of many things; laying in wait for him, and seeking to catch something out of his mouth, that they might accuse him. In the mean time, when there were gathered together an innumerable multitude of people, in so much that they trode one upon another, he began to say unto his disciples first of all, Beware of the leaven of the Pharisees, which is hypocrisy. For there is nothing covered that shall not be revealed; neither hid that shall not be known. Therefore, whatsoever ye have spoken in darkness shall be heard in the light; and that which ye have spoken in the ear in closets shall be proclaimed on the house-tops"—urging his disciples by precept and example to go on proclaiming the whole truth, regardless of the threats and persecutions of their enemies, adding the most comforting assurances of God's special care for them, saying, "My friends, be not afraid of them that kill the body, and after that have no more that they can do. But I will forewarn you whom ye shall fear: fear him which, after he hath killed, hath power to cast into hell; yea, I say unto you, fear him.

"Are not five sparrows sold for two farthings, and

not one of them is forgotten before God? But even the very hairs of your head are all numbered. Fear not, therefore; ye are of more value than many sparrows.

"Also I say unto you, Whosoever shall confess me before men, him shall the Son of man also confess before the angels of God: but he that denieth me before men, shall be denied before the angels of God."

With such comforting pledges of divine sympathy and ultimate salvation, he informs them in his discourse what they should expect to suffer for his sake, and how they should quit themselves as men of God.

His sermon on covetousness, which he illustrated by the case of the rich man, who was going to build new barns in which to store his goods, when "God said unto him, Thou fool, this night thy soul shall be required of thee," was introduced by the request of the man who said to Jesus, "Master, speak to my brother, that he divide the inheritance with me."

On another occasion: "The Pharisees and scribes murmured, saying, This man receiveth sinners, and eateth with them." Jesus then preached on the great object of his mission—to save sinners—illustrating by the lost sheep, the lost piece of money, and the prodigal son.

"And he came to Capernaum: and being in the house, he asked them, What was it that ye disputed among yourselves by the way? But they held their peace, for by the way they had disputed among themselves which should be the greatest."

The apostles still have many successors in that particular line.

He then preached to them on humility, illustrating by the little child he set in the midst of them.

"John answered him, saying, Master, we saw one casting out devils in thy name, and he followeth not us; and we forbade him, because he followeth not us." Jesus replied in a searching sermon on Christian union.

You can hardly find, my brother, a single discourse of Jesus that was not called for by the apparent demand of the occasion on which it was preached. I have illustrated this fact, simply for the sake of the bearing it has on my subject—the perfect adaptation of his teaching to the condition and wants of his hearers, and not to indicate that we may rely on the incidents or inspiration of the occasion, and neglect to prepare our discourses in advance. Yet, while we should always, as far as possible, make thorough preparation, we should never be so tied down to any subject or arrangement as not to be ready to follow the leading of the Spirit, or seize any incident or theme at the moment, which may promise greater success than our prepared discourse.

A man tied to a written sermon has but a poor opportunity of imitating the great Teacher.

We may not hope to adapt truth to the peculiar wants of our hearers, perfectly, as did the Savior, because of our ignorance of the secret workings and wants of their souls, and yet it is our duty to study well the power of Gospel remedies and the condition of the patients to whom we apply them, and make the wisest application possible.

When we have done our duty in this regard, we may claim the presence of the omniscient Spirit, who will make a searching application of truth to the conscience; "For the word of God"—in demonstration of the Spirit—"is quick and powerful, and sharper than any two-edged sword, piercing even to the dividing asunder of soul and spirit, and of the joints and marrow, and is a discerner of the thoughts and intents of the heart." Such are the perfect delineations of human experience and conduct furnished in the Scriptures, and such the searching application of the Holy Spirit accompanying the preached Gospel, that it is very common for awakened sinners to believe that the preacher had been informed of their peculiar cases, and applied his discourse personally to them.

During a revival of religion in Greenbrier county, Virginia, a man by the name of Armstrong was converted, and in relating his experience said: "Having heard of this revival, and that so many of my neighbors had obtained religion, I came, one night, to see how it was done.

"The preacher, that night, instead of preaching to the people, as I expected, got up and talked to me, and told me how I had been living, and what I had come for, and what I was thinking about, and exposed me publicly right there before all my neighbors. I never felt so much ashamed in my life before, but was mad to think that any body should be so mean as to go and tell the preacher all about me. I was sure somebody had done it, for I knew the preacher was an entire stranger to me.

"The next night I came in early, and hid behind the door. I thought if the preacher did not see me, he would let me alone and preach to the people, but the first thing he commenced on me again, and raked me so severely that I cried, and when he called for mourners I went forward and prayed. The next night God, for Christ's sake, pardoned my sins, and now I love that preacher more than any other living man."

I could multiply truthful statements of similar cases which have come under my own observation, but the point is clear and needs no further illustration.

Your success in preaching the Gospel does not depend "on enticing words of man's wisdom, but in demonstration of the Spirit and of power."

I have not written a separate letter on the necessity of constant reliance on the Holy Spirit for the success of our labors, because that subject has been long and ably defended by all our standard writers, and is generally admitted. I assume that, as an unquestionable fact in all my letters to you, and yet God does not, by his Spirit, propose to do our work for us—the work he has given us to do, as workers together with him. It is in connection with our best efforts of study and application of the truth, that we are authorized to claim the unction of the Spirit upon ourselves and upon our labors. God often uses the weak things of this world to confound the mighty, but he generally blesses with success the means which, in their nature, are best adapted to the end.

In undertaking any important work you inquire, first, what is the extent of the work, and what are the difficulties in the way of its accomplishment?

Second. Where is the power by which this great work may be done?

Third. How shall I apply the power so as to secure the desirable end?

You go to work instrumentally to "save a soul from death"—a momentous work, in comparison with which every other sinks to insignificance. You know that the Gospel, which is "the power of God unto salvation," is sufficient, and now the question turns on the *application of that power*. This opens the field in which you are to display your skill as a "workman that needeth not to be ashamed"—"wise to win souls."

You find the sinner you seek to win subject to "the law of sin and death," indulging in the unrestrained promptings of "the carnal mind, which is enmity against God, not subject to the law of God, neither indeed can be;" "led captive by the devil at his will."

It may be that, from a demoralizing education and

the force of the most vicious habits, his soul may be encompassed by peculiar disabilities and barriers. He, perhaps, entertains strong prejudices against you personally, and particularly against your cause.

To drive such a soul to Christ is out of the question. You may assist the devil in driving him from Christ, but you can not drive any soul to Christ. If such was the Gospel mode, God could do that himself without human instrumentality or any moral appliances whatever. It is our business, my brother, not to drive, but to win souls to Christ.

I deduce from the Gospel mode of procedure in the work of soul-saving three practical rules. The first involves a wise application of the law of sympathy. In approaching a soul you wish to lead to Jesus, introduce first the points of agreement between your soul and his, and not at once the points of disagreement—strike first the chords of mutual sympathy between you and the sinner, and, for a time, suspend the discordant notes of mutual repulsion. If you will thus make him your friend, or, at least, show him that you are his friend, and walk along in agreeable company with him, till you come to the point of necessary divergence, he may by that time be induced to go with you to the Savior, or, at least, will give to the message you bear from God to his soul a respectful hearing. But if you *begin* with the points of disagreement—attack his prejudices, berate him for what he considers his honest opinions, or sharply reprove him for the commission of sin, enormous in your eyes, and perhaps diminutive in his, you will most probably insult him at the very outset, close up his heart against you tighter than an oyster, and drive him, in his blindness and guilt, beyond your reach forever.

However deep a man's degradation, he is still a man—a precious soul, bought with the blood of Jesus, and traveling to eternity. The very fact that he is out of perdition, furnishes strong presumptive evidence that he has been spared for purposes of mercy, and entitles him to a claim upon our sympathies and considerate attention.

This rule involves a potent practical principle, which may be applied with great advantage to every variety of moral suasion, pertaining to all the departments and relations of life.

There is an accessible avenue to almost every man's heart. There is some chord of mutual sympathy, which, if kindly struck, will vibrate a friendly response. Study him, and learn the available avenues to his heart—what strings you may in honest propriety strike for the securement of his good behavior, his respectful attention to what you have to say, his coöperation with you in whatever work you wish his assistance, or his salvation. He has many essential attributes of humanity in common with yourself; besides, he may be from the same section of country, may have been educated in the same school with yourself, may subscribe to the same religious belief, may have had a pious mother who prayed for him in life, and with her dying breath commended him to God, or he may have been a fellow-soldier in some engagement or a fellow-sufferer in some expedition, may with you belong to the same social fraternity, or political party, or be at any rate a fellow-citizen of the same glorious commonwealth—if not, you may know some honored champion of human rights in his country, the mention of whose name will thrill his heart—he is a fellow-man, and you are bound by the golden rule to do unto him as you would have him do unto you.

Treat any man as a dog, and he will bite you if he can, unless he has such a development of Christian meekness as to return you good for evil, and then he will make you feel like a snarling cur after snapping at his master.

Treat a man as a man; show him that while you have no compromises to make with sin, you do nevertheless respect him as a fellow human being, and desire to do him good; put him on his good behavior as a man, and if he has a grain of common-sense in his head, or a spark of human sympathy in his soul, he will try to show himself a man, or at least give you a hearing, and return you a grateful grin for your kind attentions, and for the confidence you have reposed in him. "A soft answer turneth away wrath, but grievous words stir up anger."

At a camp meeting I once attended, a large company of rowdies were creating a great deal of disturbance.

The preacher in charge, learning who was their

leader, at a convenient opportunity met him, and said, as he gave him a hearty shake by the hand, "Mr. B., I'm glad to see you. I know your good father and mother, and I am glad at any time to meet a member of the family; but I wanted to see you specially at this time, to enlist your coöperation in preserving order on the encampment. There are a great many thoughtless, reckless young men on the ground, who are giving us some trouble, and from your acquaintance with them, and influence over them, I believe you can do more than any other man in maintaining the peace and quiet of the meeting, and I shall rely upon you to keep those fellows straight."

The preacher did believe it, and did not misplace his confidence. Mr. B. promised to do what he could to preserve order, and they parted good friends. There was no further disturbance during the meeting.

At one of the large encampments I attended last fall, there were a great many very rude fellows present, who seemed determined to break up, or at least seriously disturb the meeting.

The presiding elder, having charge, was firm, but kind—"harmless as a dove, and wise as a serpent." He reasoned the case with them clearly, without threatening, and then instead of administering public rebukes from the stand for any breach of order, he had his police posted on different parts of the ground, to speak personally to any who were disorderly, and kindly, but firmly, to enforce the rules of the meeting. The result was just as he intended it should be.

At another I attended last fall, the preacher in charge read his rules of order for the meeting, and added, "You see we have rules, and we intend to have them observed. We have the law on our side, and we will enforce it if necessary. You may rely upon it, we don't intend to be run over by a set of unprincipled rowdies. If they haven't sense and good-breeding enough to know how to behave themselves, we will teach them in a manner that will not be very agreeable to their feelings."

Said I to myself, "My dear brother, you have thrown down the glove, and I'm very much mistaken in my judgment of this people if you don't find plenty of fellows who will pick it up very quickly."

That night we had a great deal of disturbance, and I know not where it would have ended, but for a meek, fearless brother, who went out among the rowdies, and talked kindly to them, and finally succeeded in getting them off to his own barn to take lodgings for the night. But in one of the previous engagements of the night brother Smith was struck with a stone, which raised a bump of combativeness on his head, and roused his righteous indignation.

The next morning he went round and notified all the tent-holders that the brethren were going out at nine o'clock to arrest every rowdy on the ground, and put them through, as they deserved, and requested each tent company to furnish help.

At the appointed time the company formed, and marched out with the preacher in charge at their head. The rowdies kept out of their way, but were back in guerilla squads again at night.

The preaching was good, and the prospect for revival quite fair; but, after night preaching, while the prayer meeting with the mourners was in progress, the preacher in charge said, "Hold on a moment, brethren."

Then addressing a man away back on the ladies' side of the encampment, he said, "Young man, go over to your own side of the ground. You are violating the rules of the meeting. I tell you to go away from there."

The penitents remained on their knees, but the "whole train stood waiting" while the two belligerents held each other at bay.

"If you do n't go away from there," continued the preacher, "I'll take you away." He was fairly committed—one or the other must switch off the track, or risk a collision. The young man muttered defiance and stood his ground.

Down came the preacher, who, with rapid, undaunted steps, made for the incorrigible sinner, seized and led him away. He displayed great courage, and took his foe captive; but by that time the revival fire had gone down, the steam had escaped, and the train could not be got in motion again that night.

Upon the whole it was a great meeting for magistrates, lawyers, arrests, fines, bad feeling, loud talk, confusion, and nearly every thing but the salvation of souls.

The application of my Gospel rule would have produced a very different result.

I remember in my early ministry, in holding a meeting in Monroe county, Va., that the deputy sheriff of the county was in attendance regularly for the purpose of opposing the revival. I had no personal acquaintance with him, but frequently saw him, while penitents were being invited to the altar, going round among the people, employing his persuasive power to prevent them from seeking religion.

One day, as a large number of seekers came forward and kneeled at the altar, just as I said, "Let us all unite in prayer," I saw the sheriff start from the rear of the audience toward the mourners, and knowing that he had some evil design, I said, "Stop a little, brethren; don't kneel yet." By that time the sheriff seized the arm of a young lady who was kneeling at the altar, saying, "Eliza, you must come away from here."

Then said I, "Mr. Campbell, what do you want, sir?"

"I want this girl away from here."

"Is she your wife, sir?"

"No."

"Is she your daughter?"

"No; but she's a relation of mine, and she's in my care, and I intend to have her away from here. I don't believe in this thing of forcing people into measures."

"No, Mr. Campbell, and I don't believe in that

either, and if the young lady was forced to come forward, I shall certainly not object to your taking her away. Ask her, if you please."

He would not ask her, but a sister near said, "Eliza, did you come forward of your own accord, or were you overpersuaded?"

She replied, "I came without being asked at all. I want to try to save my soul, and I can't go away from here till I find mercy."

"She don't know what she is about," rejoined the sheriff; "she's too young to engage in any thing of this kind, and I'll have her away."

"O, Mr. Campbell," said I, "she has long since passed the line of accountability, and is entirely capable of thinking and acting for herself; but, if you assume the responsibility of thinking and deciding for her in this matter, will you stand for her in the day of judgment?"

"No, but I'll stand for her now, and I'm bound to have her away."

Eliza wept aloud, and held on so tightly to the bench over which she was kneeling that he could not get her up.

Then said I, "Mr. Campbell, if you please, sir, just take a seat by her side, and you can see that she is duly cared for, and not imposed upon." With that he let her go, and began to work his way back toward the door; but I took him gently by the arm, and said, "Mr. C., the young lady wants religion, and, as I have no ill-feeling in the world toward you, I would be most happy to see you embrace religion also. I presume you need it as much as any of us."

"Yes," said he, "I suppose I do."

Then addressing the people, I said, "Let us pray." We "kneeled before the Lord our Maker," and I told the Lord about Eliza, commended her to his special care, and begged him to pity her uncle and bring him to a knowledge of the truth.

The meeting from that moment went on gloriously. Eliza found the Savior that day, and a very wicked old companion of Mr. C.'s, and even a greater persecutor of the Methodists than he, was also, after a very hard struggle, powerfully converted that day.

As soon as I pronounced the benediction Mr. Campbell came up, and grasping my hand, said, "I want you to come and take dinner with me."

"Thank you, sir," said I, "I will go with pleasure."

On his way home he told me all about the manner in which he had been brought up, and how he became so prejudiced against the Methodists; but said he, "I see now that I am wrong, and I will never oppose them again." I prayed in his family, and afterward baptized his wife and children, and ever after found in him a warm personal friend; and though he did not embrace religion while I remained on the circuit, he embraced every opportunity to show his high regard for the Church.

At another meeting on the same circuit, a man by the name of John Carlisle, hearing that his wife had gone to the altar as a seeker of religion, raved like a maniac, swore like a pirate, and wanted to fight.

It was missionary ground, and there was not a male member of the Church in that neighborhood, except some new converts, and they did not feel like fighting, and I was not disposed to fight him; but instead of a fist and skull knock-down with him, we piled on to him a few "soft answers," and down we fetched him.

By that time his wife found mercy, ran and embraced him, and told him a wonderful story about an old neglected friend of theirs, whom they had long been slighting—the Savior of sinners.

It was not long till John was at the mourner's bench, roaring in an agony of despair. "O," said he, "I'm lost, I'm lost! I have committed the unpardonable sin. I am reprobated to all eternity." But in due time John obtained mercy, and he and his wife together joined the Church.

When Ben. Currier, whom you knew in California, heard that his wife was at a Methodist altar, he swore that if the devil would help him, he would go right into the church and whip the preacher, and every man and woman who dared to resist him in taking his wife away.

Said he, "I had about a mile to go to get to the church, and all the way along I felt as strong as Sampson. I told the devil just to back me and I would clear out the whole concern, and I believed he would do it.

"When I reached the church I found it crowded to overflowing. I could hardly get in.

"As I tried to press my way up the aisle, the preacher met me with a smile, and said, 'Mr. Currier, I'm glad to see you. Here's a good seat for you, sir. Sit over there a little, gentlemen, and make room for Mr. Currier. There, Mr. Currier, take a seat and enjoy our meeting.'

"I sat down, feeling as mean as a sheep-stealing dog. I never was so much ashamed and confounded in my life. The longer I sat the worse I felt. I was mad at myself and mad at the devil for having brought me into such a snap and leaving me in the lurch.

"I sat there about fifteeen minutes, and thought I would have given a hundred dollars to be out of the house, but feared that I could n't get out. After a desperate effort I got to the door, and left things as I found them. On my way home I abused the devil for his meanness, and told him I never would have any thing more to do with him; and as soon as I got into the house I dropped on my knees, and there prayed all that night. My wife came home happy, and prayed for me. The next day God, for Christ's sake, converted my soul."

LETTER XII.

APPROPRIATENESS—CONTINUED.

My Dear Brother,—But for the practical power of this law of kindness, how could I have got along for the last thirteen years, preaching in the streets and highways, especially in the early settlement of California?

You remember that when I commenced to preach on the Plaza in San Francisco, nearly all the gambling-houses in the city fronted on that square, and they occupied the best houses in the city.

Such was their power, that though they shot a man almost every week, there were no arrests nor investigations—no power of law that dared to touch them.

But relying on the potent forces of common-sense and Christian sympathy, and the promised presence of Jesus, I took my stand in front of their largest saloon, and sang together, I suppose, five hundred gamblers, and as many more excitables of all sorts, in less than ten minutes. That brought on the tug of war. In reading the third chapter of my *California Life Illustrated*, you have seen that I surrounded and arrested them, and, by the grace of Jesus, so committed them to my cause, that so far from disturbing, they received the word kindly and became my regular hearers; although I often preached on gambling, and showed it up with all its withering consequences.

Generally after that, whenever they shot a fellow, they sent for me to preach his funeral.

As an illustration of the rule under consideration, I will insert an extract from one of those funeral sermons, found in *Seven Years' Street Preaching*, page 82. Taking my stand in the gambling-house beside the bloody corpse of C. B., I sang:

> "That awful day will surely come,
> Th' appointed hour makes haste,
> When I must stand before my Judge,
> And pass the solemn test," etc.

The gamblers, *en masse*, crowded the saloon, and I announced as my text the last two verses of the book of Ecclesiastes: "Let us hear the conclusion of the whole matter: Fear God, and keep his commandments: for this is the whole duty of man. For God shall bring every work into judgment, with every secret thing, whether it be good, or whether it be evil."

I then addressed them as follows: "Gentlemen, in my discourses I always endeavor, so far as I can, to adapt my remarks to my audience. I take it for granted that the greater portion, if not all of you, are sportsmen; as such I shall address you. 'The conclusion of the whole matter,' the summary of life's duties, what is it? 'Fear God, and keep his commandments.' Do you understand it?

"You are not a set of ignoramuses. I know from

your appearance that you have had educational advantages. Some of you have had pious mothers, who used to put your little hands together, and teach you to say, 'Our Father who art in heaven.' Ah, those sweet days of juvenile innocency! Do you remember them?

"Many of you, I doubt not, have been brought up in the Sabbath school, and you have all had opportunity of reading the word of God, and of hearing it preached from your boyhood to the present hour. You can not plead ignorance. You know your duty— to 'keep His commandments.' How comprehensive the commandments of God, embracing every duty growing out of the relations we sustain to God and to each other!

"Had you given your hearts to God, believed in Jesus Christ, received the regenerating power of his grace in your souls, and were you to-day consecrated to his service, what happy men you would be! What an influence you might wield for God and his cause in California; help to build up good society, and make this fair land a safe and happy home for your wives and children! The little boys and girls now growing up in our midst would repeat your names with grateful hearts, and call you blessed when your bodies are in the ground, and your souls safe in the abode of angels and God.

"But what are you about? What are you doing here in California?

"Look at that bloody corpse! What will his mother

say? What will his sisters think of it? To die in a distant land, among strangers, is bad; to die unforgiven, suddenly, and unexpectedly, is worse; to be shot down in a gambling-house, at the midnight hour, O, horrible! And yet this is the legitimate fruit of the excitement and dissipation, chagrin and disappointment, consequent upon your business—a business fatal to your best interests of body and soul, for time and for eternity.

"Again: look at its influence upon society. The unwary are decoyed and ruined. Little boys, charmed by your animating music, dazzled by the magnificent paraphernalia of your saloons, are enticed, corrupted, and destroyed, to the hopeless grief of their mothers, whose wailings will be entered against you in the book of God. Remember that for all these things God will bring you into judgment. 'For God shall bring every work into judgment, with every secret thing, whether it be good, or whether it be evil.'"

Every gambler listened with profound attention.

In four years from that time the people demanded an anti-gambling law, which was granted, and every gambling-house in the state was closed by its prompt execution, and every gambler went down under the pressure of an indignant public sentiment a thousand per cent. below par.

Suppose that on the funeral occasion referred to I had commenced my discourse where I left off. They would have kicked me out of the house, and perhaps shot me, for there was no visible protection nor redress; but by adhering to the Gospel rule under discussion I was enabled to conquer their prejudices, and pour the unadulterated truth right down into their guilty hearts.

You know, my brother, and all who know me will bear record, that while I begin with the points of agreement, and not the points of disagreement, I never compromise religious principle in the application of this rule, but preach the law and the Gospel in all plainness.

I could have had as many fights as any of the pioneers of the west, and I think, from what you know of the elastic, muscular power with which God has endowed me, you will say that I could have gained as great a reputation in that line as any of them, but I do n't choose to fight in that way. I rely much more on a judicious application of the law of common-sense and Christian sympathy than upon muscular force. "It is not by might nor by power, but by my Spirit, saith the Lord," that the great Gospel achievements are to be made.

I do not mean to berate the grand old heroes, who, in leading the van of our Methodist armies westward, had an occasional knock-down with a rowdy. I will not pass judgment on the necessity that justified that course in their minds, for they were good, great, and useful men—men of God raised up for the glorious work in which they devoted their lives.

I think, however, they possessed the power which, if properly applied, would, consistently with the law of love, have conquered their enemies, in most cases, much more easily and more effectually.

When a man gets it into his head that it is necessary for him to have a fight occasionally, he can generally be accommodated with an opportunity.

When did you, my brother, ever see a short-tailed, snub-nosed bull-dog that was not covered with scars back to his massive shoulders, consequent on his great fights?

But look at the New Foundland; see the friendly wag of his huge tail, as he walks round and waits for an opportunity to rescue some drowning child. There is not a scar on him; he has plenty of friends, fares well, never had a fight in his life, and does not feel that the vindication of his courage or his carcass will ever require one.

There is a great deal, my brother, in knowing how to manage and get along peaceably with man and beast, and I will here give you a few practical hints, as they are relevant to my subject.

If you should be pursued by a furious bull—which may probably occur among your great herds of Oregon, the "Bashan" of the north-west—run from him in a straight line till he gets within a few feet of you, and then spring off at a right angle. The animal will run on in a straight line, and you can go on to your appointment.

The philosophy of it I presume to be this: when he makes a drive at an object—say in a fight with his fellow—he will, in that act, shut his eyes. So in pursuing you, when he bows his neck to give you a death-blow, he shuts his eyes and do n't see you dodge. He rushes right on, and, opening his eyes, no doubt wonders what has become of his man. Should he soon after see you, he will, by that time, have spent his wrath, and is not likely to pursue you.

If a dog bound at you to bite you, hold out your hat to him, and let him bite that. A snap at your hat will satisfy him about as well as to bite off the calf of your leg, and will be much cheaper for you. I have tried that often, and always with success.

The philosophy of it is this: a snap or two at your hat will suffice to let the steam off—the wrathful passion escapes, and having displayed the courage of his dogship, he is satisfied.

On the same principle, if an angry man attack you, just be calm, and, if possible, hold him at bay a minute and let him talk, till you apply "a soft answer" or two, and strike a few chords of mutual sympathy, and soon his wrathful steam will escape, and he will cower down before your superior, self-possessed soul. In that way you conquer him, and do it so effectually, that he is not likely ever to attack you again. I have tried this in a number of cases, and always with success.

If you keep out of his way, his passion, unless his heart is deeply corroded with malice, will soon escape and he will conquer himself; but in that case you gain no power over him.

I once saw two men, in San Francisco, who wanted

to fight each other. One of them was furious, and when he was prevented by the crowd from getting hold of his antagonist, he pulled off his own hat and tore it to pieces. That served to express his chivalry and opened a safety-valve through which the malicious gas escaped, and in a few minutes he walked away quietly about his business, feeling, as I thought, nearly as well satisfied as if he had whipped the man.

This theory accounts for the fact, that a dog that barks much, or a man or woman who talks much, is not apt to bite, because the steam escapes in the barking and talking, and they have but little desire, and less power, left for biting or fighting.

But you say, "If this law of sympathy be so potent, why did not the martyrs and the persecuted Christians, in all ages, employ it for their own protection?" In the rush of mob force there is no time, ordinarily, for the application of it. Persecution is usually carried on by an organized power, which operates beyond the reach of the moral suasion of the persecuted, and, to anticipate and prevent the effect of their moral power of speech, they have not generally been permitted to speak for themselves. When such privilege was granted them, they displayed a wisdom and power of speech which their adversaries were not able to gainsay nor resist. Wherever this law has been applied we find the clearest demonstrations of its power.

When St. Paul was brought before the Sanhedrim for trial, he perceived, during the proceedings, that about half the judges were Pharisees and the other half Sadducees, and "cried out in the council, Men and brethren, I am a Pharisee, the son of a Pharisee: of the hope and resurrection of the dead am I called in question. And when he had so said, there arose a dissension between the Pharisees and Sadducees: and the multitude was divided." He struck, and truthfully, too, a single chord of mutual sympathy or agreement that vibrated in the heart of every Pharisee in the council.

How often did Mr. Wesley quell the mob by the application of this law! Whenever he had the opportunity of speaking to them he subdued the most turbulent spirits, the leader of the mob sometimes coming right out and swearing that he would defend the preacher to the death. How many thousands of persecutors have thus been won to Christ! Allow me to present a few examples from the history of the great revival of the eighteenth century. "An innumerable multitude assailed the dwelling where Mr. Wesley was staying. 'A louder or more confused noise,' he says, 'could hardly occur at the taking of a city.' The terrified family escaped, leaving only Wesley and a servant-maid in the house. The rabble forced open the door and filled the passage. Only a wainscot partition remained between them and their victim. Wesley, supposing the wall would soon fall, showed his coolness at the moment by taking down a large looking-glass which hung against it. The mob, with terrible imprecations, began to attack the partition. 'Our lives,' he says, 'seemed hardly worth an hour's purchase.' The servant entreated him to hide himself in a closet. 'It is best,' he replied, 'for me to stand just where I am.' The crews of some privateers, which had lately arrived in the harbor, were in the street, and being impatient at the slow progress of the rioters within, drove them out, and undertook the assault themselves. Putting their shoulders against the door, and shouting, 'Avast, lads! avast!' they prostrated it upon the floor of the room. Wesley stepped forward immediately into their midst, bareheaded, and said, 'Here I am. Which of you has any thing to say to me? To which of you have I done any wrong? To you? or you? or you?' He continued speaking till he reached the middle of the street; there he took his stand, and addressed them as his 'neighbors and countrymen.' He had his usual success. Several of the crowd cried out, 'He shall speak. Yes! yes!' Others swore that no man should touch him. He was conducted in safety to a house, and soon after left the town in a boat." (Stevens's History of Methodism.)

See the power of this law illustrated in the experience of Whitefield. "At London Whitefield could no longer be content with his spacious tabernacle, but took again the open field. The most riotous scenes at Moorfields were usually during the Whitsun holidays. The devils then held their rendezvous there, he said, and he resolved 'to meet them in pitched battle.' He began early in order to secure the field before the greatest rush of the crowd. At six o'clock in the morning he found ten thousand people waiting impatiently for the sports of the day. Mounting his pulpit, and assured that he 'had for once got the start of the devil,' he soon drew the whole multitude around him. At noon he again took the field. Between twenty and thirty thousand swarmed upon it. He described it as in complete possession of Beelzebub, whose agents were in full motion. Drummers, trumpeters, merry-andrews, masters of puppet-shows, exhibitors of wild beasts, players, were all busy in entertaining their respective groups. He shouted his text, 'Great is Diana of the Ephesians,' and boldly charged home upon the vice and peril of their dissipations. The craftsmen were alarmed, and the battle he had anticipated and challenged now fairly began. Stones, dirt, rotten eggs, and dead cats were thrown at him. 'My soul,' he says, 'was among lions;' but before long he prevailed, and the immense multitude were 'turned into lambs.' At six in the evening he was again in his field pulpit. 'I came,' he says, 'and I saw; but what? Thousands and thousands more than before.' He rightly judged that Satan could not brook such repeated assaults, in such circumstances, and never, perhaps, had they been pushed more bravely home against the very citadel of his power. A harlequin was exhibiting and trumpeting on a stage, but was deserted as soon as the people saw Whitefield, in his black robes, ascend his pulpit. He 'lifted up his voice like a trumpet, and many heard the joyful sound.' At length they approached nearer, and the merry-andrew, attended by others, who complained that they had taken many pounds less that day on account of the preaching, got upon a man's shoulders, and advancing toward the pulpit, attempted several times to strike the preacher with a long, heavy whip, but always tumbled down by the violence of his motion. The mob next secured the aid of a recruiting sergeant, who, with music and straggling followers, marched directly through the crowd before the pulpit. Whitefield knew instinctively how to manage the passions and whims of the people. He called out to them to make way for the King's officer. The sergeant, with assumed official dignity, and his drum and fife, passed through the opened ranks, which closed immediately after him, and left the solid mass still in possession of the preacher. A third onslaught was attempted. Roaring like wild beasts, on the outskirts of the assembly, a large number combined for the purpose of sweeping through in solid column. They bore a long pole for their standard, and came on with the sound of drum and menacing shouts, but soon quarreled among themselves, threw down their pole, and dispersed, leaving many of their number behind, 'who were brought over to join the besieged party.' At times, however, the tumult rose like the noise of many waters, drowning the preacher's voice; he would then call upon his brethren near him to unite with him in singing, till the clamorous host were again charmed into silence.

He was determined not to retreat defeated; preaching, praying, singing, he kept his ground till night closed the strange scene. It was one of the greatest of his field days. He had won the victory, and moved off with his religious friends to celebrate it at night in the Tabernacle; and great were the spoils there exhibited. No less than a thousand notes were afterward handed up to him for prayers, from persons who had been brought 'under conviction' that day; and soon after upward of three hundred were received into the society at one time. Many of them were 'the devil's castaways,' as he called them." (Ibid.)

At a later period Charles Wesley, writing from Cornwall, said, "Their sufferings have been for the furtherance of the Gospel. The opposers behold and wonder at their steadfastness and godly conversation." "Four exhorters had been raised up among them." "Both sheep and shepherds," he adds, "had been scattered in the late cloudy day of persecution, but the Lord gathered them again, and kept them together by their own brethren, who began to exhort their companions, one or more, in every society." At a later period he says of Cornwall, "The whole country finds the benefit of the Gospel. Hundreds who follow not with us have broken off their sins, and are outwardly reformed, and, though persecutors once, will not suffer a word to be spoken against this way." At St. Ives he writes that "the whole place is outwardly changed. I walk the streets, scarce believing that it is St. Ives. It is the same throughout all the country. All opposition falls before us, or rather is fallen, and not suffered to lift up its head again." "At Sithney, fierce persecution had prevailed against the society, and women and children had been struck down and beaten in the streets; now one hundred of the former rioters gathered about him to fight for him against a threatened mob from a neighboring town." (Ibid.)

By a wise application of the law of Christian sympathy, a consistent example of meekness, and patient perseverance in well-doing, on the part of that noble band of street preachers and their zealous converts, by the merciful providence of God, and the power of his Gospel, the raving mobs of England, Ireland, and Wales were all suppressed, and hundreds of the rioters became as zealous defenders as they had been opposers of the truth.

But, whatever may be the practical value of this law for any purpose of life, it is certainly of the first importance in "winning souls to Christ." Never insult or abuse any man. Why, "Michael the archangel, when contending with the devil, he disputed about the body of Moses, durst not bring against him a railing accusation, but said, The Lord rebuke thee."

If you desire to lead a soul to Christ, I repeat, approach him gently, begin with the points of agreement, strike the chords of mutual sympathy, and you will, by the blessing of God, have an opportunity of doing him good. You may not always succeed, but if you can not by that means, you can not otherwise.

Many good men practically ignore this rule, and practice its opposite. They begin with the points of disagreement, and will show you but little kind affection till you submit and come over to their side of the question. In manifesting their righteous indignation against sin, they have nothing but frowns, hard names, opprobrious epithets and anathemas, to give to the sinner. For the purpose of curing the disease, they go to work with their instruments of death, and kill the patient. Much of the cross-firing at other Christian denominations, and especially at such as are not regarded as orthodox, and at the Catholics, is done in the same spirit.

Some of our most conscientious brethren and sisters, who sincerely feel it their duty to reprove sin, publicly and privately, think of the sins to be reproved till their holy horror is aroused, and they burn with zeal to get hold of the guilty rebels; and, finding opportunity, they go at them with their legal sledge-hammer, and batter them as if they expected to maul the grace of God into them, with or without their consent. I would advise such persons to read Rary's work on horse training. I have not seen the work myself, but have no doubt, from what I have heard of Mr. Rary, that such persons seeing the effect of the law of kindness on horses, would especially see its importance in dealing with moral agents.

If, on my first approach to a sinner, I make a

direct assault on his errors of doctrine and wickedness of life, having truth on my side, I may silence his objections and shut his mouth, but I will, in all probability, more effectually shut his heart against me. I shall have delivered my soul, and made a sinner mad. But, if I approach him as a brother, strike a few chords of mutual sympathy, cause him to feel that I love him, and thus gain his confidence, and ingratiate myself into his affections; then, if the good Spirit is pleased to bless my efforts to save a soul, he will kindly receive the plainest Gospel talk I can give him, and beg me, as his friend, to tell him all I see in him that is wrong. If I should be guilty of catering to his bad passions, I would certainly forfeit his confidence. He will expect me, as the friend of his soul, to be honest, and to deal faithfully with him, and withhold no truth necessary to his salvation, however mortifying to his feelings.

When I go into a prison, as I often do, to see what sin is doing with my guilty brethren, and to see if I may do any thing for their relief, I go to a man in chains, and taking him by the hand, say, "My dear brother, I am sorry to find you here," and the degraded man will go to weeping, just to think that he has a brother left, who can care for his soul, and pour a little sympathy into his deserted heart. An old lady, in giving directions how to dress and cook a hare, said, "The first thing is to catch it."

But you inquire, "Are we to ignore Gospel polemics, the delineation and condemnation of sin, the terrors of the law, and the coming retributions of the judgment?" No, sir; not by any means. I have told you what I consider the Gospel mode of approaching a sinner you wish to lead to Christ—*begin* with the points of agreement as I have illustrated, but declare the whole counsel of God to him before you leave him. But in pouring the terrors of the law upon him, and in the dissection of his soul and body with the sword of the Spirit, be sure that you manifest constantly the same spirit of love with which you commenced.

There are, besides the object of a *direct* effort to lead souls to Christ, according to the rule I have set forth, two leading legitimate departments of Gospel polemics in which the embassadors of Christ have to "contend for the faith." The *first* involves a collision with opposing systems of formal Christianity, heathenism, Judaism, and hydra-headed infidelity. In this contest they do not generally deal directly, so much with men as with principles, theories, and God-condemned, hoary-headed, time-honored systems of error and sin. The direct object in this case is to rescue truth from the masses of accumulated error which environ and conceal it, and to bring it out unshackled in its unadulterated simplicity, virgin beauty, and saving power—to grade down the opposing hills and mountains, fill up the valleys, "prepare the way of the Lord, and make straight in the desert a highway for our God." The *second* involves a collision with the enemies of God, scoffers and opposers, who exert themselves to overthrow the Gospel or defeat its gracious ends. In this case the direct object is not so much to save the man we encounter, as to rescue and vindicate the truth for the sake of those whom his fallacious arts may otherwise poison and destroy.

It sometimes becomes necessary, for the truth's sake, to take hold of such a man in argument without ceremony, and deal with him somewhat as David did with the bear which broke into his fold and commenced devouring his lambs. His object was not to save the bear, but to save the lambs.

St. Paul furnishes a forcible illustration of this principle. Paul and Barnabas, in a missionary tour through the island of Cyprus, preached and had a revival in the town of Paphos. Among the penitents was "the deputy of the country, Sergius Paulus, a prudent man, who called for Barnabas and Paul, and desired to hear the word of God. But Elymus, the sorcerer, a false prophet and a Jew, withstood them, seeking to turn away the deputy from the faith. Then Paul, filled with the Holy Ghost, set his eyes on him, and said, O full of all subtilty and all mischief, thou child of the devil, thou enemy of all righteousness, wilt thou not cease to pervert the right ways of the Lord? And now, behold the hand of the Lord is upon thee, and thou shalt be blind, not seeing the sun for a season. And immediately there fell on him a mist and a darkness; and he went about seeking some to lead him by the hand."

Poor wretch! perhaps that was the only thing that could bring him to repentance. "Then the deputy, when he saw what was done, believed, being astonished at the doctrine of the Lord.

In these two departments of Christian warfare, Luther, Wesley, Fletcher, Watson, and a vast host of others of different denominations, have done a great work for the Church. On the same principles it often becomes necessary still, in open debate, and otherwise, to vindicate the truth, which, however, should always be done in a Christian spirit. To these may be added the "anathema maranatha," which was applied only to incorrigible souls on whom all the winning appliances of the Gospel had been tried in vain. But these two principles, however legitimate and important, and constituting an integral part of the great system of salvation, are nevertheless different from the rule I have so largely illustrated of directly winning souls to Christ.

That you may the more clearly see that I have given you the Gospel rule on that subject, I will give a few specimen proofs from the book.

King David was guilty of a most aggravated and atrocious crime, "and the Lord sent the prophet Nathan unto him." How did the prophet approach the apostate King? Did he go into the palace boiling over with indignation, and break out against the King, saying, "Thou vile wretch, what hast thou done? Wherefore hast thou despised the commandment of the Lord, to do evil in his sight? Thou hast killed

Uriah, the Hittite, with the sword, and hast taken his wife to be thy wife, and hast slain him with the sword of the children of Ammon. Now, therefore, the sword shall never depart from thy house." Had he thus commenced on the points of disagreement, the enraged King would probably have cut the prophet's head off, and would then probably have gone straight to hell, just for spite. Nathan understood his business better than that. Calm and self-possessed, he made his best bow to the fallen King, and entertained him with an interesting story, that arrested his attention, touched his sympathies, and waked up his dormant conscience on the side of justice and righteousness; and when he got the King fully committed by a nail driven in a sure place, then he clinched it with an application that swept from him his royal robes and mantled him with sackcloth. Then the prophet mauled him with his legal sledge-hammer till the old King felt like his "bones were scattered at the grave's mouth, as when one cutteth and cleaveth wood asunder;" and he "ceased not his roaring, day and night," till the Lord pardoned his "blood-guiltiness," brought him up out of the horrible pit, established his goings, and put a new song into his mouth.

Before the Savior proclaimed the searching, withering truths contained in his sermon on the mount, he struck about a dozen of the tenderest chords of mutual sympathy, in connection with as many most affectionate benedictions.

Christ and his apostles always, so far as they could

consistently with the righteousness of their mission, behaved in the most conciliatory manner toward the Jews, conforming to all their customs and usages, civil, social, and religious, as far as possible, without a compromise of their principles.

St. Paul explains clearly the principle on which he acted in this matter, saying, "For though I be free from all men, yet have I made myself servant unto all, that I might gain the more. And unto the Jews I became as a Jew, that I might gain the Jews; to them that are under the law, as under the law, that I might gain them that are under the law; to them that are without law, as without law, being not without law to God, but under the law to Christ"—he did not compromise his fidelity to God—"that I might gain them that are without law; to the weak became I as weak, that I might gain the weak: I am made all things to all men, that I might by all means save some. And this I do for the Gospel's sake, that I might be partaker thereof with you."

St. Paul's practice conforms exactly to his theory in this matter. He even went so far as to circumcise Timothy, and went into the temple himself and had his head shaved, and observed the forms of purification, when he knew they were of no service to him whatever; but he could endure these things, and hoped to conciliate and lead others to Christ by that means. When preaching to the heathen he quoted from their poets, illustrated from their games and customs, and was made all things to them that he "might by all means save some." "He was wise as a serpent, yet harmless as a dove."

When, by permission of Captain Lysius, St. Paul addressed the mob from the stairs of the Antonian tower, he commenced thus: "Men, brethren and fathers, hear ye my defense, which I now make unto you." In the discourse which followed, he interspersed with a pure Gospel, directly antagonistic to the feelings and prejudices of his hearers, so many points of agreement between him and them as to secure their profound attention till after he had illustrated the power of the Gospel by his own wonderful experience, and gave an account of his call to the ministry, and his missionary call to the Gentiles. Then the uproar commenced again. Had he commenced his sermon where he left off, he could not have commanded a hearing for one minute. As it was, he preached a discourse which astonished Captain Lysius, who had taken him for a seditious Egyptian, and sent home the shafts of truth to the hearts of guilty thousands, and which probably resulted in the salvation of many souls.

The last sermon of St. Stephen is a fine illustration of this rule. He gave the persecuting masses, who were clamoring for his blood, the finest synopsis of Jewish history they had ever heard in their lives, and before they could break the charm of his eloquence he preached to them the whole summary of the Gospel, with the consequence of its rejection, till "they were cut to the heart." The mob, to be sure, stoned him to death, because the Lord was pleased to "receive his spirit," and make that sermon, sealed with his blood, more effectual in the salvation of sinners than the prolonging of his life would have been. It was then, doubtless, that the truth began to goad the conscience of young Saul; and although he made havoc of the Church after that, he found it very hard to kick against those goads, which, with the remembrance of the sermon and triumphant death of Stephen, continued to prick his heart. Had Stephen commenced his discourse with the points of disagreement, which stood out like gleaming bayonets near its close, the mob would not have listened to him ten seconds; but, upon the principle I am advocating, he preached one of the most powerful sermons on record. The revelations of the judgment will show the number of sinners converted as the result of it. The preacher fell—the first of an illustrious train of martyrs; but from the seed of his blood sprang up, in due time, the great apostle of the Gentiles.

I will not further detain you with proofs and illustrations of my position from the example of the great Teacher and apostolic usage. You will find them in every sermon of Jesus and his primitive embassadors.

LETTER XIII.

APPROPRIATENESS—CONTINUED.

My Dear Brother,—In illustrating to you the fifth characteristic of the Savior's model for preaching the Gospel, I proposed to deduce *three* rules necessary to effective preaching:

1. A wise application of the law of sympathy, which I have largely illustrated.
2. The law of direct appeal to the heart.
3. The law of direct approach to Christ.

The last two I will illustrate together. The great Teacher and his apostles, after getting access to a sinner's confidence, by a judicious application of the law of sympathy, made a direct assault upon his heart and conscience. They lost no time in the application of outward forms and ceremonies, nor in trying to cure him of particular sins, nor in the enforcement of special outward duties. Their object direct was to convince him of the exceeding sinfulness of sin—the extreme blackness and guilt of his heart, and strip him of all hope in any past or future performances of his own.

St. Paul describes this state of hopeless bondage revealed in the awakened soul by the convincing Spirit. Personating the convicted sinner, he says: "We know that the law is spiritual; but I am carnal, sold under sin. For that which I do, I allow not: for what I would, that do I not; but what I hate, that I do. If then I do that which I would not, I consent unto the law that it is good." I acknowledge the just claims of the law of God upon me, and I ought, and I desire, and I try to obey. "But I see another law in my members warring against the law of my mind, and bringing me into captivity to the law of sin which is in my members"—the law of sinful propensity and vicious habit. Having thus defined the hopeless bondage of a soul in its sins, he illustrates it. To appreciate the apostle's illustration, my brother, you must accompany him in your mind into a Roman prison.

Prisons, at best, are uncomfortable places. I have been in a great many—always went in voluntarily, to be sure; I go in when I have opportunity, to see how my poor, guilty brothers get along there—and I never saw one yet that struck me as a desirable place for residence; but I suppose modern prisons are palaces compared with the old Roman jails with which St. Paul had a painfully-familiar acquaintance.

As you accompany the apostle across the threshold, where hope bids adieu to many a criminal, the grating of the massive doors on their rusty hinges causes you to shudder. Dark and damp, filled with poisonous vapors stifling you with stench, you feel that you have entered the vestibule of hell. Passing down the aisle, quaking with horror at every step, your ears are saluted from the cells on each side with the clanking of chains and hideous groans. Poor prisoners! they used to walk in the light of the sun; had kind mothers and sisters to caress them. Some of them have wives and children whom they have not seen for years, and may never see again. But when you reach the dungeon—O, such hideous sounds never fell on your ears before! What upon earth is the matter? Poor fellow, he must be strangling! Take a light and peep through the iron grating. O, horrible! What a sight! Why, there's a man bound to a dead body—a decomposing human carcass, face to face, and limb to limb, securely lashed. See how he struggles! Each effort to free himself only brings him into more intimate contact with the putrefying mass. Hear the broken sobs of his choked emotions and his agonizing cries: "O wretched man that I am! who shall deliver me from this dead body?" There, sir, is the sinner's moral condition, as drawn by the pen of inspiration. What shall be done for the relief of such a case? Bring in spiritual advisers, and try and do something for him before it is eternally too late. Each one has a prescription for the poor fellow. Old Mr. Harper, whom you used to know in Virginia, after listening to the lamentation of such a soul, said to him: "If that is your condition, I don't want to have any thing to do with you. I know you must be one of the reprobates, and I can do nothing for you."

But, if you listen to the various advice of the comforters of the poor, imprisoned soul, you will hear one say, "Be composed, my friend. There is no use in so much excitement. Hold your peace, Bartimeus."

Another says, "Be of good cheer, my friend, God has commenced a good work in your heart, and he will surely carry it on."

Another, thinking his conviction not quite deep enough, talks to him of death, judgment, and hell, and says, "If the foretaste is so dreadful, my friend, what must the pains of the second death be?"—the poor fellow meantime crying, "O wretched man that I am! who shall deliver me from this dead body?"

Another says to him, "Don't be discouraged, my brother. Pray on, and relief will come by and by. The darkest hour is just before day."

Another prescribes a rule of life for him, saying, "Read the Scriptures, and pray three times each day in your closet; attend the class meetings and the public means of grace; watch the risings of your bad habits, and ask for strength to break them; and you will gradually grow in grace, and overcome the power of sin and Satan."

Another, "You had better join the Church, and identify yourself with the people of God."

Another wishes to discuss the mode of baptism with him.

Others desire to enlist his influence against certain great evils of the land which they set forth before him. One discusses the slavery question; another advocates the temperance cause, and asks him to join the society.

Others wish early to impress him with the sinful compromises of the Church, and bespeak his influence against them—sectarianism, and worldliness, and extravagance in dress. Some wish him to go against pews and organs in the churches—others try to entertain him with questions of Church government, lay representation, the presiding-elder question, and the power of the bishops.

Then comes along a good brother, saying, "'Blessed are they that mourn: for they shall be comforted.' You are already blessed, my brother. Don't you love the Savior? I think you have already found comfort, if you would only believe it." The poor fellow cries again, "O wretched man that I am! who shall deliver me from this body of death?"

Then a humble disciple, "wise to win souls," kneels beside the despairing soul, and after invoking the illumination of the Spirit, says, "This is a faithful saying, and worthy of all acceptation, that Christ Jesus came into the world to save sinners—even the chief of sinners." "He is able to save, to the uttermost, all that come unto God by him." His words, but the repetition of what the poor struggling soul had often heard, are accompanied with such an unction of the Holy Spirit that they descend into his soul like rain into the thirsty land. "Say not in thy heart, Who shall ascend into heaven? that is, to bring Christ down from above; or, Who shall descend into the deep? that is, to bring up Christ again from the dead. But what saith it?" What saith the Gospel? The Word—the living Word, in the fullness of his saving mercy—is nigh thee. The desire thou now feelest in thy heart, and express with thy mouth, is proof that he is nigh thee—"Working in thee now to will and to do his good pleasure." Submit to him, my brother; venture your soul and body on his might, his mercy, his atoning blood. "Believe in the Lord Jesus Christ, and thou shalt be saved." Laying "hold of the hope set before him," and clinging to Christ, as a drowning man to the last plank, the penitent believes in his heart, and makes confession with his mouth, exclaiming, "'I thank God through Jesus Christ our Lord,' I have redemption — 'even the forgiveness of sins.' 'There is, therefore, now no condemnation to them which are in Christ Jesus, who walk not after the flesh, but after the Spirit. For the law of the Spirit of life in Christ Jesus hath made me free from the law of sin and death'"—the law of sin which reigned in his members, and the death penalty of the moral law. "For what the law could not do, in that it was weak through the flesh"—the flesh was too weak to fill its requirement, and, therefore, it could do nothing but condemn and execute its penalty on the guilty soul; but what the law could not do, God hath done by "sending his own Son in the likeness of sinful flesh, and by a sacrifice for sin condemned sin in the flesh"—passed sentence of death upon it that it should be destroyed out of my heart by his death. "That the righteousness of the law might be fulfilled in us who walk not after the flesh, but after the Spirit."

The moral law, which demands perfect obedience and rectitude, and holds me, in default, subject to its penalty of eternal death, accepts, as an equivalent for perfect rectitude, which I never could render, the love of Christ shed abroad in my heart through faith. That is my receipt in full for all past claims of the law against me, and that is the principle of righteousness within, which the law approves. This living faith, uniting me to Christ, as the branch to the vine, works by love, purifies the heart, and manifests itself in all appropriate good works. "As the branch can not bear fruit of itself, except it abide in the vine," saith the great Teacher: "no more can ye, except ye abide in me."

The first object, then, of apostolic preaching was to pierce the sinner's heart with the sword of the Spirit, and then without delay to bring him directly to the great Physician.

Three thousand souls, under the preaching of Peter at the great Pentecost, were thus awakened, converted, baptized, and admitted into the Church in a single day.

Has the Gospel lost any of its power? It remains unchanged and unchangeable, unexhausted and inexhaustible, because Jesus Christ is its soul and grand impersonation—" the same yesterday, to-day, and forever." How often, in apostolic times, did a weary, heavy-laden sinner have to approach the Savior before he could obtain relief? Why is it that the demonstration of the Spirit does not attend the preaching of this same mighty Gospel with the same saving effect now as then? Is it not a want of faith on the part of preachers and people? Are we not, to an alarming extent, substituting for living, purifying, effective faith, a system of forms, vows, rules for holy living, and outward performances? How little do we know of those rules of direct appeal to the heart, and direct approach to Christ, so patent in apostolic times!

We know that "the springs of Jericho" ought to be healed. "The situation of the city"—the providential position of the Church—"is pleasant." "But the water is naught, and the ground is barren." We have "the new cruse" of the Gospel full "of salt," and we doubt not its healing power, but instead of casting it right into the fountain—the heart—we put it a little way down the stream, down in the outward life, where we expect to see the fruit. But you inquire, "Shall we not give attention to the outward life? reprove sin of every kind, and enforce rules for the regulation of the outward conduct?" Certainly; but the way to do that effectually is to get the heart right, to have "the cruse of salt cast into the spring," and heal the fountain. A corrupt fountain will send forth a corrupt stream. "An evil tree will bring forth evil fruit." If the fountain be pure the stream will be pure, "and there shall not be from thence any more death or barren land." 2 Kings ii, 21. "A good tree bringeth forth good fruit," but any outward fruitfulness which does not proceed from the healthy sap of grace in the soul is of the mock-orange stamp — worthless — or any exuberance of outward fruit beyond the proportion of inward sap will require such a wide circulation of the sap over so extensive a surface of half-dead branches, that it can bring forth but little fruit to perfection.

If the inward life exists in the soul, there will be no difficulty in regulating its outward appropriate manifestation. If that is lacking, every thing else is utterly unavailing. "I may speak with the tongues of men and of angels; I may have the gift of prophecy, and understand all mysteries and all knowledge; and may have all faith, so that I could remove mountains; I may give all my goods to feed the poor, and give my body to be burned, and yet all these will be but as sounding brass or a tinkling cymbal, and profit me nothing, unless I have the love of God shed abroad in my heart by the Holy Ghost given unto me."

"But how shall we get the sinner's heart right unless we begin on the outside, and convince him of his sins by setting them in dark array before him, and teach him how to overcome them, and seek Christ in trying to lead a new life?" A general, in storming a city, do n't stop to demolish every house and shanty on his way, much less to discuss questions pertaining to the municipal government of the city after he shall have taken it. Such things, however important in their place, are entirely out of order at such a time. They would divert attention from the main question of the day; consume the time on the proper use of which the victory depends, and probably result in a shameful defeat, instead of a glorious conquest. His one business is first to force a breach through the walls, and batter down as many obstructions as are necessary to give him a passage to the citadel, upon which he impetuously rushes with all his concentrated force, and carries it by storm. Having got possession of the city, he can then demolish, and build up, and regulate its government as occasion may require.

In storming a sinner's heart, my brother, heave away with the battering-ram of legal thunder till you force a breach. Do n't stop then to talk of the number and comparative turpitude of his sins, nor to introduce questions of orthodoxy or rules of holy living, but rush for the citadel—the conscience and will—and having taken that, the poor sinner will feel that the smallest sin he ever committed involves the death penalty, and what he called his good works are but "filthy rags." Then—to change the application of the figure—run with him, and show him how to flee the wrath to come, to escape the pursuing avenger, to rush into the kingdom of heaven—"the kingdom of heaven suffereth violence, and the violent take it by force." These, my brother, are but faint glimpses of those potent laws manifest in apostolic preaching, which I have denominated the law of direct appeal to the heart, and the law of direct approach to Christ.

I had a talk with aunt Ellen, some months ago, on this subject. Her hobby, you know, is plainness of dress, and she is so thoroughly posted on all the authorities on the subject, from St. Paul down, that it is no use for any body to try to oppose her, should they desire to do so. She is so strict and sensitive on the subject, that the preacher who came along wearing a satin vest, or a gold watch, or preacher's wife wearing a silk dress, had to listen to a sermon on dress they never would forget. Aunt Ellen, too, though a merchant's wife, is herself an example of plainness, and so unquestionably pious, that her words have great weight, but she talks so much on that one subject, that a person in her company can scarcely think of any thing else.

The day of our little discussion we were traveling on horseback through the woodlands from her house to grandma's. Before we got out of sight of home she introduced her favorite theme, and urged me to exert my power toward arresting the progress of pride and extravagance of dress, which were destroying the vitality of the Church, and reducing thousands of families to bankruptcy.

I was too nearly of her mind as to the enormity of the evil to admit of a dispute on the main question, but I ventured to say, that by harping on that one question, or any other pertaining to the outward life, so much, there was danger of exciting the prejudices of the persons we wish to benefit against us, so as to weaken our influence over them for good, and by making a secondary question so prominent, we might divert their attention from the vital thing of looking unto Jesus, and defeat our designs by our well-meant but misdirected zeal.

"O, brother T.," she replied, "none of the commands of God are of secondary importance. The Scriptures positively prohibit 'the putting on of gold and costly apparel,' and there is no danger of dealing too severely with sin."

I admit that every thing in the Scriptures is important, and should be carried into practical effect according to the design of the Lawgiver, but some things even in the Scriptures are more important than others. St. Paul enumerates a great many important things which we may possess, and yet be destitute of the most important thing—the inward life—the love of God in the heart. All besides profit us nothing. To produce a sound outward reformation, we must give special attention to the essential thing of getting the heart right. Gain access to the heart by some means; begin inside and work outward, instead of spending all our time in vainly trying to correct outward evils while the fountain remains impure.

One-ideaism, which is a dangerous form of fanaticism, whether it pertain to plainness of dress, or temperance, or any theological dogma—no matter how valuable in itself—almost invariably becomes so pertinacious as to divert attention from every thing else, and taking hold only on the outward life, either in reproving and trying to correct certain evils, or in the endless discussion of some dogmatical question, its effect upon the vital question of looking unto Jesus, the author and finisher of our faith, is decidedly bad. In constantly obtruding your one idea upon persons, you begin on the outside—raise the points of disagreement first—strike the discords of their souls, and thus excite their dread or hate, so that you can not lead them to Christ as you might otherwise do.

After some talk further on both sides of the question, aunt Ellen said in a surprise, "Brother T., which way are we going? We have got into the wrong path. How did we come to miss the way? Did you see where we turned off?"

"No, aunt," I replied, "my attention was occupied with the subject of our talk, and I took no notice of which way we were going. That, too, is just in accordance with my position—draw off the mind in endless discussions about secondary matters, and we are sure to get out of the path."

"Come, brother T.," she replied, "you must not be too hard with me till we get out of the woods."

On we went till, coming to a road, we met a colored man driving a wagon and team.

"Uncle Daniel," said aunt, "can you tell me the way to mother's?"

"Yes, missus; jis down dar de road crosses and go up dat ridge."

"How far is it, uncle Daniel, to where the road crosses?"

"O, jis down in dat holler. I show you." So the

kind-hearted fellow jumped off his horse and ran to show us the way.

As we passed along, said I, "Uncle Daniel, are you acquainted with Jesus?"

"O yes, bless de Lord, I knows Jesus any whars."

"How long since you got acquainted with Jesus?"

"O, praise de Lord, I knows him for years."

"How do you like him, uncle Daniel?"

"O, I likes him first-rate. He de best friend to poor colored man yet."

"He improves on acquaintance, do n't he?"

"O yes, glory to King Jesus, I loves him better and better."

"Good-by, uncle Daniel."

"O, mus' you go?"

"Yes, uncle Daniel, I must go; but we 'll meet again 'right early in the morning;' we 'll shake hands again on the 'other side of the river.' Will you meet me, uncle Daniel?"

"O yes, glory to King Jesus, I meets you up dar in de morning."

Said aunt Ellen, as we passed up the ridge, "Brother T., the colored people about here think you are more than mortal."

"Well, now, aunt Ellen, I did not think of it during my little talk with uncle Daniel, but it strikes me that this is another wayside illustration of my argument. If I had commenced on the outside of that colored man, and struck a discordant note or two to begin with, I could not have reached his heart in an hour, perhaps not at all; but I commenced on the inside of the colored brother, raised a few points of agreement, and see how the flood-tide of his heart's emotions flowed out. I could now tell him in all plainness, as a brother, whatever I should find within him, or in his conduct, contrary to the spirit of the Gospel, with the confident hope of correcting his irregularities. A foolish fondness for superfluities of dress and other forms of extravagance, and many other things in the Church, ought to be reproved and removed; but there is a right way and a wrong way to go about it. If you can not accomplish it by what I believe to be the Gospel mode, which I have been advocating, I am clearly of the opinion that you never will by any other mode. I am as much in favor of amputating the diseased members of the body as you can be, but we should always consult the inward strength and vitality of the patient, and use the knife as promptly as the sufferer can bear it without too great a hazard of life."

Aunt Ellen, without changing her views of plainness—a thing I did not wish her to do—admitted that she had not pursued the more excellent way in presenting and pressing her cause, and promised, in the future, to begin on the points of agreement, gain access to the heart, conduct that heart to Christ, and in the light of the cross, and by the purifying blood of sprinkling, reveal and remove the evils of the outward life.

LETTER XIV.

THE MASTER'S MODEL.

My Dear Brother,—In elaborating and illustrating what I believe to be the leading characteristics of the model preacher's mode of preaching the Gospel, though I have been somewhat lengthy in drawing them out in their practical application to the demands of the present times, I designed my treatment of the subject to be rather suggestive than exhaustive. I know I have not exhausted my theme, and feel incapable of doing it justice; I hope I have not exhausted your patience. While I have in part proved from divine and apostolic precedent the various essential elements of my model as I proceeded with the discussion, it remains for me now to bring out its different parts in their symmetrical combination, and compare the model as a whole with the Gospel standard; and then, in conclusion, to show, as far as my space will allow, by specimen extracts from some of the most popular pulpit orators of different centuries, that the success of the embassadors of Christ, from the call of the apostles down to the present period, has depended on their conformity to their Master's model, and that their success in moving the masses, and preaching the Gospel effectively, has been exactly proportionate to the *degree* of their conformity to it.

The leading characteristics, then, of the great Teacher's model are:

    I. CLEARNESS.
    II. EARNESTNESS.
    III. NATURALNESS.
    IV. LITERALNESS.
    V. APPROPRIATENESS, or a wise adaptation of truth to the living subject.

I need not here repeat my definition of these essential elements of pulpit power. I might have added the *unction of the Spirit* as a distinct point, but I have taken the ground that the unction of the Spirit must pervade the whole to give them efficiency in leading sinners to Christ, and then at last perform the work of applying the remedy and saving the soul.

The Holy Spirit needs, and hence employs, human instrumentality in the great business of soul-saving, but the saving effect can only be secured by the omnipotent strength of the holy Trinity. "It is God that justifieth." "It is Christ that died, yea, rather, that is risen again, who is even at the right hand of God, who also maketh intercession for us." It is the Holy Spirit that "convinces the sinner of sin," "works in him both to will and to do of his good pleasure," makes "him free from the law of sin and death," delivers him from the power of darkness, and "translates him into the kingdom" of Jesus, and finally seals him "unto the day of redemption," and then "quickens the mortal bodies" of the saints, and resurrects them in the likeness of their risen Savior.

The love of God the Father is, therefore, the originating cause of our salvation—"God so loved the world that he gave his only-begotten Son."

The atoning sacrifice of Christ is the meritorious cause. "We have redemption through his blood, even the forgiveness of sins."

The present energy of the Holy Ghost is the efficient appropriating cause. These combined forces of God the Father, God the Son, and God the Holy Ghost coöperate with the instrumental cause involved in the model I have given, and with all other moral appliances God is pleased to employ in the world. No power short of the omnipotence of the holy Trinity can save a soul from death, and yet we are by Divine appointment "workers together with God" in this business; therefore, my brother, "study to show thyself approved unto God, a workman that needeth not to be ashamed, rightly dividing the word of truth."

"The pattern given us on the holy mount"—the model I have presented—is the only one you need to work by, for all the characteristics defining that model are clearly and directly manifested in every example recorded of divine and apostolic teaching. If an exception there be to this remark, it is in *naturalness*, which, pertaining principally to manner, we have to gather mainly by implication. We know that the honest simplicity of Jesus and his apostles would not in any case permit affectation. Needless formality and unnatural stiffness in gestures or intonations are equally inconsistent with their character and calling. And from the social habits of the God-man, his familiar intercourse with the people of all classes, and the effect of his preaching upon them, we are warranted in the conclusion that his naturalness of gesture, tones of voice, forms of expression, every thing, were perfect. The direct appeals to the heart, and simple touches that intersperse the Savior's discourses, and, indeed, the spirit, tone, and attendant circumstances of every discourse, all bear testimony to the perfection of his naturalness.

The apostles, doubtless, adopted his model, and clearly manifest all its characteristics in their Gospel ministrations. The matter of their discourses differs from that of the Savior's in that, while he preached the Gospel in its incipiency, they added the startling facts of the crucifixion, resurrection, and ascension of their Lord, and the descent of the Holy Ghost, with the signs following, and preached the Gospel in its full development.

Jesus built the Gospel arch, and by his death prepared the keystone, which, after his resurrection, he fitted in its place, binding the whole arch. The Holy Spirit descended and cleared away the scaffolding and rubbish, and reflected the divine glory upon it, and anointed his embassadors, according to the promise contained in the last words of their ascending Sovereign, to go forth as "witnesses of these things throughout Judea, and Samaria, and Galilee, and to the uttermost parts of the earth," "to preach the Gospel to every creature," and invite a world of sinners lost to enter through this "new and living way" into the Eden of love to the tree of life, and obtain inheritance among the sanctified in heaven.

When you familiarize your mind, my brother, with the points I have named contained in the Savior's model, you will see them standing out so prominently in every recorded sermon in the Bible that I need hardly make another selection from the book in proof or illustration of their correctness; and yet I may be permitted to hold up my model by the light of a few more specimens of Gospel sermonizing, that you may see more clearly its conformity to the divine pattern. I do not propose to introduce any new mode, but simply to define and bring more clearly to light the good old mode that worked so well eighteen hundred years ago.

Once when Jesus was preaching, "Behold a certain lawyer stood up and tempted him, saying, Master, what shall I do to inherit eternal life?" The Master, to test his knowledge of the moral law, and to commit him to that standard—it is no use to argue with a man unless he will subscribe to some test-standard—proposed to him this question: "What is written in the law? how readest thou? And he, answering, said, Thou shalt love the Lord thy God with all thy heart, and with all thy soul, and with all thy strength, and with all thy mind, and thy neighbor as thyself. And he said unto him, Thou hast answered right; this do, and thou shalt live. But he, willing to justify himself, said unto Jesus, And who is my neighbor?" If Jesus had produced an abstract argument to prove that his neighbors were not confined to his own sect, the Jewish Church, but also embraced the members of other nations, he might have argued for an hour without getting the lawyer to concede a single point. If he had said to the legal gentleman, "A Samaritan is your neighbor," he would have taken it as an insult. What! a dog my neighbor? But the wise Teacher brought out the point of his argument with irresistible force by a simple literal illustration, saying, "A certain man went down from Jerusalem to Jericho, and fell among thieves, which stripped him of his raiment, and wounded him, and departed, leaving him half dead." The attention of every hearer was wide awake now to hear about the tragedy on that dangerous road. (But what had that to do with the question?) "And by chance there came down a priest that way." Ah! he will help his poor bleeding brother. No. "When he saw him he passed by on the other side." (A surprise.) "And likewise a Levite, when he was at the place, came and looked on him." Ah! the sight will affect his heart, and he will pity and help his dying brother. Nay; he turned his back upon him, "and passed by on the other side." (Another surprise.) "But a certain Samaritan, as he journeyed, came where he was." Ah! there is such relentless hate existing between the Jews and Samaritans that he will show him no mercy. If his own brethren will not even speak a word of comfort to his dying ears, we may expect his enemy to give him a kick as he passes, and mutter malicious satisfaction over his downfall. Nay: "When the Samaritan saw him he had compassion on him, and went to him, and bound up his wounds, pouring in oil and wine, and set him on his own beast, and brought him to an inn, and took care of him. And on the morrow, when he departed, he took out two pence and gave them to the host, and said unto him, Take care of him, and whatsoever thou spendest more, when I come again I will repay thee." The greatest surprise of all; for though hated as a dog by the Jews, he did not simply say, "I'm sorry for thee, my friend;" nor, "Here's a penny, and if every body else will do as much for thee, thou wilt do well." Nay, he did for him every thing that he needed—was physician and nurse; put him on his own horse, and walked along side and held him on; did not send him off to some alms-house or charity-hospital, but took him to the inn, and watched with him that night till he saw him out of danger, and became responsible for his board at the hotel till he should entirely recover. Then inquired Jesus of the lawyer, "Which, now, of these three, thinkest thou, was neighbor unto him that fell among the thieves? And he said, He that showed mercy on him"—an admission from the lawyer that even a Samaritan was a neighbor. "Then said Jesus unto him, Go and do thou likewise"—be a neighbor, not to your own people simply, but to all men—not to friends only, but to enemies.

Do you not see, my brother, the clearness, the earnestness, the naturalness, the literalness, and appropriateness of this specimen of the Savior's preaching? You may select any other example you please, and the result will be the same.

Take an example of apostolic preaching: Peter preached to vast multitudes in Solomon's porch. He had a literal illustration of his subject in the person of the lame man, who had just been healed at the beautiful gate of the temple. He had "leaped, and walked, and praised God," till the audience, drawn together by his shouts, "were filled with wonder and amazement at that which had happened unto him."

Peter's sermon on the occasion is thus reported by Dr. Luke: "Ye men of Israel, why marvel ye at this? or why look ye so earnestly on us, as though by our own power or holiness we had made this man to walk? The God of Abraham, and of Isaac, and of Jacob, the God of our fathers [he begins with the points of agreement] hath glorified his Son Jesus, whom ye delivered up, and denied him in the presence of Pilate, when he was determined to let him go. But ye denied the Holy One and the Just, and desired a murderer to be granted unto you; and killed the Prince of life, whom God hath raised from the dead; whereof we are witnesses." Great principles and arguments couched in *literal facts* versus *abstract* principles, terms, and theories. "And his name, through faith in his name, hath made this man strong, whom ye see and know: yea, the faith which is by him hath given him this perfect soundness in the presence of you all." Plain dealing that. It would be well to strike another chord of mutual sympathy now between people and preacher, lest the repulsion should drive them away from him. Peter understood that, and continues in great tenderness, "And now, brethren, I wot that through ignorance ye did it, as did also your rulers." But still ye did not defeat the purpose of God concerning the sacrifice of his Son. "But those things which God before had shewed by the mouth of all his prophets, that Christ should suffer, he hath so fulfilled. Repent ye, therefore, and be converted, that your sins may be blotted out, when the times of refreshing shall come from the presence of the Lord. And he shall send Jesus Christ, which before was preached unto you; whom the heaven must receive till the times of restitution of all things, which God hath spoken by the mouth of all his holy prophets since the world began. For Moses truly said unto the fathers, A prophet shall the Lord your God raise up unto you of your brethren, like unto me; him shall ye hear in all things whatsoever he shall say unto you. And it shall come to pass, that every soul which will not hear that prophet shall be destroyed from among the people. Yea, and all the prophets from Samuel, and those that follow after, as many as have spoken, have likewise foretold of these days." Would it not be well to strike another chord of mutual sympathy, and draw the people a little closer to the preacher? O, yes; the preacher, though his earnest zeal swept like

Niagara, had a heart full of love, and understood his business, and continues, "Ye are the children of the prophets, and of the covenant which God made with our fathers, saying unto Abraham, And in thy seed shall all the kingdoms of the earth be blessed. Unto you first, God having raised up his Son Jesus, sent him to bless you, in turning away every one of you from his iniquities."

Though he dealt so plainly, he held the people to the last; but "the priests, and the captain of the temple, and the Sadducees, came upon them, being grieved that they taught the people, and preached through Jesus the resurrection from the dead. And they laid hands on them, and put them in hold till the next day; for it was now eventide." "Howbeit, many of them which heard the word believed." Ah, that sermon did execution among the sinners, and yet our reporter do n't make a great noise over it, as though it was an extraordinary thing. It was just what their faith in the mighty Gospel anticipated.

Well, Dr. Luke, how "many of them which heard the word believed?"

"The number of the men was about five thousand."

Amazing! Why, in these days of modern improvements, if we get one hundred converted during a month's hard labor, we think we have done a wonderful business, and publish the news all over the continent.

The next day Peter and John, accompanied by their living literal illustration of Gospel power, stood before the Sanhedrim, and Peter, in his defense, preached the Gospel to them. "When they had set them in the midst," says Dr. Luke, "they asked, By what power, or by what name have ye done this?

"Then Peter, filled with the Holy Ghost, said unto them, Ye rulers of the people, and elders of Israel, if we this day be examined of the good deed done to the impotent man"—he "pleaded guilty" to a "good deed"—"by what means he is made whole: be it known unto you all, and to all the people of Israel, that by the name of Jesus Christ of Nazareth, whom ye crucified, whom God raised from the dead, even by him doth this man stand here before you whole. This is the stone which was set at naught of your builders, which is become the head of the corner. Neither is there salvation in any other; for there is none other name under heaven given among men, whereby we must be saved. Now, when they saw the boldness of Peter and John, and perceived that they were unlearned and ignorant men, they marveled"—if they were so ignorant, why did not some of their learned doctors put in a rejoinder, that would confound and silence them?—"and they took knowledge of them, that they had been with Jesus." Yes, and they were graduates in the school of Christ. "And beholding the man which was healed standing with them, they could say nothing against it." Finding that they had so bad a cause, they commanded the sheriff to take the men out of court, till the judges could hold a consultation; and when they had gone "aside out of the council, they conferred among themselves, saying, What shall we do with these men? for that indeed a notable miracle hath been done by them, is manifest to all them that dwell in Jerusalem; and we can not deny it. But that it spread no further among the people, let us straightly threaten them, that they speak henceforth to no man in this name. And they called them, and commanded them not to speak at all nor teach in the name of Jesus. But Peter and John answered and said unto them, Whether it be right in the sight of God to hearken unto you more than unto God, judge ye. For we can not but speak the things which we have seen and heard. So, when they had further threatened them, they let them go, finding nothing how they might punish them, because of the people: for all men glorified God for that which was done. For the man was above forty years old on whom this miracle of healing was showed."

The preacher's *clearness*, in both the specimens just given, shines out luminously in his terms, propositions, arguments, proofs—in the directness of his appeals of application—every thing. His *earnestness* was that of a devoted hero who had a life to lay down for his cause, not on the altar of ambition, but on the altar of human redemption, on which his divine Master, "who for the joy that was set before him"—the joy of saving perishing sinners—poured out his heart's blood; no worldly honors taken into the account, but love, all-conquering love to God and man, constituted the motive power that carried him with resistless energy over the combined forces of earth and hell; and yet his earnestness, in the impetuosity of its flow, did not destroy his *naturalness,* and his *literalness* stands out in every word. He did not need in that case to multiply literal figures to arrest attention, or to illustrate his subject; he had a literal figure in the person of the happy man, healed of his impotency, standing up before his audience, a living illustration of Gospel power—St. Paul was fond of such illustrations, and called them "living epistles known and read of all men"—but his facts were of the most definite, personal, literal character—nothing abstract, nor ambiguous, nor redundant; and his *wise adaptation of truth to the hearers* is seen in the effect produced. He struck the chords of mutual sympathy, to begin with, and restruck them as often as necessary, to draw the people within reach of his Gospel sword, and also strikingly exemplified what I have called the laws of direct appeal to the heart and of direct approach to Christ—no irrelevancy, no unnecessary circumlocution, nor formality. With means perfectly adapted to the end, he plied them, by the power of the Holy Spirit, with definiteness, promptness, and efficiency. He was a preacher after the model of his Master.

"And Peter and John, after their release, went to their own company, and reported all that the chief priests and elders had said unto them." The company of disciples immediately engaged in a prayer meeting, and returned thanks to God. Dr.

Luke has reported a specimen of their prayers, which is marked by the same clearness, earnestness, naturalness, literalness, and appropriateness which characterized their preaching.

Naturalness in prayer is not the familiar colloquial style common in addressing an equal or an inferior. Such a style would be very unnatural in pleading for the life of a criminal at the bar, or in presenting a petition to a sovereign, and such addressed to God grates very irreverently on my ear. Judah's style, in pleading his cause before the governor of Egypt, was doubtless perfectly natural, and yet it was very different from his address to his father.

The law of naturalness which I have in part illustrated, applying to every kind of address to God or men, does not tie us down to any set of tones or forms. Its manifestations vary with the heart's emotions, and are regulated by the law of appropriateness, indicated by the circumstances of the occasion, and the instincts of common-sense.

Carefully examine this specimen of prayer: "And when they heard that, they lifted up their voice to God with one accord, and said, Lord, thou art God, which hast made heaven, and earth, and the sea, and all that in them is: who, by the mouth of thy servant, hast said, Why did the heathen rage, and the people imagine vain things? The kings of the earth stood up, and the rulers were gathered together against the Lord, and against his Christ. For of a truth against thy holy child Jesus, whom thou hast anointed, both Herod, and Pontius Pilate, with the Gentiles, and the people of Israel, were gathered together, for to do whatsoever thy hand and thy counsel determined before to be done. And now, Lord, behold their threatenings: and grant unto thy servants, that with all boldness they may speak thy word, by stretching forth thine hand to heal; and that signs and wonders may be done by the name of thy holy child Jesus. And when they had prayed, the place was shaken where they were assembled together; and they were filled with the Holy Ghost, and they spake the word of God with boldness."

No abstract generalizing in that prayer; no stereotyped quotations, thrown in to fill up or to ornament the performance; no prayer for every body in general and nobody in particular; no stiff formality. It was profoundly reverent, yet simple, natural, clear, earnest, literal, and well-timed in every particular, and brought down the power. In a revival I always put the new converts to praying in public as early as practicable; because, having learned no form of prayer, and having adopted no stiff, unnatural, inappropriate modes, they come right to the subject, and in all simplicity pray with personal definiteness for their brothers, and sisters, and friends, and ask directly for "whatsoever they desire."

I once conducted a revival in Virginia, and organized a large class, in a new field, where there was not one old member to furnish a stereotyped formula for the young soldiers to work by, and hence they all talked and prayed in appropriate simplicity, which seldom ever failed to wake my heart's emotions, and waked up all saints and sinners who attended our meetings. It is a great thing to have fathers and mothers in Israel, if they can truthfully be called "nursing fathers and mothers," who can develop the growing powers of the babes in Christ, and not wrap them up like Egyptian mummies in the swaddling bands of lifeless forms and stiff, unnatural modes.

An old fellow, by the name of Ratcliff, was converted at a meeting I held once, and when he went to class the first time, never having heard any one speak in class, and being called on at the opening of the meeting to state his experience, he arose and told it just as it was, and sat down. The next one that spoke closed in the old way, "Remember me at a throne of grace when it goes well with you, that I may be kept faithful till death, and at last receive a crown of life." Brother Ratcliff listened attentively till the last sentence closed, and sprang to his feet, saying, "I declare, brothers and sisters, I forgot that, but any of you, when it goes well with you, please to remember me in your prayers, that I may be kept faithful till death, and also get a crown of life."

You observe, my brother, that while the essential elements of power embraced in the Gospel model for preaching, are definite, and invariably successful in the results of their application, they are so general as not to tie us down to any set of forms, but are like the Gospel itself, equally well adapted to all ages, all countries, all languages, and all the natural and moral varieties of human kind. Nor do they require that all persons should pursue the same plan for presenting and enforcing truth. One may be naturally adapted to excel in argument, another in exhortation, another in illustration. All the diversity of gifts found in the Church, both in the ministry and in the laity, may, in all their variety, be directed and effectively applied by this model.

St. Paul, to-day, would be "made all things to all men, that by all means he might save some," with the same facility of adaptation that he exhibited eighteen hundred years ago.

The great Teacher, who always adapted his illustrations to the occasion and to the condition of his hearers, would to-day, on the same principles which characterize his model, illustrate his sermons by every striking, familiar object of these times—railroads, steamships, telegraphs—every familiar thing which he could lay under contribution to convey Gospel truth to the heart, and fix it on the memory of his hearers.

The Gospel, with the divinely-instituted mode of proclaiming it, should produce the same saving effect to-day that it did when preached by St. Peter.

The miracle-working power of that day gave them an advantage that we do not enjoy; but the cumulative fruits of the effectual working of the Spirit in the salvation of successive millions ought to make up fully for our deficiency in that particular, for the power of the Holy Ghost in raising dead souls, creating them anew in Christ Jesus, is much greater than the power necessary to raise dead bodies. Jesus, on one occasion, sent out his apostles two and two, on a missionary tour, and when on their return, in presenting their report, they spoke of the miracle-working power which they had been enabled to exercise, saying, "Even the devils are subject unto us;" to which he replied, "Rejoice not at this, but rather rejoice that your names are written in heaven"—teaching them that to have their names written in heaven was much more a matter of rejoicing than the power to work miracles. The regenerating, sanctifying, sealing power of the Spirit is as available now as then. The power to work miracles was but incidental to this, and would still be continued as manifestly as ever, were it necessary to the great purpose of saving the world; but their perpetuation visibly to the observation of men would have classed them long ago with other marvelous things, as the result of some uniform law of nature, and would thus have defeated the very object for which they were instituted. But all the exhaustless resources of Gospel grace, in all their saving power, are just as available now for the salvation of the world, as they were under the preaching of St. Paul.

If you will take the Savior's model for preaching, my brother, and carefully review the history of the Church, you will find that the success of God's ministers has always been proportionate to the degree of their comformity to it.

Why was it that Whitefield had such power over the masses, and preached the Gospel with such success? Because, as a man of great natural force, and called of God to the work of the ministry, he conformed to the Master's model. He had clearness—a clear conception of his points, arguments, and illustrations, and hence presented them clearly. He had earnestness—a soul of fire, thrilled with "the burden of the Lord" to perishing sinners, and the tidings of mercy for stricken hearts. He had naturalness. He used to say that he talked to the people in their "market language." He had literalness. He brought great Gospel principles to light through literal facts and figures, and had but little to do with metaphysics in the pulpit. He wisely adapted the truth to the condition of his hearers.

The same is true of Wesley. He had greater clearness than Whitefield, equal earnestness of soul, though less physical force and vehemence of manner. He also possessed an equal degree of naturalness and literalness. Wesley used many literal figures of illustration, but more literal facts. Metaphysical abstractions in the pulpit were out of the question in his ministry. His wise adaptation of truth to the occasion and circumstances of his hearers was a leading feature of his preaching.

Summerfield is another example. That is the secret of Spurgeon's success. "O, but is he not a high-toned Calvinist? And does he not run into a great many extravagant eccentricities of style?" I admit all that, and reply, If with these defects his approximate conformity to the Savior's model give him so much pulpit power, what would he not accomplish were his conformity so perfect as to remove all these defects?

James Caughey is another example. "Ah, but he can't preach." Yet his efforts in trying to preach embrace the essential elements of power contained in the Savior's model; and if they secure such wonderful success in soul-saving by the ministry of a man who "can't preach," as no other man in modern days can claim, what might not some of our learned D. D.'s, who can preach, accomplish if they but conformed to the Gospel model?

Henry Ward Beecher is another example. Though not so successful in saving sinners as the others I have mentioned, yet he conforms to the model sufficiently to give him extraordinary power over the masses, and is, I believe, accomplishing a good work.

John B. Gough, as a temperance lecturer, is a good illustration of the truth of my position. Listen to one of his master-speeches, and you will say, "Clearness, earnestness, naturalness, literalness, and appropriateness constitute the essential and sole elements of his power."

A great many preachers have a considerable degree of clearness, and a still greater degree of earnestness, and hence have great power, and accomplish much good, for these are essential elements of power, as before shown; but they, being defective in naturalness and literalness, wield perhaps but half the power for good their capacity and position would warrant, were their naturalness and literalness equal to their clearness and earnestness. Some have a degree of all these characteristics of the great model, and in the same proportion they have power. Any single one of those elements will give a man power; all of them, in any considerable degree, will constitute what is called "a man of mark." I suppose that means a man who is "making his mark" in the world.

These rules do not apply exclusively to ministers alone, but to witnesses of Jesus in all their variety.

It is said that a celebrated minister prepared and preached a course of sermons against infidelity for the purpose specially of convincing and bringing over to Christianity an intelligent infidel neighbor, who was a regular attendant at his Church. Just after the close of the said series of sermons, the infidel professed to experience religion, and the preacher was anxious to know which of his sermons did the execution.

Soon after the new convert, in relating his experience, said: "The instrument God was pleased to use for my awakening and conversion was not the preaching of those sermons against infidelity, but the simple remark of a poor old colored woman. In going down the steps of the church one night, seeing that the poor old woman was lame, I gave her my hand, and assisted her.

"She looked up at me with a peculiar expression of grateful pleasure, saying, 'Thank you, sir. Do you love Jesus, my blessed Savior?'

"I was dumb. I could not answer that question.

"She said 'Jesus, my blessed Savior,' with so much earnest confidence, that I could not deny that she had a blessed Savior, and felt ashamed to confess that I did not love him. I could not dismiss the subject from my mind, and the more I thought of it the clearer my convictions became that the old colored sister had a Jesus, a blessed Savior; and I thought of how kind a Savior he must be to impart such joy and comfort to such poor, neglected creatures as she was; and I soon began to weep over my base ingratitude in denying and rejecting such a Savior. I earnestly sought that Savior, and found him; and now I can say, I do love Jesus, my blessed Savior."

In that simple remark of the old colored woman there was clearness of faith, a joyous confidence that shook the foundation of the infidel's refuge of lies. It had earnestness in it. The old sister was very grateful for a small favor, and very solicitous about the soul of the kind stranger. You may be sure there was naturalness in it; and as for its literalness, the address was personal, the question was personal, her testimony to having a Jesus her Savior was personal and real—nothing indefinite or abstract about it; and the Holy Spirit gave the whole an appropriateness of appli cation which knocked the underpinning out of his infidel fort, and the walls that withstood the "great guns" of the preacher tumbled down as suddenly as the walls of Jericho at the blast of the rams' horns.

George W., a strong Cincinnati lawyer, attended a revival meeting held by Rev. H. Hayes, a friend of mine, for the avowed purpose of showing up the fallacy of revealed religion, but before the meeting closed George was powerfully converted to God.

Brother Hayes had fired his Gospel gun at him a number of times, and thought he had hit him. All were desirous to know the instrumentality God had used in his conversion.

There was at the meeting a man called "Bud Thomas," who was but one remove above an idiot, but was very pious, and lived round among the people.

George, in relating the circumstances of his awakening, said: "I attended this meeting several days as a confirmed infidel, but at the love-feast, when I heard 'Bud Thomas' talk with so much clearness and confidence about his mother in heaven, and how she used to pray for her poor, afflicted boy, and how much he loved Jesus, and of his bright hopes of meeting his dear mother in heaven, I wept, and I saw in his simple experience the truth and beauty of religion with such clearness that my infidelity went like the mist of the morning before the rising sun."

I mention these cases simply to show,

1. That, while the Holy Spirit often uses the most simple means, he always uses appropriate means, con-

taining some or all of the elements of power so manifest in the model of Jesus.

2. That, while literary education is all-important, there are very many who, in their literary wisdom, overlook the simple, essential elements of power on which their success depends.

3. That, while willful ignorance is a sin, the most illiterate should not be discouraged in trying to be a witness for Jesus, and a worker together with God in the great business of saving the world, seeing he often uses the weak things of this world to confound the mighty by the wonderful success with which he crowns their simple efforts.

It was my design to furnish you with a specimen sermon from each of the most celebrated preachers of different ages; but I now find that my space will not admit of many entire sermons, and I must content myself with giving a few specimen extracts from the sermons of some of the most remarkable preachers of different periods of the history of the Church, to show that, in a considerable degree, they conformed to the Master's model, and to establish at least a clear presumption that their success was consequent on that fact, and proportionate to the degree of their conformity to it.

LETTER XV.

PULPIT ORATORS.

My Dear Brother,—If my space would admit of it, I would like to insert a specimen sermon from each of the most celebrated preachers of ancient and modern times, that you might see that they all, in a considerable degree, conformed to the Savior's model, and to establish a clear presumption, too, that their success depended on that fact, and was proportionate to the degree of their conformity to it, but my space will only allow me to present a few extracts from a small number of the most distinguished preachers. (There is a work, in two octavo volumes, by Rev. Henry C. Fish, published by M. W. Dodd, New York, entitled "Masterpieces of Pulpit Eloquence," which contains one sermon each from the greatest preachers, ancient and modern, from which I select a few extracts.) I will begin with

CHRYSOSTOM.

"John, called, for at least the last twelve centuries, *Chrysostom*—golden-mouthed—was the brightest ornament of the ancient Greek Churches. He was born probably about the year 347, at Antioch, in Syria, where he spent most of his public life, and died on the 14th of September, 407, with his favorite expression on his lips, '*God be praised for every thing.*' For overpowering popular eloquence Chrysostom had no equal among the fathers. He has been called the Homer of orators. Ferrarius quotes Suidas, as saying that Chrysostom had *a tongue flowing like the Nile:* and when he was banished, his people said that 'it were better that the *sun* should cease to shine, than that his mouth should be shut.' Gibbon's testimony to his eloquence—Decline and Fall of the Roman Empire, period 398–403—is worthy of particular note, especially considering its source. Speaking of the various works that remain of this father, the principal of which are about one thousand sermons or homilies, he says they authorize the critics to appreciate his genuine merit: and that they unanimously attribute to him 'the free command of an elegant and copious language; the judgment to conceal the advantages which he derived from the knowledge of rhetoric and philosophy; an inexhaustible fund of metaphors and similitudes, of ideas and images, to vary and illustrate the most familiar topics; the happy art of engaging the passions in the service of virtue; and of exposing the folly as well as the turpitude of vice, almost with the truth and spirit of a dramatic representation.'"

See how the testimony of Gibbon bears on the fact which I assume—that Chrysostom conformed in a most efficient degree to his Master's model. Such testimony is the more valuable in this case, from the fact, that you can have but a very limited idea of a man's preaching from a portion of a single sermon. This remark will apply to all whom I may try to represent by the specimens I may furnish from their published sermons. I presume no man's pulpit power can be fully represented by a printed sermon, and especially when it has been handed down for ages, through different languages.

The subject of the sermon, from which I now present an extract, is

EXCESSIVE GRIEF AT THE DEATH OF FRIENDS.

"But I would not have you to be ignorant, brethren, concerning them which are asleep, that ye sorrow not." 1 Thess. iv, 13.

* * * * * * *

We ought here, at the outset, to inquire why, when he is speaking of Christ, he employs the word *death;* but when he is speaking of our decease he calls it *sleep,* and not *death.* For he did not say, Concerning them that are dead: but what did he say? Concerning them that are asleep. And again, Even so them also which sleep in Jesus will God bring with him. He did not say, Them that have died. Still again, We who are alive and remain unto the coming of the Lord shall not go before them that sleep. Here, too, he did not say, Them that are dead; but a third time bringing the subject to their remembrance, he for the third time called death a sleep. Concerning Christ, however, he did not speak thus: but how? For if we believe that Jesus *died.* He did not say, Jesus slept, but he died. Why now did he use the term *death* in reference to Christ, but in reference to us the term *sleep?* For it was not casually, or negligently, that he employed this expression, but he had a wise and great purpose in so doing. In speaking of Christ, he said *death*, so as to confirm the fact that Christ had actually suffered death; in speaking of us, he said *sleep*, in order to impart consolation. For where a resurrection had already taken place, he mentions death with plainness; but where the resurrection is still a matter of hope, he says *sleep*, consoling us by this very expression, and cherishing our valuable hopes. For he who is only asleep will surely awake; and death is no more than a long sleep.

Say not, a dead man hears not, nor speaks, nor sees, nor is conscious. It is just so with a sleeping person. If I may speak somewhat paradoxically, even the soul of a sleeping person is in some sort asleep; but not so the soul of a dead man; that is awake.

But you say, a dead man experiences corruption, and becomes dust and ashes. And what then, beloved hearers? For this very reason we ought to rejoice. For when a man is about to rebuild an old and tottering house, he first sends out its occupants, then tears it down, and rebuilds anew a more splendid one. This occasions no grief to the occupants, but rather joy; for they do not think of the demolition which they see, but of the house which is to come, though not yet seen. When God is about to do a similar work, he destroys our body, and removes the soul which was dwelling in it as from some house, that he may build it anew and more splendidly, and again bring the soul into it with greater glory. Let us not, therefore, regard the tearing down, but the splendor which is to succeed.

If, again, a man has a statue decayed by rust and age, and mutilated in many of its parts, he breaks it up and casts it into a furnace, and after the melting, he receives it again in a more beautiful form. As then the dissolving in the furnace was not a destruction, but a renewing of the statue, so the death of our bodies is not a destruction, but a renovation. When, therefore, you see us in a furnace, our flesh flowing away to corruption, dwell not on that sight, but wait for the recasting. And be not satisfied with the extent of this illustration, but advance in your thoughts to a still higher point; for the statuary, casting into the furnace a brazen image, does not furnish you in its place a golden and undecaying statue, but again makes a brazen one. God does not thus; but casting in a mortal body formed of clay, he returns to you a golden and immortal statue; for the earth, receiving a corruptible and decaying body, gives back the same, incorruptible and undecaying. Look not, therefore, on the corpse, lying with closed eyes and speechless lips, but on the man that is risen, that has received glory unspeakable and amazing, and direct your thoughts from the present sight to the future hope.

But do you miss his society, and therefore lament and mourn? Now is it not unreasonable, that, if you should have given your daughter in marriage, and her husband should take her to a distant country and should there enjoy prosperity, you would not think the circumstance a calamity, but the intelligence of their prosperity would console the sorrow occasioned by her absence; and yet here, while it is not a man, nor a fellow-servant, but the Lord himself who has taken your relative, that you should grieve and lament?

And how is it possible, you ask, not to grieve, since I am only a man? Nor do I say that you should not grieve: I do not condemn dejection, but the intensity of it. To be dejected is natural; but to be overcome by dejection is madness, and folly, and unmanly weakness. You may grieve and weep, but give not way to despondency, nor indulge in complaints. Give thanks to God, who has taken your friend, that you have the opportunity of honoring the departed one, and of dismissing him with becoming obsequies. If you sink under depression, you withhold honor from the departed, you displease God who has taken him, and you injure yourself; but if you are grateful, you pay respect to him, you glorify God, and you benefit yourself. Weep, as wept your Master over Lazarus, observing the just limits of sorrow, which it is not proper to pass. Thus also said Paul, I would not have you to be ignorant concerning them which are asleep, that ye sorrow not as others who have no hope. Grieve, says he; but not as the Greek, who has no hope of a resurrection, who despairs of a future life.

Believe me, I am ashamed and blush to see unbecoming groups of women pass along the mart, tearing their hair, cutting their arms and cheeks—and all this under the eyes of the Greeks. For what will they not say? What will they not utter concerning us? Are these the men who philosophize about a resurrection? Indeed! How poorly their actions agree with their opinions! In words, they philosophize about a resurrection: but they act just like those who do not acknowledge a resurrection. If they fully believed in a resurrection, they would not act thus; if they had really persuaded themselves that a deceased friend had departed to a better state, they would not thus mourn. These things, and more than these, the unbelievers say when they hear those lamentations. Let us then be ashamed, and be more moderate, and not occasion so much harm to ourselves and to those who are looking on us.

For on what account, tell me, do you thus weep for one departed? Because he was a bad man? You ought on that very account to be thankful, since the occasions of wickedness are now cut off. Because he was good and kind? If so, you ought to rejoice; since he has been soon removed, before wickedness had corrupted him: and he has gone away to a world where he stands ever secure, and there is no room even to mistrust a change. Because he was a youth? For that, too, praise Him that has taken him, because he has speedily called him to a better lot. Because he was an aged man? On this account, also, give thanks and glorify Him that has taken him. Be ashamed of your manner of burial. The singing of psalms, the prayers, the assembling of the spiritual fathers and brethren—all this is not that you may weep, and lament, and afflict yourselves, but that you may render thanks to Him who has taken the departed. For as when men are called to some high office, multitudes with praises on their lips assemble to escort them at their departure to their stations, so do all with abundant praise join to send forward, as to greater honor, those of the pious who have departed. Death is rest, a deliverance from the exhausting labors and cares of this world. When, then, thou seest a relative departing, yield not to despondency; give thyself to reflection; examine thy conscience; cherish the thought that after a little while this end awaits thee also. Be more considerate; let another's death excite thee to salutary fear; shake off all indolence; examine your past deeds; quit your sins, and commence a happy change.

We differ from unbelievers in our estimate of things. The unbeliever surveys the heaven and worships it, because he thinks it a divinity; he looks to the earth and makes himself a servant to it, and longs for the things of sense. But not so with us. We survey the heaven, and admire him that made it; for we believe it not to be a god, but a work of God. I look on the whole creation, and am led by it to the Creator. He looks on wealth, and longs for it with earnest desire; I look on wealth, and contemn it. He sees poverty, and laments; I see poverty, and rejoice. I see things in one light; he in another. Just so in regard to death. He sees a corpse, and thinks of it as a corpse; I see a corpse, and behold sleep rather than death. And as in regard to books, both learned persons and unlearned see them with the same eyes, but not with the same understanding—for to the unlearned the mere shapes of letters appear, while the learned discover the sense that lies within those letters—so in respect to affairs in general, we all see what takes place with the same eyes, but not with the same understanding and judgment. Since, therefore, in all other things we differ from them, shall we agree with them in our sentiments respecting death?

Consider to whom the departed has gone, and take comfort. He has gone where Paul is, and Peter, and the whole company of the saints. Consider how he shall arise, with what glory and splendor. Consider, that by mourning and lamenting thou canst not alter the event which has occurred, and that thou wilt in the end injure thyself.

BISHOP LATIMER.

HUGH LATIMER was born about the year 1480, and on the 16th of October, 1555, was burned alive at the stake, by the decree of bloody Mary, uttering those memorable and truly-prophetic words to his companion in the flames, "*Be of good comfort, brother Ridley, and play the man; we shall this day light such a* candle, by God's grace, in *England*, as, I trust, nev r shall be put out."

His sermons were not learned, and many of his anecdotes and illustrations would not suit the modern taste. But he always insisted on the cardinal doctrine, that justification is not by works, and that Christ, by the one only oblation of his body, sanctified forever those that believe. In *courage*, too, Latimer has never been excelled.

As a *powerful* preacher Latimer has been rarely equaled, and perhaps never excelled. His enemies, "though swelling, blown full, and puffed up, like Æsop's frog, with envy and malice against him," as Bacon has it, returned from hearing him with the words of exaggeration, "Never man spake like this man." His style is lively and cheerful, and though in his sermons we meet with many quaint, odd, and coarse things, yet we every-where discover the traces of his homely wit, his racy manner, his keen observation, his manly freedom, his playful temper, and his simplicity and sincerity of heart. Says a well-known English divine, "If a combination of sound Gospel doctrine, plain Saxon language, boldness, liveliness, directness, and simplicity, can make a preacher, few, I suspect, have ever equaled old Latimer."

It was customary with the preachers of Latimer's day, oftentimes, to seize upon some singular topic to engage the attention of their hearers, which may account for the odd title of the sermon which follows. It was preached in 1548, when Latimer must have been nearly seventy years of age, and, perhaps, in no one of his discourses—of which the very rare extant editions contain forty-five—does the great martyr-preacher appear to better advantage.

SERMON OF THE PLOW.

"For whatsoever things were written aforetime, were written for our learning." Rom. xv, 4.

All things that are written in God's book, in the Bible book, in the book of the holy Scripture, are written to be our doctrine. I told you in my first sermon, honorable audience, that I proposed to declare unto you two things: the one, what seed should be sown in God's field, in God's plow-land; and the other, who should be the sowers.

That is to say, what doctrine is to be taught in Christ's Church and congregation, and what men should be the teachers and preachers of it. The first part I have told you in the three sermons past, in which I have essayed to set forth my plow, to prove what I could do. And now I shall tell you who are the plowers; for God's word is seed to be sown in God's field—that is, the faithful congregation—and the preacher is the sower. And it is said in the Gospel: "He that soweth," the husbandman, the plowman, "went forth to sow his seed." So that a preacher is compared to a plowman, as it is in another place: "No man that putteth his hand to the plow, and looketh back, is apt for the kingdom of God." Luke ix. That it is to say, let no preacher be negligent in doing his office. This is one of the places that has been racked, as I told you of racking Scriptures, and I have been one of them myself that have racked it— I cry God mercy for it; and have been one of them that have believed, and have expounded it against religious persons that would forsake their order which they had professed, and would go out of their cloister; whereas, indeed, it relates not to monkery, nor makes at all for any such matter; but it is directly spoken of diligent preaching of the word of God. For preaching of the Gospel is one of God's plowworks, and the preacher is one of God's plowmen.

Be not offended with my similitude, in that I compare preaching to the labor and work of plowing, and the preacher to a plowman; ye may not be offended with this, my similitude, though I have been unjustly slandered by some persons for such thing. . . . . . But as preachers must be wary and circumspect, that they give not any just occasion to be slandered and ill-spoken of by the hearers, so the auditors must not be offended without cause. For heaven is in the Gospel likened unto a mustard seed: it is compared, also, to a piece of leaven; and Christ saith, that at the last day he will come like a thief; and what dishonor is this to God? Or what derogation is this to heaven? You should not then, I say, be offended with my similitude, because I liken preaching to a plowman's labor, and a prelate to a plowman. But now you will ask me whom I call a prelate? A prelate is that man, whatsoever he is, that has a flock to be taught by him; whosoever has any spiritual charge in the faithful congregation, and whosoever he is that has a cure of souls.

Well may the preacher and the plowman be likened together; first, for their labor at all seasons of the year; for there is no time of the year in which the plowman has not some special work to do; as in my country in Leicestershire, the plowman has a time to set forth, and to assay his plow, and other times for other necessary works to be done. And they also may be likened together for the diversity of works and variety of offices that they have to do. For as the plowman first sets forth his plow, and then tills the land, and breaks it in furrows, and sometimes ridges it up again; and at another time harrows it and clotteth it, and sometimes dungs it and hedges it, digs it and weeds it, and makes it clean; so the prelate, the preacher, has many diverse offices to do. He has first a busy work to bring his parishioners to a right faith, as Paul calleth it; and not a swerving faith, but to a faith that embraces Christ, and trusts to his merits; a lively faith, a justifying faith; a faith that makes a man righteous, without respect of works; as you have it very well declared and set forth in the homily. He has then a busy work, I say, to bring his flock to a right faith, and then to confirm them in the same faith. Now casting them down with the law, and with threatenings of God for sin; now ridging them up again with the Gospel, and with the promises of God's favor. Now weeding them by telling them their faults, and making them forsake sin; now clotting them, by breaking their stony hearts and by making them supple-hearted, and making them to have hearts of flesh; that is, soft hearts, and apt for doctrine to enter in. Now teaching to know God rightly, and to know their duty to God and their neighbors. Now exhorting them when they know their duty, that they do it, and be diligent in it; so that they have a continual work to do. Great is their business, and therefore great should be their hire. They have great labors, and therefore they ought to have good livings, that they may commodiously feed their flock; for the preaching of the word of God unto the people is called meat; Scripture calls it meat; not strawberries, that come but once a year, and tarry not long, but are soon gone; but it is meat, it is not dainties. The people must have meat that is familiar and continual, and daily given unto them to feed upon. Many make a strawberry of it, ministering it but once a year; but such do not the office of good prelates. For Christ saith, "Who think you is a wise and a faithful servant? He that giveth meat in due time." So that he must, at all times convenient, preach diligently; therefore saith he, "Who, think ye, is a faithful servant?" He speaks as though it were a rare thing to find such a one, and as though he should say, there are but few of them to be found in the world. And how few of them there are throughout this realm that give meat to their flock as they should do, the visitors can best tell. Too few, too few, the more is the pity, and never so few as now.

By this then it appears that a prelate, or any that has the cure of souls, must diligently and substantially work and labor. Therefore, saith Paul to Timothy, "He that desireth to have the office of a bishop, or a prelate, that man desireth a good work." Then if it is a good work, it is work; you can make but a work of it. It is God's work, God's plow, and that plow God would have still going. Such then as loiter and live idly are not good prelates, or ministers. And of such as do not preach and teach, and do their duties, God saith by his prophet Jeremy, "Cursed be the man that doth the work of God fraudulently, guilefully, or deceitfully;" some books have it "negligently or slackly." How many such prelates, how many such bishops, Lord, for thy mercy, are there now in England? And what shall we in this case do? shall we company with them? O Lord, for thy mercy! shall we not company with them? O Lord, whither shall we flee from them? But "cursed be he that doth the work of God negligently or guilefully." A sore word for them that are negligent in discharging their office, or have done it fraudulently; for that is the thing which makes the people ill.

But it must be true that Christ saith, "Many are called, but few are chosen." Matt. xxii. Here I have an occasion by the way to say somewhat unto you; yea, for the place that I alleged unto you before out of Jeremy, the forty-eighth chapter. And it was spoken of a spiritual work of God, a work that was commanded to be done, and it was of shedding blood, and of destroying the cities of Moab. For, saith he, "Cursed be he that keepeth back his sword from shedding of blood." As Saul, when he kept back the sword from shedding of blood, at the time he was sent against Amalek, was refused of God for being disobedient to God's commandment, in that he spared Agag the king. So that place of the prophet was spoken of them that went to the destruction of the cities of Moab, among which there was one called Nebo, which was much reproved for idolatry, superstition, pride, avarice, cruelty, tyranny, and hardness of heart; and these sins were plagued of God and destroyed.

Now what shall we say of these rich citizens of London? what shall I say of them? Shall I call them proud men of London, malicious men of London, merciless men of London? No, no, I may not say so; they will be offended with me then. Yet must I speak. For is there not reigning in London as much pride, as much covetousness, as much cruelty, as much oppression, and as much superstition, as there was in Nebo? Yes, I think, and much more too. Therefore, I say, Repent, O London! repent, repent! Thou hearest thy faults told thee; amend them, amend them. I think, if Nebo had had the preaching that thou hast, they would have converted. And you, rulers and officers, be wise and circumspect, look to your charge, and see you do your duties; and rather be glad to amend your ill living than be angry when you are warned or told of your fault. What ado was there made in London at a certain man, because he said—and indeed at that time on a just cause—"Burgesses," quoth he, "nay, butterflies!" What ado there was for that word! and yet would that they were no worse than butterflies! Butterflies do but their nature; the butterfly is not covetous, is not greedy of other men's goods; is not full of envy and hatred, is not malicious, is not cruel, is not merciless. The butterfly glories not in her own deeds, nor prefers the traditions of men before God's word; it commits not idolatry, nor worships false gods. But London can not abide to be rebuked; such is the nature of men. If they are pricked, they will kick; if they are galled, they will wince; but yet they will not amend their faults, they will not be ill spoken of. But how shall I speak well of them? If you would be content to receive and follow the word of God, and favor good preachers, if you could bear to be told of your faults, if you could amend when you hear of them, if you could be glad to reform that which is amiss; if I might see any such inclination in you, that you would leave off being merciless, and begin to be charitable, I would then hope well of you, I would then speak well of you. But London was never so ill as it is now. In times past men were full of pity and compassion, but now there is no pity; for in London their brother shall die in the streets for cold, he shall lie sick at the door, and perish there for hunger. Was there ever more unmercifulness in Nebo? I think not. In times past, when any rich man died in London, they were wont to help the poor scholars of the universities with exhibitions. When any man died, they would bequeath great sums of money toward the relief of the poor. When I was a scholar in Cambridge myself, I heard very good report of London, and knew many that had relief from the rich men of London; but now I hear no such good report, and yet I inquire of it, and hearken for it; but now charity is waxen cold, none helps the scholar nor yet the poor. And in those days, what did they when they helped the scholars? They maintained and gave them livings who were very Papists, and professed the Pope's doctrine: and now that the knowledge of God's word is brought to light, and many earnestly study and labor to set it forth, now hardly any man helps to maintain them.

O, London, London! repent, repent; for I think God is more displeased with London than ever he was with the city of Nebo. Repent, therefore; repent, London, and remember that the same God liveth now that punished Nebo, even the same God, and none other; and he will punish sin as well now as he did then: and he will punish the iniquity of London as well as he did them of Nebo. Amend, therefore. And you that are prelates, look well to your office; for right prelating is busy laboring, and not lording. Therefore, preach and teach, and let your plow be going. Ye lords, I say, that live like loiterers, look well to your office—the plow is your office and charge.

If you live idle and loiter, you do not your duty, you follow not your vocation; let your plow, therefore, be going, and not cease, that the ground may bring forth fruit.

But now methinks I hear one say unto me, "Wot ye what you say? Is it a work? Is it a labor? How, then, hath it happened that we have had for so many hundred years so many unpreaching prelates, lording loiterers, and idle ministers?" You would have me here to make answer, and to show the cause thereof. Nay, this land is not for me to plow—it is too stony, too thorny, too hard for me to plow. They have so many things that make for them, so many things to say for themselves, that it is not for my weak team to plow them. They have to say for themselves long customs, ceremonies, and authority, placing in Parliament, and many things more. And I fear this land is not yet ripe to be plowed; for, as the saying is, it lacketh weathering; it lacketh weathering, at least it is not for me to plow. For what shall I look for among thorns, but pricking and scratching? What among stones, but stumbling? What, I had almost said, among serpents, but stinging? But this much I dare say, that since lording and loitering hath come up, preaching hath come down, contrary to the apostles' time; for they preached and lorded not, and now they lord and preach not. For they that are lords will ill go to plow: it is no meet office for them; it is not seeming for their estate. Thus came up lording loiterers—thus crept in unpreaching prelates, and so have they long continued. For how many unlearned prelates have we now at this day! And no marvel; for if the plowmen that now are were made lords, they would give over plowing; they would leave off their labor and fall to lording outright, and let the plow stand: and then both plows not walking, nothing should be in the commonweal but hunger. For ever since the prelates were made lords and nobles, their plow standeth—there is no work done—the people starve. They hawk, they hunt, they card, they dice, they pastime in their prelacies with gallant gentlemen, with their dancing minions, and with their fresh companions, so that plowing is set aside. And by the lording and loitering, preaching and plowing are clean gone. And thus, if the plowmen of the country were as negligent in their office as prelates are, we should not long live, for lack of sustenance. And as it is necessary to have this plowing for the sustentation of the body, so must we have also the other for the satisfaction of the soul, or else we can not live long spiritually. For as the body wastes and consumes away for lack of bodily meat, so the soul pines away for default of spiritual meat. But there are two kinds of inclosing, to hinder both these kinds of plowing; the one is an inclosing to hinder the bodily plowing, and the other to hinder the holy day plowing—the Church plowing.

The bodily plowing is taken in and inclosed for the gain of individuals. For what man will let go or diminish his private advantage for a commonwealth?

And who will sustain any damage for public benefit? The other plow, also, no man is diligent to set forward, and no man will hearken to it. But to hinder it all men's ears are open; yea, and there are a great many of this kind of plowmen, who are very busy, and would seem to be very good workmen. I fear some are rather mock-gospelers than faithful plowmen. I know many myself that profess the Gospel, and live nothing thereafter. I know them, and have been conversant with some of them. I know them, and I speak it with a heavy heart, there is as little charity and good living in them as in any others, according to that which Christ said in the Gospel to the great number of people that followed him; as though they had an earnest zeal for his doctrine, whereas, indeed, they had it not. "Ye follow me," saith he, "not because ye have seen the signs and miracles that I have done, but because ye have eaten the bread and refreshed your bodies; therefore ye follow me." So that I think many nowadays profess the Gospel for the living's sake, not for the love they bear to God's word. But they that will be true plowmen must work faithfully for God's sake, for the edifying of their brethren. And as diligently as the husbandman ploweth for the sustentation of the body, so diligently must the prelates and ministers labor for the feeding of the soul; both the plows must still be going, as most necessary for man. And wherefore are magistrates ordained, but that the tranquillity of the commonweal may be confirmed, limiting both plows?

But now for the fault of unpreaching prelates, methinks I could guess what might be said for excusing of them. They are so troubled with lordly living—they are so placed in palaces, couched in courts, ruffling in their rents, dancing in their dominions, burdened with embassages, pampering themselves like a monk that maketh his jubilee, and moiling in their gay manors and mansions, and so troubled with loitering in their lordships, that they can not attend it. They are otherwise occupied; some in the King's matters, some are embassadors, some of the privy council, some to furnish the court, some are lords of the Parliament, some are presidents, and some controllers of mints.

Well, well; is this their duty? Is this their office? Is this their calling? Should we have ministers of the Church to be controllers of the mints? Is this a meet office for a priest that hath cure of souls? Is this his charge? I would here ask one question: I would fain know who controlleth the devil at home in his parish, while he controlleth the mint? If the apostles might not leave the office of preaching to the deacons, shall one leave it for minting? I can not tell you; but the saying is, that since priests have been minters, money hath been worse than it was before. And they say that the evilness of money hath made all things dearer. And in this behalf I must speak to England. "Hear, my country, England," as Paul said in his first epistle to the Corinthians, the sixth chapter—for Paul was no sitting bishop, but a walking and a preaching bishop—but when he went from them he left there behind him the plow going still; for he wrote unto them, and rebuked them for going to law, and pleading their causes before heathen judges—"Is there," saith he, "among you no wise man, to be an arbitrator in matters of judgment? What! not one of all that can judge between brother and brother; but one brother goeth to law with another, and that before heathen judges? Appoint those for judges that are most abject and vile in the congregation;" which he speaks to rebuke them; "For," saith he, "I speak it to your shame." So, England, I speak it to thy shame. Is there never a nobleman to be a lord-president but it must be a prelate? Is there never a wise man in the realm to be a controller of the mint? I speak it to your shame. If there be never a wise man, make a water-bearer, a tinker, a cobbler, a slave, a page, controller of the mint: make a mean gentleman, a groom, a yeoman, or a poor beggar, lord-president.

Thus I speak, not that I would have it so, but to your shame, if there is never a gentleman meet or able to be lord-president. For why are not the noblemen and young gentlemen of England so brought up in knowledge of God, and in learning, that they may be able to execute offices in the commonweal? The King has a great many wards, and I trow there is a court of wards; why is there not a school for the wards, as well as there is a court for their lands? Why are they not set in schools where they may learn? Or why are they not sent to the universities, that they may be able to serve the King when they come to age? If the wards and young gentlemen were well brought up in learning, and in the knowledge of God, they would not, when they come to age, so much give themselves to other vanities. And if the nobility be well trained in godly learning, the people would follow the same train; for truly, such as the noblemen are such will the people be. And now, the only cause why noblemen are not made lord-presidents, is because they have not been brought up in learning.

Therefore, for the love of God, appoint teachers and schoolmasters, you that have charge of youth; and give the teachers stipends worthy their pains, that they may bring them up in grammar, in logic, in rhetoric, in philosophy, in the civil law, and in that which I can not leave unspoken, of the word of God. Thanks be unto God, the nobility otherwise is very well brought up in learning and godliness, to the great joy and comfort of England; so that there is now good hope in the youth, that we shall another day have a flourishing commonweal, considering their godly education. Yea, and there are already noblemen enough, though not so many as I would wish, able to be lord-presidents, and wise men enough for the mint. And as unmeet a thing it is for bishops to be lord-presidents, or priests to be minters, as it was for the Corinthians to plead matters of variance before heathen judges. It is also a slander to the noblemen, as though they lacked wisdom and learning to be able for such offices, or else were no men of conscience, or else were not meet to be trusted, and able for such offices. And a prelate has a charge and cure otherwise; and therefore he can not discharge his duty and be a lord-president too. For a presidentship requireth a whole man; and a bishop can not be two men. A bishop has his office, a flock to teach, to look unto; and therefore he can not meddle with another office, which alone requires a whole man; he should therefore give it over to whom it is meet, and labor in his own business; as Paul writes to the Thessalonians, "Let every man do his own business, and follow his calling." Let the priest preach, and the nobleman handle the temporal matters. Moses was a marvelous man, a good man: Moses was a wonderful man, and did his duty, being a married man: we lack such as Moses was. Well, I would all men would look to their duty, as God hath called them, and then we should have a flourishing Christian commonweal.

And now I would ask a strange question: who is the most diligent bishop and prelate in all England, that passes all the rest in doing his office? I can tell, for I know who it is; I know him well. But now I think I see you listening and hearkening that I should name him. There is one that passes all the other, and is the most diligent prelate and preacher in all England. And will ye know who it is? I will tell you—it is the devil. He is the most diligent preacher of all others; he is never out of his diocese; he is never from his cure; you shall never find him unoccupied; he is ever in his parish; he keeps residence at all times; you shall never find him out of the way; call for him when you will he is ever at home. He is the most diligent preacher in all the realm; he is ever at his plow; no lording nor loitering can hinder him; he is ever applying his business; you shall never find him idle I warrant you. And his office is to hinder religion, to maintain superstition, to set up idolatry, to teach all kinds of Popery. He is ready as can be wished for to set forth his plow; to devise as many ways as can be to deface and obscure God's glory. Where the devil is resident, and has his plow going, there away with books and up with candles; away with Bibles and up with beads; away with the light of the Gospel and up with the light of candles, yea, at noonday. Where the devil is resident, that he may prevail, up with all superstition and idolatry; censing, painting of images, candles, palms, ashes, holy water, and new service of men's inventing; as though man could invent a better way to honor God with than God himself hath appointed. Down with Christ's cross, up with purgatory pickpurse—up with him, the Popish purgatory, I mean. Away with clothing the naked, the poor and impotent; up with decking of images, and gay garnishing of stocks and stones; up with man's traditions and his laws, down with God's traditions and his most holy word. Down with the old honor due to God, and up with the new god's honor. Let all things be done in Latin: there must be nothing but Latin, not so much as "Remember, man, that thou art ashes, and into ashes shalt thou return:" which are the words that the minister speaketh unto the ignorant people, when he gives them ashes upon Ash-Wednesday, but it must be spoken in Latin. God's word may in no wise be translated into English.

O that our prelates would be as diligent to sow the corn of good doctrine, as Satan is to sow cockle and darnel! And this is the devilish plowing which worketh to have things in Latin, and hinders the fruitful edification. But here some man will say to me, What, sir, are you so privy to the devil's counsel that you know all this to be true? True, I know him too well, and have obeyed him a little too much in condescending to some follies; and I know him as other men do; yea, that he is ever occupied, and ever busy in following his plow. I know by St. Peter, who saith of him, "He goeth about like a roaring lion, seeking whom he may devour." I would have this text well viewed and examined, every word of it: "He goeth about" in every corner of his diocese; he goeth on visitation daily, he leaves no place of his cure unvisited: he walks round about from place to place, and ceases not. "As a lion," that is, strongly, boldly, and proudly; stately and fiercely, with haughty looks, with his proud countenances, with his stately braggings. "Roaring," for he lets not any occasion slip, to speak or to roar out when he seeth his time. "He goeth about seeking," and not sleeping, as our bishops do; but he seeketh diligently, he searcheth diligently all corners, where he may have his prey. He roveth abroad in every place of his diocese; he standeth not still, he is never at rest, but ever in hand with his plow, that it may go forward. But there was never such a preacher in England as he is. Who is able to tell his diligent preaching, which every day, and every hour, labors to sow cockle and darnel, that he may bring out of form, and out of estimation and renown, the institution of the Lord's supper and Christ's cross? For there he lost his right; for Christ said, "Now is the judgment of this world, and the prince of this world shall be cast out. And as Moses did lift up the serpent in the wilderness, so must the Son of man be lift up. [John iii.] And when I shall be lift up from the earth, I will draw all things unto myself." For the devil was disappointed of his purpose; for he thought all to be his own: and when he had once brought Christ to the cross, he thought all was sure.

But there lost he all reigning: for Christ said, "I will draw all things to myself." He means, drawing of man's soul to salvation. And that he said he would do by his own self; not by any other sacrifice. He meant by his own sacrifice on the cross, where he offered himself for the redemption of mankind; and not the sacrifice of the mass, to be offered by another. For who can offer him but himself? He was both the Offerer and the Offering. And this is the mark at which the devil shooteth, to evacuate the cross of Christ, and to mangle the institution of the Lord's supper; which, although he can not bring to pass, yet he goes about by his sleights and subtile means to frustrate the same: and these fifteen hundred years he has been a doer, only purposing to make Christ's death of small efficacy and virtue. For whereas Christ, "according as the serpent was lifted up in the wilderness," so would he himself be exalted; that thereby as many as trusted in him should have salvation; but the devil would none of that. They would have us saved by a daily oblation propitiatory; by a sacrifice expiatory or remissory.

Now propitiatory, expiatory, remissory, or satisfactory, signify all one thing in effect, and it is nothing else but whereby to obtain remission of sins, and to have salvation. And this way the devil used to evacuate the death of Christ, that we might have affiance in other things, as in the daily sacrifice of the priest; whereas Christ would have us to trust in his sacrifice alone. So he was "the Lamb that hath been slain from the beginning of the world; and therefore he is called a "continual sacrifice;" and not for the continuance of the mass, as the blanchers have blanched it, and wrested it, and as I myself did once mistake it. But Paul saith, "By himself, and by none other, Christ made purgation and satisfaction for the whole world."

WILLIAM CHILLINGWORTH.

He was born in 1602, and died in 1644. The fame of Chillingworth, as an author and controversialist, is world-wide. His excellence, says Barlow, consisted in "his logic, both natural and acquired." Warren, in his Law Studies, says, "Chillingworth is the writer whose works are recommended for exercitations of the student." Lord Mansfield pronounced him to be a perfect model of argumentation. Tillotson calls him, "incomparable, the glory of his age and nation." Locke proposes, for the attainment in right reasoning, the constant reading of Chillingworth, who, by his example, "will teach both perspicuity and the way of right reasoning better than any book that I know." His sermons are nine in number, of which the following is, by common consent, admitted to be the masterpiece:

THE FORM OF GODLINESS WITHOUT ITS POWER.

"This know also, that in the last days perilous times shall come. For men shall be lovers of their own selves, covetous, boasters, proud, blasphemers, disobedient to parents, unthankful, unholy, without natural affection, truce-breakers, false accusers, incontinent, fierce, despisers of those that are good, traitors, heady, high-minded, lovers of pleasures more than lovers of God; having a form of godliness, but denying the power thereof." 2 TIM. iii 1-5.

To a discourse upon these words, I can not think of any fitter introduction than that wherewith our Savior sometime began a sermon of his, "This day is this Scripture fulfilled." And I would to God there were not great occasion to fear that a great part of it may be fulfilled in this place.

Two things are contained in it: First, the real wickedness of the generality of the men of the latter times, in the first four verses. For by "men shall be lovers of themselves, covetous, boasters, proud," etc., I conceive is meant, men generally shall be so; otherwise this were nothing peculiar to the last, but common to all times; for in all times, some, nay many, have been "lovers of themselves, covetous, boasters, proud," etc. Secondly, we have here the formal and hypocritical godliness of the same times, in the last verse: "Having a form of godliness, but denying the power thereof;" which latter ordinarily and naturally accompanies the former. For, as the shadows are longest when the sun is lowest, and as vines and other fruit-trees bear the less fruit when they are suffered to luxuriate and spend their sap upon superfluous suckers, and abundance of leaves; so, commonly, we may observe, both in civil conversation, where there is great store of formality, there is little sincerity; and in religion, where there is a decay of true cordial piety, there men entertain and please themselves, and vainly hope to please God, with external formalities and performances, and great store of that righteousness for which Christ shall judge the world.

It were no difficult matter to show that the truth of St. Paul's prediction is by experience justified in both parts of it; but my purpose is to restrain myself to the latter, and to endeavor to clear unto you that,

that in our times is generally accomplished: that almost in all places the power of godliness is decayed and vanished; the form and profession of it only remaining; that the spirit, and soul, and life of religion, is for the most part gone; only the outward body or carcass, or rather the picture or shadow of it, being left behind. This is the doctrine which at this time I shall deliver to you; and the use, which I desire most heartily you shall make of it, is this: to take care that you confute, so far as it concerns your particulars, what I fear I shall prove true in general.

[Chillingworth here alludes, in few words, to the promises and professions of many which are disregarded, and condemning particularly their vain pretensions in *prayer*, proceeds thus:]

And then, for the Lord's prayer, the plain truth is, we lie unto God for the most part clean through it; and for want of desiring indeed what in word we prayed for, tell him to his face as many false tales as we make petitions. For who shows by his endeavors that he desires heartily that God's name should be hallowed—that is, holily and religiously worshiped and adored by all men? That his kingdom should be advanced and enlarged; that his blessed will should be universally obeyed? Who shows, by his forsaking sin, that he desires, so much as he should do, the forgiveness of it? Nay, who doth not revenge, upon all occasions, the affronts, contempts, and injuries put upon him, and so upon the matter curse himself, as often as he says, "Forgive us our trespasses, as we forgive them that trespass against us?" How few depend upon God only for their "daily bread"—namely, the good things of this life—as upon the only Giver of them, so as neither to get nor keep any of them, by any means, which they know or fear to be offensive unto God! How few desire in earnest to avoid temptation! Nay, who almost is there that takes not the devil's office out of his hand, and is not himself a tempter both to himself and others? Lastly, who almost is there that desires heartily, and above all things, so much as the thing deserves, to be delivered from the greatest evil; sin, I mean, and the anger of God? Now, beloved, this is certain; he that employs not requisite industry to obtain what he pretends to desire, does not desire indeed, but only pretends to do so: he that desires not what he prays for, prays with tongue only, and not with his heart: indeed does not pray to God, but play and dally with him. And yet this is all which men generally do, and therefore herein also accomplish this prophecy, "Having a form of godliness, but denying the power thereof."

And this were ill enough were it in private; but we abuse God Almighty also with our public and solemn formalities; we make the Church a stage whereon to act our parts, and play our pageantry; there we make a profession every day of confessing our sins with humble, lowly, and obedient hearts; and yet, when we have talked after this manner twenty, thirty, forty years together, our hearts for the most part continue as proud, as impenitent, as disobedient, as they were in the beginning. We make great protestations "when we assemble and meet together to render thanks to God Almighty, for the benefits received at his hands;" and if this were to be performed with words, with hosannas and halleluiahs, and gloria patris, and psalms and hymns, and such like outward matters, peradventure we should do it very sufficiently; but, in the mean time, with our lives and actions we provoke the Almighty, and that to his face, with all variety of grievous and bitter provocations; we do daily and hourly such things as we know, and he hath assured us, to be as odious unto him, and contrary to his nature, as any thing in the world is to the nature of any man in the world; and all this upon poor, trifling, trivial, no temptations. If a man whom you have dealt well with should deal so with you, one whom you had redeemed from the Turkish slavery, and instated in some indifferent good inheritance, should make you fine speeches, entertain you with panegyrics, and have your praises always in his mouth; but all this while do nothing that pleases you, but upon all occasions put all affronts and indignities upon you: would you say this was a thankful man? Nay, would you not make heaven and earth ring of his unthankfulness, and detest him almost as much for his fair speeches as his foul actions? Beloved, such is our unthankfulness to our God and Creator, to our Lord and Savior; our tongues ingeminate, and cry aloud, Hosanna, hosanna, but the louder voice of our lives and actions is, "Crucify him, crucify him." We court God Almighty, and compliment with him, and profess to esteem his service perfect freedom; but if any thing be to be done, much more if any thing be to be suffered for him, here we leave him. We bow the knee before him, and put a reed in his hand, and a crown upon his head, and cry, "Hail, King of the Jews;" but then, with our customary sins, we give him gall to eat and vinegar to drink; we thrust a spear in his side, nail him to the cross, and crucify to ourselves the Lord of glory. This is not the office of a friend to bewail a dead friend with vain lamentations; *sed quæ voluerit meminisse, quæ mandaverit exequi*—to remember what he desires, and to execute what he commands. So said a dying Roman to his friend, and so say I to you. To be thankful to God is not to say, God be praised, or God be thanked; *but to remember what he desires, and execute what he commands.* To be thankful to God is certainly to love him, and to love him is to keep his commandments: so saith our Savior, "If ye love me, keep my commandments." If we do so, we may justly pretend to thankfulness, which, believe me, is not a word, nor to be performed with words: but, if we do not so, as generally we do not, our talk of thankfulness is nothing else but mere talk, and we accomplish St. Paul's prophecy herein also: having a form of thankfulness, but not the reality, nor the power of it.

If I should reckon up unto you how many direct lies every wicked man tells to God Almighty, as often as he says amen to this "form of godliness" which our Church hath prescribed; if I should present unto you all our acting of piety, and playing of humiliation, and personating of devotion, in the psalms, the litanies, the collects, and generally in the whole service, I should be infinite; and, therefore, I have thought good to draw a vail over a great part of our hypocrisy, and to restrain the remainder of the discourse to the contrariety between our profession and performance only in two things; I mean faith and repentance.

And, first, for faith: we profess, and indeed generally, because it is not safe to do otherwise, that we believe the Scripture to be true, and that it contains the plain and only way to infinite and eternal happiness; but if we did generally believe what we do profess, if this were the language of our hearts as well as our tongues, how comes it to pass that the study of it is so generally neglected?

Let a book that treats of the philosopher's stone promise never so many mountains of gold, and even the restoring of the golden age again, yet were it no marvel if few should study it; and the reason is, because few would believe it. But if there were a book extant, and ordinary to be had, as the Bible is, which men did generally believe to contain a plain and easy way for all men to become rich, and to live in health and pleasure, and this world's happiness, can any man imagine that this book would be unstudied by any man? And why then should I not believe that, if the Scripture were firmly and heartily believed, the certain and only way to happiness, which is perfect and eternal, it would be studied by all men with all diligence? Seeing, therefore, most Christians are so cold and negligent in the study of it, prefer all other business, all other pleasures before it, is there not great reason to fear that many who pretend to believe it firmly believe it not at all, or very weakly and faintly? If the general of an army, or an embassador to some prince or state, were assured by the king his master that the transgressing any point of his commission should cost him his life, and the exact performance of it be recompensed with as high a reward as were in the king's power to bestow upon him; can it be imagined that any man who believes this, and is in his right mind, can be so supinely and stupidly negligent of this charge, which so much imports him, as to oversee, through want of care, any one necessary article or part of his commission, especially if it be delivered to him in writing, and at h s pleasure to peruse it every day? Certainly this absurd negligence is a thing without example, and such as peradventure will never happen to any sober man to the world's end; and, by the same reason, if we were firmly persuaded that this book doth indeed contain that charge and commission which infinitely more concerns us, it were not in reason possible but that to such a persuasion our care and diligence about it should be in some measure answerable. Seeing, therefore, most of us are so strangely careless, so grossly negligent of it, is there not great reason to fear that though we have professors and protestors in abundance, yet the faithful, the truly and sincerely faithful, are, in a manner, failed from the children of men? What but this can be the cause that men are so commonly ignorant of so many articles and particular mandates of it, which yet are as manifest in it as if they were written with the beams of the sun? For example, how few of our ladies and gentlewomen do or will understand that a voluptuous life is damnable and prohibited to them! Yet St. Paul saith so very plainly, "She that liveth in pleasure is dead while she liveth." I believe that this case directly regards not the sex; he would say *he*, as well as *she*, if there had been occasion. How few of the gallants of our time do or will understand that it is not lawful for them to be as expensive and costly in apparel as their means, or perhaps their credit, will extend unto! Which is to sacrifice unto vanity that which by the law of Christ is due unto charity; and yet the same St. Paul forbids plainly this excess, even to women— "Also let women"—he would have said it much rather to men—"array themselves in comely apparel, with shamefacedness and modesty, not with embroidered hair, or gold, or pearls, or costly apparel." And, to make our ignorance the more inexcusable, the very same rule is delivered by St. Peter also.

How few rich men are or will be persuaded, that the law of Christ permits them not to heap up riches forever, nor perpetually to add house to house, and land to land, though by lawful means; but requires of them thus much charity at least, that ever, while they are providing for their wives and children, they should, out of the increase wherewith God hath blessed their industry, allot the poor a just and free proportion! And when they have provided for them in a convenient manner—such as they themselves shall judge sufficient and convenient in others—that then they should give over making purchase after purchase; but with the surplusage of their revenue beyond their expense, procure, as much as lies in them, that no Christian remain miserably poor; few rich men, I fear, are or will be thus persuaded, and their daily actions show as much; yet undoubtedly, either our Savior's general command, of loving our neighbors as ourselves, which can hardly consist with our keeping vainly, or spending vainly, what he wants for his ordinary subsistence, lays upon us a necessity of this high liberality: or his special command concerning this matter: *Quod superest date pauperibus*, "That which remains give to the poor:" or that which St. John saith, reacheth home unto it: "Whosoever hath this world's good, and seeth his brother have need, and shutteth up the bowels of his compassion from him, how dwelleth the love of God in him?" Which is, in effect, as if he had said, he that keepeth from any brother in Christ that which his brother wants, and he wants not, doth but vainly think that he loves God; and, therefore, vainly hopes that God loves him.

Where almost are the men that are or will be persuaded, the Gospel of Christ requires of men humility, like to that of little children, and that under the highest pain of damnation? That is, that we should no more overvalue ourselves, or desire to be highly esteemed by others; no more undervalue, scorn, or despise others; no more affect pre-eminence over others, than little children do, before we have put that pride into them, which afterward we charge wholly upon their natural corruption; and yet our blessed Savior requires nothing more rigidly, nor more plainly, than this high degree of humility: "Verily"—saith he—"I say unto you"—he speaks to his disciples affecting high places, and demanding which of them should be greatest—"except you be converted, and become as little children, ye shall not enter into the kingdom of heaven."

Would it not be strange news to a great many, that not only adultery and fornication, but even uncleanness and lasciviousness; not only idolatry and witchcraft, but hatred, variance, emulations, wrath, and contentions; not only murders, but envyings; not drunkenness only, but revelings, are things prohibited to Christians, and such as, if we forsake them not, we can not inherit the kingdom of heaven? And yet these things, as strange as they may seem, are plainly written; some of them by St. Peter; but all of them by St. Paul: "Now the works of the flesh are manifest, which are these, adultery, fornication, uncleanness, lasciviousness," etc., "of the which I tell you before, as I have told you in times past, that they who do such things, shall not inherit the kingdom of God."

If I should tell you that all bitterness and evil-speaking—nay, such is the modesty and gravity which Christianity requires of us,—foolish talk and jesting, are things not allowed to Christians, would not many cry out, "These are hard and strange sayings—who can hear them?" And yet, as strange as they may seem, they have been written well-nigh one thousand six hundred years, and are yet extant in very legible characters in the epistle to the Ephesians, the end of the fourth and the beginning of the fifth chapter.

[Chillingworth deprecates briefly and incidentally the course of the party who were taking up arms against the King, and then pursues his discourse thus:]

You see, beloved, how many instances and examples I have given you of our gross ignorance of what is necessary and easy for us to know; and to these it were no difficult task to add more. Now, from whence can this ignorance proceed but from supine negligence? And from whence this negligence, but from our not believing what we pretend to believe? For did we believe firmly and heartily that this book was given us by God for the rule of our actions, and that obedience to it were the certain and only way to eternal happiness, it were impossible we should be such enemies to ourselves, such traitors to our own souls, as not to search it at least with so much diligence that no necessary point of our duty plainly taught in it could possibly escape us. But it is certain and apparent to all the world that the greatest part of Christians, through gross and willful negligence, remain utterly ignorant of many necessary points of their duty to God and man; and, therefore, it is much to be feared that this book, and the religion of Christ contained in it, among an infinity of professors, labors with great penury of true believers.

JOHN BUNYAN.

The "Shakspeare among divines," as Bunyan has been justly termed, was born in the year 1628, at Elstow, in Bedfordshire, the son of a traveling tinker. In his youth he led a wandering and dissipated life; and though frequently convicted of sin, it was not till twenty-five years of age that he found peace in believing; at which time he joined a dissenting Baptist Church in Bedford. Three years subsequent he became a preacher of the Gospel; and after the Restoration, in common with many others, he suffered much from the cruel persecutions under the reign of that unprincipled tyrant, Charles the Second, and was finally thrown into Bedford jail, where he was immured for nearly thirteen years, and where he wrote, among other works, "The Pilgrim's Progress." Upon his release he resumed preaching, and was very popular, attracting immense congregations, whether in his own meeting-house at Bedford or on his visits to London and other places. After sixty years of hardship, persecution, and unwearied toil, he ended his labors

August 31, 1688, and went up to sit down with the shining ones of the Celestial City.

The following is from one of his very long discourses, and is a fair example of his style of preaching:

THE BARREN FIG-TREE; OR, THE DOOM AND DOWNFALL OF THE FRUITLESS PROFESSOR.

"And he, answering, said unto him, Lord, let it alone this year also, till I shall dig about it, and dung it; and if it bear fruit, well; and if not, then after that thou shalt cut it down." LUKE xiii, 8, 9.

These are the words of the Dresser of the vineyard, who, I told you, is Jesus Christ—for "he made intercession for the transgressors"—and they contain a petition presented to offended Justice, praying that a little more time and patience might be exercised toward the barren cumber-ground fig-tree.

In this petition there are six things considerable. 1. That justice might be deferred. "O that justice might be deferred! Lord, let it alone," etc., "awhile longer." 2. Here is time prefixed, as a space to try if more means will cure a barren fig-tree. "Lord, let it alone this year also." 3. The means to help it are propounded: "till I shall dig about it, and dung it." 4. Here is also an insinuation of a supposition that, by thus doing, God's expectation may be answered: "and if it bear fruit, well." 5. Here is a supposition that the barren fig-tree may yet abide barren, when Christ has done what he will unto it: "and if it bear fruit," etc. 6. Here is at last a resolution, that if thou continue barren, hewing days will come upon thee: "and if it bear fruit, well; and if not, then after that thou shalt cut it down."

But to proceed according to my former method, by way of exposition.

Lord, let it alone this year also. Here is astonishing grace indeed! Astonishing grace, I say, that the Lord Jesus should concern himself with a barren fig-tree; that he should step in to stop the blow from a barren fig-tree! True, he stopped the blow but for a time; but why did he stop it at all? Why did he not fetch out the ax? Why did he not do execution? Why did he not cut it down? Barren fig-tree, it is well for thee that there is a Jesus at God's right hand—a Jesus of that largeness of bowels as to have compassion for a barren fig-tree, else justice had never let thee alone to cumber the ground as thou hast done. When Israel also had sinned against God, down they had gone, but that Moses stood in the breach. "Let me alone," said God to him, "that I may consume them in a moment, and I will make of thee a great nation." Barren fig-tree, dost thou hear? Thou knowest not how oft the hand of divine Justice hath been up to strike, and how many years since thou hadst been cut down had not Jesus caught hold of his Father's ax. "Let me alone! let me fetch my blow!" or, "Cut it down! why cumbereth it the ground?" Wilt thou not hear yet, barren fig-tree? Wilt thou provoke still? Thou hast wearied men, and provoked the justice of God; and wilt thou weary my God, also?

Lord, let it alone THIS YEAR. "Lord, a little longer! Let us not lose a soul for want of means. I will try—I will see if I can make it fruitful. I will not beg a long life, nor that it might still be barren, and so provoke thee. I beg, for the sake of the soul, the immortal soul, Lord, spare it one year only—one year longer—this year also. If I do any good to it, it will be in little time. Thou shalt not be overwearied with waiting; one year, and then!"

Barren fig-tree, dost thou hear what a striving there is between the vine-dresser and the husbandman for thy life? "Cut it down," saith one; "Lord, spare it," saith the other. "It is a cumber-ground," saith the Father. "One year longer," prays the Son. "Let it alone this year also."

Till I shall dig about it, and dung it. The Lord Jesus, by these words, supposeth two things as causes of the want of fruit in a barren fig-tree, and two things he proposeth as a remedy. The things that are a cause of the want of fruit, are, 1. It is earth-bound: "Lord, the fig-tree is earth-bound." 2. A want of warmer means, or fatter means.

Wherefore accordingly he propoundeth, 1. To loosen the earth, to dig about it. 2. And then to supply it with manure: "to dig about it, and dung it."

Lord, let it alone this year also, till I shall dig about it. I doubt it is too much earth-bound. The love of this world, and the deceitfulness of riches, lie too close to the roots of the heart of this professor. The love of riches, the love of honors, the love of pleasures, are the thorns that choke the word. "For all that is in the world, the lust of the flesh, and the lust of the eyes, and the pride of life, is not of the Father, but of the world." How then—where these things bind up the heart—can there be fruit brought forth to God?

Barren fig-tree! see how the Lord Jesus, by these very words, suggesteth the cause of thy fruitlessness of soul. The things of this world lie too close to thy heart; the earth with its things has bound up thy roots; thou art an earth-bound soul, thou art wrapped up in thick clay. "If any man love the world, the love of the Father is not in him;" how then can he be fruitful in the vineyard? This kept Judas from the fruit of caring for the poor. This kept Demas from the fruit of self-denial. And this kept Ananias and Sapphira his wife from the goodly fruit of sincerity and truth. What shall I say? These are "foolish and hurtful lusts, which drown men in destruction and perdition; for the love of money is the root of all evil." How then can good fruit grow from such a root, the root of all evil, "which, while some coveted after, they have erred from the faith, and pierced themselves through with many sorrows?" It is an evil root, nay, it is the root of all evil. How then can the professor that hath such a root, or a root wrapped up in such earthly things, as the lusts, and pleasures, and vanities of this world, bring forth fruit to God?

1. *Till I shall* DIG *about it.* "Lord, I will loosen his roots; I will dig up this earth, I will lay his roots bare. My hand shall be upon him by sickness, by disappointments, by cross providences. I will dig about him till he stands shaking and tottering, till he be ready to fall; then, if ever, he will seek to take faster hold." Thus, I say, deals the Lord Jesus ofttimes with the barren professor; he diggeth about him, he smiteth one blow at his heart, another blow at his lusts, a third at his pleasures, a fourth at his comforts, another at his self-conceitedness: thus he diggeth about him. This is the way to take bad earth from the roots, and to loosen his roots from the earth. Barren fig-tree! see here the care, the love, the labor, and way, which the Lord Jesus, the dresser of the vineyard, is fain to take with thee, if haply thou mayest be made fruitful.

2. *Till I shall dig about it, and* DUNG *it.* As the earth, by binding the roots too closely, may hinder the tree's being fruitful, so the want of better means may also be a cause thereof. And this is more than intimated by the Dresser of the vineyard: "till I shall dig about it, and dung it." "I will supply it with a more fruitful ministry, with a warmer word. I will give them pastors after mine own heart. I will dung them." You know dung is a more warm, more fat, more hearty and succoring matter, than is commonly the place in which trees are planted.

I will "dig about it, and dung it." That is, "I will bring it under a heart-awakening ministry; the means of grace shall be fat and good. I will also visit it with heart-awakening, heart-warming, heart-encouraging considerations. I will apply warm dung to its roots. I will strive with him by my Spirit, and give him some tastes of the heavenly gift, and the power of the world to come. I am loth to lose him for want of digging." "Lord, let it alone this year also, till I shall dig about it, and dung it."

And if it bear fruit, well. "And if the fruit of all my labor doth make this fig-tree fruitful, I shall count my time, my labor, and means, well bestowed upon it. And thou, also, O my God, shalt be therewith much delighted. For thou art gracious and merciful, and repentest thee of the evil which thou threatenest to bring upon a people."

These words, therefore, inform us that if a barren fig-tree, a barren professor, shall now at last bring forth fruit to God, it shall go well with that professor. It shall go well with that poor soul. His former barrenness, his former tempting of God, his abuse of God's patience and long-suffering, his misspending year after year, shall now be all forgiven him. Yea, God the Father, and our Lord Jesus Christ, will now pass by, and forget all, and say, Well done, at the last. "When I say to the wicked, O wicked man, thou shalt surely die; if he then do that which is lawful and right, if he walk in the statutes of life, without committing iniquity, he shall surely live, he shall not die."

Barren fig-tree! dost thou hear? The ax is laid to thy roots; the Lord Jesus prays God to spare thee. Hath he been digging about thee? Hath he been manuring thee? O barren fig-tree! now thou art come to the point. If thou shalt now become good; if thou shalt, after a gracious manner, suck in the Gospel, and if thou shalt bring forth fruit unto God, well; but if not, the fire is the last. Fruit or the fire; fruit or the fire, barren fig-tree! "If it bear fruit, well."

And IF NOT, *then after that Thou shalt cut it down.* "And if not," etc. The Lord Jesus, by this *if*, giveth us to understand that there is a generation of professors in the world that are incurable, that will not, that can not repent, nor be profited by the means of grace; a generation, I say, that will retain a profession, but will not bring forth fruit; a generation that will wear out the patience of God, time and tide, threatenings and intercessions, judgments and mercies, and after all will be unfruitful.

O the desperate wickedness that is in thy heart! Barren professor, dost thou hear? The Lord Jesus stands yet in doubt about thee; there is an *if* stands yet in the way. I say, the Lord Jesus stands yet in doubt about thee, whether or no at last thou wilt be good; whether he may not labor in vain; whether his digging and dunging will come to more than lost labor. "I gave her space to repent, and she repented not." "I digged about, I dunged it; I granted time, and supplied it with means; but I labored here in vain, and spent my strength for naught and in vain." Dost thou hear, barren fig-tree? There is yet a question whether it will be well with thy soul at last?

And if not, AFTER THAT *Thou shalt cut it down.* There is nothing more exasperating to the mind of a man than to find all his kindness and favor slighted. Neither is the Lord Jesus so provoked with any thing, as when sinners abuse his means of grace. "If it be barren and fruitless under my Gospel; if it turn my grace into wantonness; if after digging and dunging, and waiting, it yet remain unfruitful, I will let thee cut it down."

Gospel-means applied, is the last remedy for a barren professor. If the Gospel, if the grace of the Gospel will not do, there can be nothing expected, but "cut it down." "Then after that thou shalt cut it down." "O Jerusalem, Jerusalem, thou that killest the prophets, and stonest them that are sent unto thee, how often would I have gathered thy children together, as a hen gathereth her chickens under her wings, and ye would not! Behold your house is left unto you desolate." Yet it can not be but that this Lord Jesus who at first did put a stop to the execution of his Father's justice, because he desired to try more means with the fig-tree; I say it can not be but that a heart so full of compassion as his is, should be touched to behold this professor must now be cut down. "And when He was come near, he beheld the city, and wept over it, saying, If thou hadst known, *even thou,* at least in this thy day, the things which belong unto thy peace! But now they are hid from thine eyes."

After that THOU SHALT CUT IT DOWN. When Christ

giveth thee over, there is no intercessor or mediator, no more sacrifice for sin. All is gone but judgment, but the ax, but "a certain fearful looking-for of judgment, and fiery indignation, which shall devour the adversaries."

Barren fig-tree! take heed that thou comest not to these last words, for these words are a give-up, a cast-up, a cast-up of a castaway. "After that thou shalt cut it down." They are as much as if Christ had said, "Father, I begged for more time for this barren professor; I begged till I should dig about it, and dung it; but now, Father, the time is out, the year is ended, the summer is ended, and no good done. I have also tried with my means, with the Gospel; I have digged about it; I have laid also the fat and hearty dung of the Gospel to it; but all comes to nothing. Father, I deliver up this professor to thee again; I have done. I have done all, I have done praying and endeavoring, I will hold the head of thine ax no longer; take him into the hands of justice. Do justice! Do the law! I will never beg for him more." "After that thou shalt cut it down." "Woe unto them when I depart from them!"

GEORGE WHITEFIELD.

When he was preaching from the text, "Wherefore glorify ye the Lord in the fires," Isa. xxiv, 15, he said, "When I was some years ago at Shields, I went into a glass house, and standing very attentively

I saw several masses of burning glass of various forms. The workman took one piece of glass and put it into one furnace, then he put it into a second, then into a third. I asked him, 'Why do you put that into so many fires?' He answered me, 'O, sir, the first was not hot enough, nor the second, and therefore we put it into the third, and that will make it transparent.' O, thought I, does this man put this glass into one furnace after another that it may be rendered perfect? O my God, put me into one furnace after another, that my soul may be transparent, that I may see God as he is."

I will add the closing paragraphs of his sermon on

THE KINGDOM OF GOD.

"For the kingdom of God is not meat and drink; but righteousness, and peace, and joy in the Holy Ghost." Rom. xiv, 17.

* * * * * * * * *

Here, then, we will put the kingdom of God together. It is "righteousness," it is "peace," it is "joy in the Holy Ghost." When this is placed in the heart, God there reigns, God there dwells and walks—the creature is a son or daughter of the Almighty. But, my friends, how few are there here who have been made partakers of this kingdom! Perhaps the kingdom of the devil, instead of the kingdom of God, is in most of our hearts. This has been a place much favored of God; may I hope some of you can go along with me and say, "Blessed be God, we have got righteousness, peace, and joy in the Holy Ghost!"

Have you so? Then you are kings, though beggars; you are happy above all men in the world—you have got heaven in your hearts; and when the crust of your bodies drops, your souls will meet with God, your souls will enter into the world of peace, and you shall be happy with God for evermore. I hope that there is none of you who will fear death; fie for shame, if ye do! What, afraid to go to Jesus, to your Lord? You may cry out, "O death, where is thy sting? O grave, where is thy victory?" You may go on your way rejoicing, knowing that God is your friend; die when you will, angels will carry you safe to heaven.

But, O, how many are here in this church-yard, who will be laid in some grave erelong, who are entire strangers to this work of God upon their souls! My dear friends, I think this is an awful sight. Here are many thousands of souls that must shortly appear with me, a poor creature, in the general assembly of all mankind before God in judgment. God Almighty knows whether some of you may not drop down dead before you go out of the church-yard; and yet, perhaps most are strangers to the Lord Jesus Christ in their hearts. Perhaps curiosity has brought you out to hear a poor babbler preach. But, my friends, I hope I came out of a better principle. If I know any thing of my heart, I came to promote God's glory, and if the Lord should make use of such a worthless worm, such a wretched creature, as I am, to do your precious souls good, nothing would rejoice me more than to hear that God makes the foolishness of preaching a means of making many believe. I was long myself deceived with a form of godliness, and I know what it is to be a factor for the devil, to be led captive by the devil at his will, to have the kingdom of the devil in my heart; and I hope I can say, through free grace, I know what it is to have the kingdom of God erected in me. It is God's goodness that such a poor wretch as I am converted; though sometimes when I am speaking of God's goodness I am afraid he will strike me down dead. Let me draw out my soul and heart to you, my dear friends, my dear guilty friends, poor bleeding souls, who must shortly take your last farewell, and fly into endless eternity. Let me entreat you to lay these things seriously to heart this night. Now, when the Sabbath is over, and the evening is drawing near, methinks the very sight is awful—I could almost weep over you, as our Lord did over Jerusalem—to think in how short a time every soul of you must die—some of you to go to heaven, and others to go to the devil for evermore.

O my dear friends, these are matters of eternal moment. I did not come to tickle your ears; if I had a mind to do so, I would play the orator: no, but I came, if God should be pleased, to touch your hearts. What shall I say to you? Open the door of your heart, that the King of glory, the blessed Jesus, may come in and erect his kingdom in your soul. Make room for Christ; the Lord Jesus desires to sup with you to-night; Christ is willing to come into any of your hearts, that will be pleased to open and receive him. Are there any of you made willing Lydias? There are many women here, but how many Lydias are there here? Does power go with the word to open your heart? and find you a sweet melting in your soul? Are you willing? Then Christ Jesus is willing to come to you. But you may say, Will Christ come to my wicked, polluted heart? Yes, though you have many devils in your heart, Christ will come and erect his throne there; though the devils be in your heart, the Lord Jesus will scourge out a legion of devils, and his throne shall be exalted in thy soul. Sinners, be ye what you will, come to Christ, you shall have righteousness and peace. If you have no peace, come to Christ, and he will give you peace. When you come to Christ, you will feel such joy that it is impossible for you to tell. O, may God pity you all! I hope this will be a night of salvation to some of your souls.

My dear friends, I would preach with all my heart till midnight, to do you good, till I could preach no more. O, that this body might hold out to speak more for my dear Redeemer! Had I a thousand lives, had I a thousand tongues, they should be employed in inviting sinners to come to Jesus Christ! Come, then, let me prevail with some of you to come along with me. Come, poor, lost, undone sinner, come just as you are to Christ, and say, If I be damned, I will perish at the feet of Jesus Christ, where never one perished yet. He will receive you with open arms; the dear Redeemer is willing to receive you all. Fly, then, for your lives. The devil is in you while unconverted; and will you go with the devil in your heart to bed this night? God Almighty knows if ever you and I shall see one another again. In one or two days more I must go, and, perhaps, I may never see you again till I meet you at the judgment-day. O my dear friends, **think of that solemn meeting**; think of that important hour, when the heavens shall pass away with a great noise, when the elements shall melt with **fervent heat**, when the sea and the grave shall be giving up their dead, and all shall be summoned to appear before the great God. What will you do then, if the kingdom of God is not erected in your hearts? You must go to the devil—like must go to like—if you are not converted. Christ hath asserted it in the strongest manner: "Verily, verily, I say unto you, except a man be born again, he can not enter into the kingdom of God." Who can dwell with devouring fire? Who can dwell with everlasting burnings? O, my heart is melting with love to you. Surely God intends to do good to your poor souls. Will no one be persuaded to accept of Christ? If those who are settled Pharisees will not come, I desire to speak to you who are drunkards, Sabbath-breakers, cursers and swearers—will you come to Christ? I know that many of you come here out of curiosity: though you come only to see the congregation, yet if you come to Jesus Christ, Christ will accept of you. Are there any cursing, swearing soldiers here? Will you come to Jesus Christ, and list yourselves under the banner of the dear Redeemer? You are all welcome to Christ. Are there any little boys or little girls here? Come to Christ, and he will erect his kingdom in you. There are many little children whom God is working on, both at home and abroad. O, if some of the little lambs would come to Christ, they shall have peace and joy in the day that the Redeemer shall set up his kingdom in their hearts. Parents tell them that Jesus Christ will take them in his arms, that he will dandle them on his knees. All of you, old and young, you that are old and gray-headed, come to Jesus Christ, and you shall be kings and priests to your God. The Lord will abundantly pardon you at the eleventh hour. "Ho, every one of you that thirsteth." If there be any one of you ambitious of honor, do you want a crown, a scepter? Come to Christ, and the Lord Jesus Christ will give you a kingdom that no man shall take from you.

CHRISTMAS EVANS.

This great pulpit orator was born at Ysgarwen, Cardiganshire, South Wales, on the 25th of December, 1766. On the sixteenth of July, 1838, he preached at Swansea, and said, as he sat down, "This is my last sermon;" and so it proved; for that night he was taken violently ill, and died three days afterward, in his seventy-third year, and the fifty-fourth of his ministry.

Evans's descriptive powers were perhaps never excelled. His imagination was of the imperial order, and absolutely knew no bounds; and his facility in the ready use of language altogether wonderful. Besides this, he was a man of the liveliest sensibilities, and always spoke out of a full heart, sometimes storming his hearers with his impassioned earnestness, and sometimes himself overwhelmed with the magnitude and grandeur of his theme. Add to this his pre-eminent faith and holiness of life, and we discover the secret of his astonishing pulpit eloquence—which, according to Robert Hall, entitles him to be ranked among the first men of his age. The best edition of Evans's sermons is that by Joseph Cross. Of course no translator can do him full justice, but the wide popularity of these discourses is the best evidence of their real merit, though in a foreign dress. Perhaps there is no one, upon the whole, superior to that which is here given. It contains one or two passages, which, for originality and brilliancy of conception, and for force of utterance, are absolutely unrivaled.

THE FALL AND RECOVERY OF MAN.

"For if, through the offense of one, many be dead; much more the grace of God, and the gift by grace, which is by one man, Jesus Christ, hath abounded unto many." ROMANS v, 15.

Man was created in the image of God. Knowledge and perfect holiness were impressed upon the very nature and faculties of his soul. He had constant access to his Maker, and enjoyed free communion with him, on the ground of his spotless moral rectitude. But, alas! the glorious diadem is broken; the crown of righteousness is fallen. Man's purity is gone, and his happiness is forfeited. "There is none righteous; no, not one." "All have sinned, and come short of the glory of God." But the ruin is not hopeless. What was lost in Adam is restored in Christ. His blood redeems us from bondage, and his Gospel gives us back the forfeited inheritance. "For if, through the offense of one, many be dead; much more the grace of God, and the gift by grace, which is by one man, Jesus Christ, hath abounded unto many." Let us consider: *first*, the corruption and condemnation of man; and, *secondly*, his gracious restoration to the favor of his offended God.

1. To find the cause of man's corruption and condemnation we must go back to Eden. The eating of the "forbidden tree" was "the offense of one," in consequence of which "many are dead." This was the "sin," the act of "disobedience," which "brought death into the world, and all our woe." It was the greatest ingratitude to the divine bounty, and the boldest rebellion against the divine sovereignty. The royalty of God was contemned; the riches of his goodness slighted; and his most desperate enemy preferred before him, as if he were a wiser counselor than Infinite Wisdom. Thus man joined in

league with hell, against heaven; with demons of the bottomless pit, against the almighty Maker and Benefactor; robbing God of the obedience due to his command, and the glory due to his name; worshiping the creature, instead of the Creator; and opening the door to pride, unbelief, enmity, and all wicked and abominable passions. How is the "noble vine," which was planted "wholly a right seed," "turned into the degenerate plant of a strange vine!"

Who can look for pure water from such a fountain? "That which is born of the flesh is flesh." All the faculties of the soul are corrupted by sin; the understanding dark; the will perverse; the affections carnal; the conscience full of shame, remorse, confusion, and mortal fear. Man is a hard-hearted and stiff-necked sinner; loving darkness rather than light, because his deeds are evil; eating sin like bread, and drinking iniquity like water; holding fast deceit, and refusing to let it go. His heart is desperately wicked; full of pride, vanity, hypocrisy, covetousness, hatred of truth, and hostility to all that is good.

This depravity is universal. Among the natural children of Adam there is no exemption from the original taint. "The whole world lieth in wickedness." "We are all as an unclean thing, and all our righteousness is as filthy rags." The corruption may vary in the degrees of development, in different persons; but the elements are in all, and their nature is every-where the same; the same in the blooming youth, and the withered sire; in the haughty prince, and the humble peasant; in the strongest giant, and the feeblest invalid. The enemy has "come in like a flood." The deluge of sin has swept the world. From the highest to the lowest, there is no health or moral soundness. From the crown of the head to the soles of the feet, there is nothing but wounds, and bruises, and putrefying sores. The laws, and their violation, and the punishments every-where invented for the suppression of vice, prove the universality of the evil. The bloody sacrifices and various purifications of the pagans show the handwriting of remorse upon their consciences; proclaim their sense of guilt, and their dread of punishment. None of them are free from the fear which hath torment, whatever their efforts to overcome it, and however great their boldness in the service of sin and Satan. "Mene! Tekel!" is written on every human heart. "Wanting! wanting!" is inscribed on heathen fanes and altars; on the laws, customs, and institutions of every nation; and on the universal consciousness of mankind.

This inward corruption manifests itself in outward actions. "The tree is known by its fruit." As the smoke and sparks of a chimney show that there is fire within; so all the "filthy conversation" of men, and all "the unfruitful works of darkness" in which they delight, evidently indicate the pollution of the source whence they proceed. "Out of the abundance of the heart the mouth speaketh." The sinner's speech betrayeth him. "Evil speaking" proceeds from malice and envy. "Foolish talking and jesting" are evidence of impure and trifling thoughts. The mouth full of cursing and bitterness, the throat an open sepulcher, the poison of asps under the tongue, the feet swift to shed blood, destruction and misery in their paths, and the way of peace unknown to them, are the clearest and amplest demonstration that men "have gone out of the way," "have together become unprofitable." We see the bitter fruit of the same corruption in robbery, adultery, gluttony, drunkenness, extortion, intolerance, persecution, apostasy, and every evil work—in all false religions; the Jew, obstinately adhering to the carnal ceremonies of an abrogated law; the Mohammedan, honoring an impostor, and receiving a lie for a revelation from God; the Papist, worshiping images and relics, praying to departed saints, seeking absolution from sinful men, and trusting in the most absurd mummeries for salvation; the pagan, attributing divinity to the works of his own hands, adoring idols of wood and stone, sacrificing to malignant demons, casting his children into the fire or the flood as an offering to imaginary deities, and changing the glory of the incorruptible God into the likeness of the beast and the worm.

"For these things' sake the wrath of God cometh upon the children of disobedience." They are under the sentence of the broken law; the malediction of eternal Justice. "By the offense of one, judgment came upon all men unto condemnation." "He that believeth not is condemned already." "The wrath of God abideth on him." "Cursed is every one that continueth not in all things written in the book of the law, to do them." "Woe unto the wicked; it shall be ill with him, for the reward of his hands shall be given him." "They that plow iniquity, and sow wickedness, shall reap the same." "Upon the wicked the Lord shall rain fire, and snares, and a horrible tempest; this shall be the portion of their cup." "God is angry with the wicked every day; if he turn not, he will whet his sword; he hath bent his bow, and made it ready."

Who shall describe the misery of fallen man! His days, though few, are full of evil. Trouble and sorrow press him forward to the tomb. All the world, except Noah and his family, are drowning in the deluge. A storm of fire and brimstone is fallen from heaven upon Sodom and Gomorrah. The earth is opening her mouth to swallow up alive Korah, Dathan, and Abiram. Wrath is coming upon "the Beloved City," even "wrath unto the uttermost." The tender and delicate mother is devouring her darling infant. The sword of men is executing the vengeance of God. The earth is emptying its inhabitants into the bottomless pit. On every hand are "confused noises, and garments rolled in blood." Fire and sword fill the land with consternation and dismay. Amid the universal devastation, wild shrieks and despairing groans fill the air. God of mercy! is thy ear heavy, that thou canst not hear? or thy arm shortened, that thou canst not save? The heavens above are brass, and the earth beneath is iron; for Jehovah is pouring his indignation upon his adversaries, and he will not pity or spare.

Verily, "the misery of man is great upon him!" Behold the wretched fallen creature! The pestilence pursues him. The leprosy cleaves to him. Consumption is wasting him. Inflammation is devouring his vitals. Burning fever has seized upon the very springs of life. The destroying angel has overtaken the sinner in his sins. The hand of God is upon him. The fires of wrath are kindling about him, drying up every well of comfort, and scorching all his hopes to ashes. Conscience is chastising him with scorpions. See how he writhes! Hear how he shrieks for help! Mark what agony and terror are in his soul, and on his brow! Death stares him in the face, and shakes at him his iron spear. He trembles, he turns pale, as a culprit at the bar, as a convict on the scaffold. He is condemned already. Conscience has pronounced the sentence. Anguish has taken hold upon him. Terrors gather in battle array about him. He looks back, and the storms of Sinai pursue him; forward, and hell is moved to meet him; above, and the heavens are on fire; beneath, and the world is burning. He listens, and the judgment trump is calling; again, and the brazen chariots of vengeance are thundering from afar; yet again, and the sentence penetrates his soul with anguish unspeakable—"Depart! ye accursed! into everlasting fire, prepared for the devil and his angels!"

Thus, "by one man, sin entered into the world, and death by sin; and so death passed upon all men, for that all have sinned." They are "dead in trespasses and sins;" spiritually dead, and legally dead; dead by the mortal power of sin, and dead by the condemnatory sentence of the law; and helpless as sheep to the slaughter, they are driven fiercely on by the ministers of wrath to the all-devouring grave, and the lake of fire!

But is there no mercy? Is there no means of salvation? Hark! amidst all this prelude of wrath and ruin, comes a still small voice, saying: "much more the grace of God, and the gift by grace, which is by one man, Jesus Christ, hath abounded unto many."

2. This brings us to our second topic, man's gracious recovery to the favor of his offended God.

I know not how to represent to you this glorious work, better than by the following figure. Suppose a vast graveyard, surrounded by a lofty wall, with only one entrance, which is by a massive iron gate, and that is fast bolted. Within are thousands and millions of human beings, of all ages and classes, by one epidemic disease bending to the grave. The graves yawn to swallow them, and they must all perish. There is no balm to relieve, no physician there. Such is the condition of man as a sinner. All have sinned; and it is written, "The soul that sinneth shall die." But while the unhappy race lay in that dismal prison, Mercy came and stood at the gate, and wept over the melancholy scene, exclaiming, "O that I might enter! I would bind up their wounds; I would relieve their sorrows; I would save their souls!" An embassy of angels, commissioned from the court of heaven to some other world, paused at the sight, and heaven forgave that pause. Seeing Mercy standing there, they cried: "Mercy! canst thou not enter? Canst thou look upon that scene and not pity? Canst thou pity, and not relieve?" Mercy replied: "I can see!" and in her tears she added, "I can pity, but I can not relieve!" "Why canst thou not enter?" inquired the heavenly host. "O!" said Mercy, "Justice has barred the gate against me, and I must not—can not unbar it!" At this moment Justice appeared, as if to watch the gate. The angels asked, "Why wilt thou not suffer Mercy to enter?" He sternly replied: "The law is broken, and it must be honored! Die they or Justice must!" Then appeared a form among the angelic band like unto the Son of God. Addressing himself to Justice, he said: "What are thy demands?" Justice replied: "My demands are rigid; I must have ignominy for their honor, sickness for their health, death for their life. Without the shedding of blood there is no remission!" "Justice," said the Son of God, "I accept thy terms! On me be this wrong! Let Mercy enter, and stay the carnival of death!" "What pledge dost thou give for the performance of these conditions?" "My word; my oath!" "When wilt thou perform them?" "Four thousand years hence, on the hill of Calvary, without the walls of Jerusalem!" The bond was prepared, and signed and sealed in the presence of attendant angels. Justice was satisfied, the gate was opened, and Mercy entered, preaching salvation in the name of Jesus. The bond was committed to patriarchs and prophets. A long series of rites and ceremonies, sacrifices and oblations, was instituted to perpetuate the memory of that solemn deed. At the close of the four thousandth year, when Daniel's "seventy weeks" were accomplished, Justice and Mercy appeared on the hill of Calvary. "Where," said Justice, "is the Son of God?" "Behold him," answered Mercy, "at the foot of the hill!" And there he came, bearing his own cross, and followed by his weeping Church. Mercy retired, and stood aloof from the scene. Jesus ascended the hill, like a lamb for the sacrifice. Justice presented the dreadful bond, saying, "This is the day on which this article must be canceled." The Redeemer took it. What did he do with it? Tear it in pieces, and scatter it to the winds? No! He nailed it to his cross, crying, "It is finished!" The Victim ascended the altar. Justice called on holy fire to come down and consume the sacrifice. Holy fire replied: "I come! I will consume the sacrifice, and then I will burn up the world!" It fell upon the Son of God, and rapidly consumed his humanity; but when it touched his Deity, it expired. Then was there darkness over the whole land, and an earthquake shook the mountain, but the heavenly host broke forth in rapturous song—

"Glory to God in the highest! on earth peace, good-will to man!"

Thus grace has abounded, and the free gift has come upon all, and the Gospel has gone forth proclaiming redemption to every creature. "By grace ye are saved, through faith; and that not of yourselves; it is the gift of God; not of works, lest any man should boast." By grace ye are loved, redeemed, and justified. By grace ye are called, converted, reconciled, and sanctified. Salvation is wholly of grace. The plan, the process, the consummation, are all of grace.

> "Grace all the work shall crown
> Through everlasting days;
> It lays in heaven the topmost stone,
> And well deserves the praise."

"Where sin abounded, grace hath much more abounded." "Through the offense of one, many were dead." And as men multiplied, the offense abounded. The waters deluged the world, but could not wash away the dreadful stain. The fire fell from heaven, but could not burn out the accursed plague. The earth opened her mouth, but could not swallow up the monster sin. The law thundered forth its threat from the thick darkness on Sinai, but could not restrain, by all its terrors, the children of disobedience. Still the offense abounded and multiplied as the sands on the sea-shore. It waxed bold, and pitched its tent on Calvary, and nailed the Lawgiver to a tree. But in that conflict sin received its mortal wound. The Victim was the Victor. He fell, but in his fall he crushed the foe. He died unto sin, but sin and death were crucified upon his cross. Where sin abounded to condemn, grace hath much more abounded to justify. Where sin abounded to corrupt, grace hath much more abounded to purify. Where sin abounded to harden, grace hath much more abounded to soften and subdue. Where sin abounded to imprison men, grace hath much more abounded to proclaim liberty to the captives. Where sin abounded to break the law and dishonor the Lawgiver, grace hath much more abounded to repair the breach and efface the stain. Where sin abounded to consume the soul as with unquenchable fire and a gnawing worm, grace hath much more abounded to extinguish the flame and heal the wound. Grace hath abounded! It hath established its throne on the merit of the Redeemer's sufferings. It hath put on the crown, and laid hold of the golden scepter, and spoiled the dominion of the prince of darkness, and the gates of the great cemetery are thrown open, and there is the beating of a new life-pulse throughout its wretched population, and Immortality is walking among the tombs!

This abounding grace is manifested in the gift of Jesus Christ, by whose mediation our reconciliation and salvation are effected. With him, believers are dead unto sin and alive unto God. Our sins were slain at his cross and buried in his tomb. His resurrection hath opened our graves and given us an assurance of immortality. "God commendeth his love toward us, in that, while we were yet sinners, Christ died for us; much more, then, being now justified by his blood, we shall be saved from wrath through him, for if, when we were enemies, we were reconciled to God by the death of his Son, much more, being reconciled, we shall be saved by his life."

"The carnal mind is enmity against God; it is not subject to the law of God, neither indeed can be." Glory to God for the death of his Son, by which this enmity is slain, and reconciliation is effected between the rebel and the law! This was the unspeakable gift that saved us from ruin—that wrestled with the storm and turned it away from the devoted head of the sinner. Had all the angels of God attempted to stand between these two conflicting seas, they would have been swept to the gulf of destruction. "The blood of bulls and goats, on Jewish altars slain," could not take away sin—could not pacify the conscience. But Christ the gift of divine Grace, "Paschal Lamb by God appointed," a "sacrifice of nobler name and richer blood than they," bore our sins and carried our sorrows, and obtained for us the boon of eternal redemption. He met the fury of the tempest, and the floods went over his head; but his offering was an offering of peace, calming the storms and the waves, magnifying the law, glorifying its Author, and rescuing its violator from wrath and ruin. Justice hath laid down his sword at the foot of the cross, and amity is restored between heaven and earth.

Hither, O ye guilty! come and cast away your

weapons of rebellion! Come with your bad principles and wicked actions—your unbelief, and enmity, and pride, and throw them off at the Redeemer's feet! God is here, waiting to be gracious. He will receive you—he will cast all your sins behind his back, into the depths of the sea, and they shall be remembered against you no more forever. By Heaven's "unspeakable gift," by Christ's invaluable atonement, by the free and infinite grace of the Father and the Son, we persuade you, we beseech you, we entreat you, "be ye reconciled to God!"

It is by the work of the Holy Spirit within us, that we obtain a personal interest in the work wrought on Calvary for us. If our sins are canceled, they are also crucified. If we are reconciled in Christ, we fight against our God no more. This is the fruit of faith. "With the heart man believeth unto righteousness." May the Lord inspire in every one of us that saving principle!

But those who have been restored to the divine favor may sometimes be cast down and dejected. They have passed through the sea, and sung praises on the shore of deliverance, but there is yet between them and Canaan "a waste howling wilderness," a long and weary pilgrimage, hostile nations, fiery serpents, scarcity of food, and the river Jordan. Fears within and fightings without; they may grow discouraged, and yield to temptation, and murmur against God, and desire to return to Egypt. But fear not, thou worm Jacob! Reconciled by the death of Christ;

much more, being reconciled, thou shalt be saved by his life. His death was the price of our redemption; his life insures liberty to the believer. If by his death he brought you through the Red Sea in the night, by his life he can lead you through the river Jordan in the day. If by his death he delivered you from the iron furnace in Egypt, by his life he can save you from all the perils of the wilderness. If by his death he conquered Pharaoh, the chief foe, by his life he can subdue Sihon, King of the Amorites, and Og, the King of Bashan. "We shall be saved by his life." "Because he liveth, we shall live also." "Be of good cheer!" The work is finished; the ransom is effected; the kingdom of heaven is opened to all believers. "Lift up your heads and rejoice," "ye prisoners of hope!" There is no debt unpaid, no devil unconquered, no enemy within your own hearts that has not received a mortal wound! "Thanks be unto God, who giveth us the victory, through our Lord Jesus Christ!"

SPURGEON.

The following is an extract from one of Spurgeon's sermons. (Fourth Series: Sheldon & Co., New York.)

"Therefore let us not sleep, as do others; but let us watch and be sober." 1 Thess. v, 6.

*   *   *   *   *   *   *   *   *

II. Thus I have occupied a great deal of time in explaining the first point—What was the sleep which the apostle meant? And now you will notice that the word "therefore" implies that there are CERTAIN REASONS FOR THIS. I shall give you these reasons; and if I should cast them somewhat into a dramatic form, you must not wonder; they will the better, perhaps, be remembered. "Therefore," says the apostle, "let us not sleep."

We shall first look at the chapter itself for our reasons. The first reason precedes the text. The apostle tells us that " we are all the children of *the light and of the day; therefore* let us not sleep, as do others." I marvel not when, as I walk through the streets after nightfall, I see every shop closed, and every window-blind drawn down; and I see the light in the upper room, significant of retirement to rest. I wonder not that a half an hour later my footfall startles me, and I find none in the streets. Should I ascend the staircase, and look into the sleepers' placid countenances, I should not wonder; for it is night, the proper time for sleep. But if, some morning, at eleven or twelve o'clock, I should walk down the streets and find myself alone, and notice every shop closed, and every house straitly shut up, and hearken to no noise, I should say, " 'T is strange, 't is passing strange, 't is wonderful." What are these people at? 'T is day-time, and yet they are all asleep. I should be inclined to seize the first rapper I could find and give a double knock, and rush to the next door and ring the bell, and so all the way down the street; or go to the police station, and wake up what men I found there, and bid them make a noise in the street; or go for the fire-engine, and bid the firemen rattle down the road and try to wake these people up. For I should say to myself, "There is some pestilence here; the angel of death must have flown through these streets, during the night, and killed all these people, or else they would have been sure to have been awake." Sleep in the day-time is utterly incongruous. "Well, now," says the apostle Paul, "ye people of God, it is day-time with you; the Sun of righteousness has risen upon you with healing in his wings; the light of God's Spirit is in your conscience; ye have been brought out of darkness into marvelous light; for you to be asleep, for a Church to slumber, is like a city abed in the day, like a whole town slumbering when the sun is shining. It is untimely and unseemly."

And now, if you look to the text again, you will find there is another argument. "Let us, who are of the day, be sober, putting on the breastplate of faith and love." So, then, it seems, it is *war-time;* and therefore, again, it is unseemly to slumber. There is a fortress, yonder, far away in India. A troop of those abominable Sepoys have surrounded it. Bloodthirsty hell hounds, if they once gain admission, they will rend the mother and her children, and cut the strong man in pieces. They are at the gates: their cannon are loaded, their bayonets thirst for blood, and their swords are hungry to slay. Go through the fortress, and the people are all asleep. There is the warder on the tower, nodding on his bayonet. There is the captain in his tent, with his pen in his hand, and his dispatches before him, asleep at the table. There are soldiers lying down in their tents, ready for the war, but all slumbering. There is not a man to be seen keeping watch; there is not a sentry there. All are asleep. Why, my friends, you would say, "Whatever is the matter here? What can it be? Has some great wizard been waving his wand, and put a spell upon them all? Or are they all mad? Have their minds fled? Sure, to be asleep in war-time is indeed outrageous. Here! take down that trumpet; go close up to the captain's ear, and blow a blast, and see if it does not awake him in a moment. Just take away that bayonet from the soldier that is asleep on the walls, and give him a sharp prick with it, and see if he does not awake." But surely, surely, nobody can have patience with people asleep, when the enemy surround the walls and are thundering at the gates.

Now, Christians, this is your case. Your life is a life of warfare; the world, the flesh, and the devil—that hellish trinity—and your poor flesh is a wretched mudwork behind which to be intrenched. Are you asleep? Asleep, when Satan has fire-balls of lust to hurl into the windows of your eyes—when he has arrows of temptation to shoot into your heart—when he has snares into which to trap your feet? Asleep, when he has undermined your very existence, and when he is about to apply the match with which to destroy you, unless sovereign grace prevents? O, sleep not, soldier of the cross! To sleep in war-time is utterly inconsistent. Great Spirit of God, forbid that we should slumber.

But now, leaving the chapter itself, I will give you one or two other reasons that will, I trust, move Christian people to awake out of their sleep. *"Bring out your dead! Bring out your dead! Bring out your dead!"* Then comes the ringing of a bell. What is this? Here is a door marked with a great white cross. Lord, have mercy upon us! All the houses down that street seem to be marked with that white death cross. What is this? Here is the grass growing in the streets; here are Cornhill and Cheapside deserted; no one is found treading the solitary pavement; there is not a sound to be heard but those horse-hoofs like the hoofs of death's pale horse upon the stones, the ringing of that bell that sounds the death-knell to many, and the rumbling of the wheels of that cart, and the dreadful cry, "Bring out your dead! Bring out your dead! Bring out your dead!" Do you see that house? A physician lives there. He is a man who has great skill, and God has lent him wisdom. But a little while ago, while in his study, God was pleased to guide his mind, and he discovered the secret of the plague. He was plague-smitten himself, and ready to die; but he lifted the blessed phial to his lips, and he drank a draught and cured himself. Do you believe what I am about to tell you? Can you imagine it? That man has the prescription that will heal all these people; he has it in his pocket. He has the medicine which, if once distributed in those streets, would make the sick rejoice, and put that dead-man's bell away. And he is asleep! He is asleep! He is asleep! O ye heavens! why do ye not fall and crush the wretch? O earth! how couldst thou bear this demon upon thy bosom? Why not swallow him up quick? He has the medicine; he is too lazy to go and tell forth the remedy. He has the cure, and is too idle to go out and administer it to the sick and dying! No, my friends, such an inhuman wretch could not exist! But I can see him here to-day. There are you! You know the world is sick with the plague of sin, and you yourself have been cured by the remedy which has been provided. You are asleep, inactive, loitering. You do not go forth to

"Tell to others round,
What a dear Savior you have found."

There is the precious Gospel; you do not go and put it to the lips of a sinner. There is the all-precious blood of Christ; you never go to tell the dying what they must do to be saved. The world is perishing with worse than plague; and you are idle! And you are a minister of the Gospel; and you have taken that holy office upon yourself; and you are content to preach twice on a Sunday, and once on a week-day, and there is no remonstrance within you. You never desire to attract the multitudes to hear you preach; you had rather keep your empty benches, and study propriety, than you would once, at the risk of appearing overzealous, draw the multitude and preach the word to them. You are a writer; you have great power in writing; you devote your talents alone to light literature, or to the production of other things which may furnish amusement, but which can not benefit the soul. You know the truth, but you do not tell it out. Yonder mother is a converted woman; you have children, and you forget to instruct them in the way to heaven. You, yonder, are a young man, having nothing to do on the Sabbath-day, and there is the Sunday school; you do not go to tell those children the sovereign remedy that God has provided for the cure of sick souls. The death-bell is ringing e'en now; hell is crying out, howling with hunger for the souls of men. "Bring out the sinner! Bring out the sinner! Bring out the sinner! Let him die and be damned!" And there are you, professing to be a Christian, and doing nothing which might make you the instrument of saving souls—never putting out your hand to be the means, in the hand of the Lord, of plucking sinners as brands from the burning! O, may the blessing of God rest on you, to turn you from such an evil way, that you may not sleep as do others, but may watch and be sober! The world's imminent danger demands that we should be active and not be slumbering.

Hark how the mast creaks! See the sails there, rent to ribbons. Breakers ahead! She will be on the rocks directly. Where is the captain? Where is the boatswain? Where are the sailors? Ahoy there!

Where are you? Here's a storm come on. Where are you? You are down in the cabin. And there is the captain in a soft, sweet slumber. There is the man at the wheel, as sound asleep as ever he can be; and there are all the sailors in their hammocks. What! and the breakers ahead? What! the lives of two hundred passengers in danger, and here are these brutes asleep? Kick them out. What is the good of letting such men as these be sailors, in such a time as this especially? Why, out with you! If you had gone to sleep in fine weather we might have forgiven you. Up with you, captain! What have you been at? Are you mad? But hark! the ship has struck; she will be down in a moment. Now you will work, will you? Now you will work, when it is of no use, and when the shrieks of drowning women shall toll you into hell for your most accursed negligence in not having taken care of them. Well, that is very much like a great many of us, in these times too.

This proud ship of our commonwealth is reeling in a storm of sin; the very mast of this great nation is creaking under the hurricane of vice that sweeps across the noble vessel; every timber is strained, and God help the good ship, or, alas! none can save her. And who are her captain and her sailors, but ministers of God, the professors of religion? These are they to whom God gives grace to steer the ship. "Ye are the salt of the earth;" ye preserve and keep it alive, O children of God. Are ye asleep in the storm? Are ye slumbering now? If there were no dens of vice, if there were no harlots, if there were no houses of profanity, if there were no murders and no crimes, O, ye that are the salt of the earth, ye might sleep; but to-day the sin of London crieth in the ears of God. This behemoth city is covered with crime, and God is vexed with her. And are we asleep, doing nothing? Then God forgive us! But sure of all the sins he ever doth forgive, this is the greatest, the sin of slumbering when a world is damning—the sin of being idle when Satan is busy, devouring the souls of men. "Brethren, let us not sleep" in such times as these; for if we do, a curse must fall upon us, horrible to bear.

There is a poor prisoner in a cell. His hair is all matted over his eyes. A few weeks ago the judge put on the black cap, and commanded that he should be taken to the place from whence he came, and hung by the neck till dead. The poor wretch has his heart broken within him, while he thinks of the pinion, of the gallows, and of the drop, and of after-death. O, who can tell how his heart is rent and racked, while he thinks of leaving all, and going he knoweth not where! There is a man there, sound asleep upon a bed. He has been asleep there these two days, and under his pillow he has that prisoner's free pardon. I would horsewhip that scoundrel, horsewhip him soundly, for making that poor man have two days of extra misery. Why, if I had had that man's pardon, I would have been there, if I rode on the wings of lightning to get at him, and I should have thought the fastest train that ever run but slow, if I had so sweet a message to carry, and such a poor heavy heart to carry it to. But that man, that brute, is sound asleep, with a free pardon under his pillow, while that poor wretch's heart is breaking with dismay! Ah! do not be too hard with him: he is here to-day. Side by side with you this morning there is sitting a poor penitent sinner; God has pardoned him, and intends that you should tell him that good news. He sat by your side last Sunday, and he wept all the sermon through, for he felt his guilt. If you had spoken to him then, who can tell? He might have had comfort; but there he is now—you do not tell him the good news. Do you leave that to me to do? Ah! sirs, but you can not serve God by proxy; what the minister does is naught to you; you have your own personal duty to do, and God has given you a precious promise. It is now on your heart. Will you not turn round to your next neighbor, and tell him that promise? O, there is many an aching heart that aches because of our idleness in telling the good news of this salvation. "Yes," says one of my members, who always comes to this place on a Sunday, and looks out for young men and young women whom he has seen in tears the Sunday before, and who brings many into the Church, "yes, I could tell you a story." He looks a young man in the face, and says, "Have n't I seen you here a great many times?" "Yes." "I think you take a deep interest in the service, do you not?" "Yes, I do: what makes you ask me that question?" "Because I looked at your face last Sunday, and I thought there was something at work with you." "O, sir," he says, "nobody has spoken to me ever since I have been here till now, and I want to say a word to you. When I was at home with my mother, I used to think I had some idea of religion; but I came away, and was bound apprentice with an ungodly lot of youths, and have done every thing I ought not to have done. And now, sir, I begin to weep, I begin to repent. I wish to God that I knew how I might be saved! I hear the word preached, sir, but I want something spoken personally to me by somebody." And he turns round; he takes him by the hand, and says, "My dear young brother, I am so glad I spoke to you; it makes my poor old heart rejoice to think that the Lord is doing something here still. Now, do not be cast down; for you know, 'This is a faithful saying, and worthy of all acceptation, that Christ Jesus came into the world to save sinners.'" The young man puts his handkerchief to his eyes, and after a minute, he says, "I wish you would let me call and see you, sir." "O, you may," he says. He talks with him, he leads him onward, and at last by God's grace the happy youth comes forward and declares what God has done for his soul, and owes his salvation as much to the humble instrumentality of the man that helped him as he could do to the preaching of the minister.

Beloved brethren, the Bridegroom cometh! Awake! Awake! The earth must soon be dissolved, and the heavens must melt! Awake! Awake! O Holy Spirit, arouse us all, and keep us awake.

III. And now I have no time for the last point, and, therefore, I shall not detain you. Suffice me to say in warning, there is AN EVIL HERE LAMENTED. There are some that are asleep, and the apostle mourns it.

My fellow-sinner, thou that art this day unconverted, let me say six or seven sentences to thee, and thou shalt depart. Unconverted man! unconverted woman! you are asleep to-day, as they that sleep on the top of the mast in time of storm; you are asleep, as he that sleeps when the water floods are out, and when his house is undermined and being carried down the stream far out to sea; you are asleep, as he who in the upper chamber, when his house is burning and his own locks are singeing in the fire, knows not the devastation around him; you are asleep—asleep as he that lies upon the edge of a precipice, with death and destruction beneath him. One single start in his sleep would send him over, but he knows it not. Thou art asleep this day; and the place where thou sleepest has so frail a support that when once it breaks thou shalt fall into hell: and if thou wakest not till then, what a waking it will be! "In hell he lifted up his eyes, being in torment;" and he cried for a drop of water, but it was denied him. "He that believeth in the Lord Jesus Christ and is baptized, shall be saved; he that believeth not, shall be damned." This is the Gospel. Believe ye in Jesus, and ye shall "rejoice with joy unspeakable and full of glory."

CAUGHEY.

Take as a specimen of Caughey's preaching his sermon on

THE OMNIPOTENCE OF FAITH.

"Therefore I say unto you, What things soever ye desire when ye pray, believe that ye receive them, and ye shall have them." MARK xi, 24.

The congregation will recollect that these words were spoken by the Savior as he was passing from the Mount of Olives to Jerusalem. By the wayside he saw a fig-tree which looked beautiful, and doubtless gave signs of fruit upon it; and being hungry, he looked up among the leaves for fruit, but there was none, and he said, "No man eat fruit of thee henceforth forever." He killed the tree, but taught a great doctrine. The next morning, as Christ and his disciples were passing by, Peter remembered that the tree had been cursed: he looked at it, and said, "Master, it is withered"—withered from top to bottom—dried up from the roots—cursed. Jesus said unto them, "Have faith in God; for verily I say unto you, That whosoever shall say unto this mountain, Be thou removed, and be thou cast into the sea, and shall not doubt in his heart, but shall believe that those things which he saith shall come to pass, he shall have whatsoever he saith. Therefore I say unto you, What things soever ye desire when ye pray, believe that ye receive them, and ye shall have them." I should like to say to this audience, that whenever our Savior said, "Verily, verily," he was about to deliver some very important truth. He was now teaching the omnipotence of faith.

In Manchester, within the last few days, many things have been said about sudden conversion. An old lady said to me, "Why, Mr. C., I hear that you are converting them by scores and by hundreds. I don't understand this sudden conversion." I answer, there is no such a thing in the Scriptures as gradual conversion or gradual purity; there must be a last moment when sin exists, and a first moment when it does not; and this must take place in time, for one moment after death would be too late, unless we believe in purgatory. Pardon and purity are doctrines clearly taught in the Bible, and, in the very nature of things, they must be sudden in their attainment. Our text is the great polar-star of our salvation. You will remember it is recorded in the Life of Napoleon, when he was contemplating the Russian campaign, his uncle, Cardinal Fesch, endeavored to dissuade him from it. Napoleon's words are these: "Am I to blame because the great degree of power I have already attained forces me to assume the dictatorship of the world? My destiny is not yet accomplished; my present situation is but a sketch of the picture which I must finish. There must be one universal European code—one court of appeal. The same money, the same weights and measures, the same laws, must have currency throughout Europe. I must make one nation out of all the European states, and Paris must be the capital of the world." His uncle remonstrated with him, and conjured him not to tempt Providence—not to defy heaven and earth, the wrath of man, and the fury of the elements: at the same time he also expressed his fear that he would sink under the difficulties. The only answer which Napoleon gave was in keeping with his character. He led the Cardinal to the window, and opening the casement, he pointed upward, and asked him, "If he saw yonder star?" "No, sire," answered the astonished Cardinal. "But I see it," answered Napoleon. We point you to our text as the great polar-star of faith—the great charter for believing, containing a principle on which slumbers omnipotence—as the medium that links man to the throne of the great Eternal, connecting man with God.

Archimedes, when he discovered the power of the lever, said, "If you can find me a fulcrum to rest my lever upon, I can move the world." "What is a fulcrum?" says one. I answer, a point or center on which a lever turns. "And what is a lever?" I answer, a bar, or mechanical power by which great weights are moved.

Our text is the fulcrum—faith is the lever; and with it we can move two worlds at once, and hell into the bargain. "What things soever ye desire when ye pray, believe that ye receive them, and ye shall have them."

Before we discuss this subject, we want to ask a few questions. There are, perhaps, persons here belonging to other denominations. You may be Calvinists, and as good, I hope, as any of us. You may, however, differ from me on doctrinal points; and, to do you good, I should have to argue with you half an hour, and then perhaps leave you as I found you. Well, I leave all controversy with the pastors; but I want to beg just two things of you: First, go with me as far as you can; and the second is, get all the good you can.

There are also some backsliders here. Are you willing to come back? "Yes," says one, "I am, I am; for I have had a miserable life of it."

And you who are seeking pardon, I want to ask you a question. "Pardon!" says one; "why, my heart is as hard as a flint." Well, if God shall convert your soul before I leave this place, will you meet me in the school-room at the close of this service to let me know it? Will you do it? Well, I believe you will.

And you who are seeking the witness of the Spirit and purity of heart, if God shall purify your heart before I leave this place, will you meet me at the close of this service and let me know it? You will all do it, will you? Well, I will trust to your honor. Says one, "Then you are expecting souls to be saved before you leave the pulpit, are you?" I am, I am expecting it; and heaven expects it, and hell expects it. I believe we shall have souls saved ere I leave this place. Lord, help! Holy Ghost, help! "What things soever ye desire when ye pray, believe that ye receive them, and ye shall have them."

I. Is there any difference between faith and believing?

I answer, yes; just as much as between water at rest and water in motion—wind at rest and wind in motion. Believing is the application of faith to some truth. Believing is faith in motion. There may be ever so much faith, and no believing. It is not enough that there be a general conviction that God is true; that the Bible is a revelation from him; that the invisible things of which the Bible speaks are realities: there may be all this, and yet no salvation. God has given us his testimony that Jesus Christ died a sacrifice for the sins of every man, and, consequently, for me. Faith, then, is putting confidence in God's testimony; it is to be understood in a plain, common-sense way. The Bible was written for the people—the common people—the mass; and if God has not meant the word faith to be understood in a common-sense way, he would have prefaced the Bible with a dictionary, and have explained the nature of believing; but, as there is no such an explanation given, we infer that we are to understand it just as it is understood in ordinary language among men. As to the mystery of faith, there is no mystery about it. Just put confidence in God as you would in a friend. Unbelief is the great sin of the age—the sin that shuts up heaven—the plague-spot of eternal death on the soul—the *sinner's mittimus* to hell, written in his heart—the sin that *damns* the soul. On the other hand, faith opens the hand of God, secures salvation, conquers hell, and places the soul on the throne of God. Believing, then, is faith in motion—faith laying hold on the testimony of God.

II. Is FAITH THE GIFT OF GOD?

There is a great deal of controversy in the world on this question—in America, in England, and especially in Scotland. Is faith the gift of God, or is it not? I answer, every thing that is good in man is from God; and every thing that is bad in him is from the devil and himself. I am exceedingly jealous of every thing that seems to rob God of a particle of the glory of a sinner's salvation. But in what sense is faith the gift of God? I answer, believing is the gift of the God of grace, just in the same sense as breathing, walking, eating, hearing, seeing, are the gifts of the God of nature. It is plain to every man's common-sense, that while the power to perform these acts is from God, the acts themselves are purely his own. As God does not breathe, walk, eat, hear, see for us, neither does he believe for us. God has given man a capacity to believe; namely, a mind to weigh evidence, and to receive truth when supported by evidence. He has given the object of faith; namely, the Lord Jesus Christ, which is like a great sun risen upon our world.

We infer then, as God has given the capacity, the evidence, the object, and as he has laid the responsibility on man, as the sentence of the last judgment turns on this point, as salvation or damnation is suspended on believing or non-believing, the act of faith must be possible—must be a man's own. O, how important it is that you understand what is God's part, and what is your part in this matter!—that you should see the folly of indulging in unbelief, under the delusion that God has not given you faith! How many on this vital point have been deceived! How many of the slain has the grave closed over! How many, as they rushed into eternity, and as the gleams of immortal light flashed upon them, and dispelled the delusions that ruined them, uttered a *death-howl*, went *down damned*, and more than blood was shed! What could God have done to enable you to believe, that he has not done? If all things be ready, then, why tarry? Why wait? Believe and be saved. "What things soever ye desire when ye pray, believe that ye receive them, and ye shall have them."

III. How can you account for it, that there is in some a greater aptness to believe than in others?

Some account for it on the ground of constitutional differences. I don't believe a word of it; I don't believe that one man is born with greater constitutional tendency to believe than another. Others account for it on the ground of divine partiality. I answer, there is no partiality in God, except such as you make yourselves. God is partial to them that believe his word; hence it is written, "He that believeth shall be saved." We may, in some measure, account for this inaptness to believe, on the ground of the pride of intellect. "O!" says one, "I am not like one of the simple herd of mankind, who can receive for truth every silly notion announced to them. I must have evidence—good, sound argument; I must be convinced before I can believe." "Well," say you, "do you despise me for that?" No; I honor a thinking man; but you pride yourself above the common mass, and you will not come down to receive God's plain, simple testimony. God says, "What things soever ye desire when ye pray, believe that ye receive them, and ye shall have them," and you refuse to believe this testimony. "Well," says another, "some have a weak faith, and some a strong faith; how do you account for that?" I answer, the one has an exercised faith, and the other has a non-exercised faith, and that is the reason why there is a greater aptness to believe in one than in another. Look yonder at that blacksmith, wielding the heavy sledge-hammer from hour to hour, and that without any injury or inconvenience. Were you to labor with that hammer for one half an hour, you would be so stiff the next morning that you would scarcely be able to lift your hand to your head; but the blacksmith is up and at it, the next morning, as lively as ever; exercise has made the difference. Take another illustration. Suppose a mother to bandage her son till he is thirteen years old, beginning at his feet, bandaging him up clear to his chin, like an Egyptian mummy. At the age of thirteen she removes the bandage, and says, "Now, my son, run forth and play with other children." Why, it can not move; its joints are stiff; it is a complete cripple. Ah, some of you have been in bandages all your life; you are spiritual cripples. Glory be to God, if you will but believe, he will set your joints all right, and put strength in your limbs. "What things soever ye desire when ye pray, believe that ye receive them, and ye shall have them." What does another mother do with her weakly child? Why, she sets him on his feet, and holds out one finger to him, and says, "Now, my dear, try." Down he tumbles. She sets him up again—"Come, come, my son, try, try again." (Ah, you see he is very weakly yet!) He tries again, and down he goes. "Come, come, my son; try once more. There, now—that's better." Soon he reaches from chair to chair, and if you do n't take care of him, he is out of doors among the wheels. That mother knows the philosophy of getting strength. He gets strength. "Whatsoever things ye desire when ye pray, believe that ye receive them, and ye shall have them."

IV. ARE THE OBJECTS OF FAITH LIMITED?

Can I believe for what I like and have it? I answer, no; on temporal matters you must put in an *if*. I was coming, the other day, from Ireland, in a steamer; I generally suffer dreadfully from seasickness. I therefore asked the Lord to let us have a calm sea; yet I did not know but that many ships might be lying outside the port loaded with corn, and would want a wind to blow them up to give food to the starving people, and I would not have the people perish to save me from sickness; therefore I had to put in an *if*. Still, I believe we may get the full assurance of faith, even for temporal matters. That mother may, for the safety of her son; that wife, for the deliverance of her husband. There's an instance in the Life of Luther of the assurance of faith in prayer. Miconius was ill, with a swelling in his throat, given up by the medical men, and appeared to be on the borders of death. Luther prayed for him, and said, "Lord, Miconius is necessary to thy Church; thy work can not go on without him." He felt he had hold of God, and said, "Miconius shall not die, but live." Intimation of the confidence of Luther for Miconius was sent to the latter, and he was so excited, that the swelling burst and his life was spared.

In a German work there is a circumstance recorded of a mother who was lying on what seemed to be the bed of death. Her little daughter, about five years of age, was heard to pray, "O, dear Lord Jesus, make my mother better!" The little child was heard to repeat to herself, "Yes, I will make your mother better!" Some would call this the child's superstition, but I would call it her faith. The mother recovered. There was once a man who had cancer in his eyes, and his eyes were being eaten out with the disease. This poor man cried to the Lord, and said, "O Lord, wilt thou let the cancer eat out mine eyes? Thou wilt not, Lord; thou wilt put greater honor on thy servant than that." And to the astonishment of medical men, his eyes were spared. And, if we walk closely with God, we shall often get the full assurance of faith even for temporal blessings. But in reference to justification and holiness we may pray with unlimited faith. "Be it unto thee according to thy faith," is the law of the kingdom. The kingdom of his grace is thrown open to you, and a voice from the throne says, "Be it unto thee even as thou wilt." The veracity of God, the blood of Christ, yea, every attribute of the Deity, every person in the Godhead, are pledged to the fulfillment of this promise. If you abandon sin, give up yourselves to him, trust in the blood of his Son, he will save you; nay, he doth save you. There must be no *ifs* here, no peradventures. Let there be an uncompromising, unreserved trust in the blood of Christ; and if the Bible be a revelation from heaven, if there be a covenant of mercy, if there be virtue in the blood of Christ, power in the Holy Ghost, truth in God, you will be saved. "What things soever ye desire when ye pray, believe that ye receive them, and ye shall have them."

V. HOW CAN WE RECONCILE THE PHRASEOLOGY OF THE TEXT, AND BELIEVE THAT WE HAVE IN THE PRESENT WHAT IS SPOKEN OF IN THE FUTURE TENSE?

I was greatly perplexed on this point, till one day I happened to be in company with two ministers; one was a Methodist, and the other a Baptist brother. The Methodist said to his Baptist brother, "I have been thinking much about that text, 'What things soever ye desire when ye pray, believe that ye receive them, and ye shall have them.' I think there must be some mistake about the translation. Have you a Greek Testament?" A good old Greek Testament was reached down; the Greek lexicon and grammar were also produced, to examine the root and tense of the verb. The words πιστευετε—believe—and λαμβανετε—receive—were carefully examined. The Baptist fixed his finger on the words, and said, "It must be in the first future." "No," said the Methodist, "see, πιστευσετε, the first future, has a different termination." "Then," said he, "it must be in the first Aorist." "No, brother; see, επιστευσε, the first Aorist, has a prefix to it; therefore it can not be that." The Baptist said, "I see I must give it up. The words are rightly translated." He remembered it was written—Isa. lxv, 24—"And it shall come to pass, that before they call, I will answer; and while they are yet speaking, I will hear." And had not Charles Wesley an eye to that when he penned that hymn,

"I take the blessing from above,
And wonder at thy boundless love?"

The Greek scholar can examine for himself; and though he may have all the knowledge of an archangel, I defy him to say that the passage is wrongly translated. It is there, "What things soever ye desire when ye pray, believe that ye receive them, and ye shall have them." Then you are not to believe that it was done some time ago—not that He will do it at some future period, but believe that he doth it now.

VI. What preparation must a man have in order to believe?

"What do you mean," says one, "by a preparation?" I answer: I mean, how many tears a man must shed—how deep must be his conviction—how soft must be his heart—what amount of godly sorrow must he feel—how long must he remain in a state of repentance? I have read this blessed Bible through on my knees, every word of it, and I find no standard in it; God has set up none. There is not a word said about how many tears a man must shed, how soft or hard the heart must be; nothing of the kind; and as God has set up no standard, I'll be the last man in the world to make one. I believe there are far too many creeds and standards floating about the Christian Church already. No, there is no spiritual barometer or thermometer; and I'm glad of it, for it would greatly perplex a minister, and it would also greatly distress penitent souls. Some persons could not shed a tear, if you gave them the world—still the heart may bleed, while the eyes are dry. Glory be to God, he has put the power in *believing*—purifying their hearts by *faith*. It is no where said purifying them by tears, by feelings, by soft hearts or hard ones, by deep convictions or shallow ones. He has, however, said, "What things soever ye desire when ye pray, *believe* that ye receive them, and ye shall have them." O! it is by faith, by confidence in God. And this method will meet all cases— the case of the farmer, of the doctor, of the lawyer, of the president of the college, of the servant, of the master, of the subject, of the sovereign, of the little child, of the venerable sage, of the man of A. B. C., of the philosopher—yes, of all grades of mind, from the first dawn of reason up to intellectual noon. "You do not mean to say," says one, "that no preparation is necessary?" I answer no, I do not; for when sin is indulged, God will never save. Sin must be given up.

* * * * * * * * *

The Methodists have clear, Scriptural views of these doctrines; but I tell you, you are holding on to things that will damn you: God would as soon sanctify the devil as to sanctify you. I know what I say; I speak advisedly. "Lift up holy hands, without wrath and doubting." Lift them up to show that there is no iniquity in them. You may leave the chapel as soon as you like; or, if you have patience to tarry, you may; but I tell you, it is of no use; God will never purify your hearts till you give up the sins to which you are clinging. See that poor fellow wandering on through the wilderness: the night is dark, he stumbles, and falls into some deep, dark pit: he sets up a cry for help: his cry breaks on the stillness of the night, and is heard echoing on through the wilderness. See those three men passing on, now, as the moon just glimmers through the cloud. See! see! they are standing listening, they have heard that cry for help: now they are making way to that spot whence the cry proceeds: one of them is standing on the edge of that deep pit: he listens, and the cry is heard again.

"Who is down there?"

"O, sir, I have fallen into this dreadful place; my feet are stuck in the mire."

"Be of good courage, my friend; there are two strong fellows here besides myself; we'll soon have you up."

Now the rope is being let down. "There, take hold of that rope, man, take fast hold: now, give a strong pull." Up comes the rope; the man in the pit has let it slip. "Why, what's the matter down there? Come, come, now take a firmer hold. Now, comrades, give another pull."

Up comes the rope again. "Why, man, you must surely have something in your hands."

"I have a few things, sir, that I should like to bring up with me, down here."

"Come, cast them away, and take hold of the rope, and not trifle in this way!"

Now he casts the things out of one of his hands, and they try again: but up comes the rope again. "I tell you, man, if you do n't cast away those things, and take hold, we will leave you to your fate." Now he casts them all away, and takes firm hold, and *up he comes!*

* * * * * * * * *

LETTER XVI.

PULPIT ORATORS—CONTINUED.

My Dear Brother,—The foregoing specimens have been presented, not as models, but simply to show that the men who have wielded the greatest pulpit power were those who conformed most nearly to the model of the Master.

Some excel in clearness and earnestness; others add to these a very effective degree of naturalness, literalness, and appropriateness. Many, no doubt, possessed a much higher degree of naturalness of manner than their published sermons indicate.

Chrysostom, Latimer, Massillon, Bunyan, Christmas Evans, and Whitefield combined with a high degree of clearness and earnestness, an equal degree of naturalness, literalness, and appropriateness. Chillingworth excelled in the first, second, and fifth. I think Chalmers was of the same type of Chillingworth. He had great clearness and earnestness, and wonderful power of application. The following notice of him I clip from the *Western Christian Advocate:*

The editor of the British Standard recently published a series of letters in favor of preaching extemporaneously, which he considered the only simple, natural, and truly-effective style of pulpit oratory.

He thus disposes of the greatest apparent exception to his rule, Chalmers, the prince of Scottish preachers:

"I have heard all the greatest pulpit readers of my time, and not one of them has formed an exception to the rule. Even Chalmers, their chief and head, whose mighty ministrations I have very frequently attended, matchless reader though he was, came most fully within the rule. That distinguished man, indeed, made no attempt to look at his audience such as is made by a multitude of readers; the finger of either hand was never for a moment removed from the MS.; there was nothing beyond a passing flash of the eye as he occasionally darted his head upward. Once fairly in motion, he rushed along like a locomotive of the highest power at full speed, heedless of every thing before, behind, or around him, with a sort of blind, though inspired fury. He could, I verily believe, have performed the magnificent feat equally well in Westminster Abbey alone, and with the doors shut! The fires which, on these occasions, raged so strongly within him, were wholly independent of external circumstances. As a consequence of this, power, all-subduing power, was the prime characteristic of the achievement. He was generally altogether wanting in pathos, that ethereal something which, proceeding from a melted heart, has the power of melting all around it. The effect of his sublime effusion was a feeling of intense excitement, ofttimes of overwhelming admiration, from which the auditor was often strongly tempted to clap his hands and shout applause; but he was rarely visited with compunction or moved to tears. Even in his death-scenes he awakened in the assembly scarcely any emotions other than those of awe or horror; the most sympathetic even of the gentler sex seldom wept. The most striking exception I ever remember was on the occasion of his farewell sermon on leaving Glasgow for St. Andrews. The discourse on that occasion was a sublime affair, not in its matter, for he was obviously by no means well prepared, but in its delivery; and the prayer was even more touching than the sermon. The discourse appears in his Collected Works, where it occupies but a very secondary place.

"How great soever, in a certain way, Chalmers might be with MS., he would have been incomparably greater with free speech; he was so in his partial attempts at extemporizing. Nothing I ever listened to might be likened to his off-hand flights, whether in the pulpit or the class-room, the social meeting or the General Assembly of the Church of Scotland. The style was then much more natural and idiomatic, much less figurative, and the matter much more simple, condensed, and business-like, and the intonation in keeping with it. It was nature perfected. On these occasions he was scarcely at all Ciceronian, ofttimes quite Demosthenic.

"Again, in the case of Chalmers, there was a most material circumstance which greatly abated the offensiveness of the MS. to the public, as well as lessened its inconvenience to himself. His discourses were written in short-hand—which he read with a facility almost miraculous—on a sheet of foolscap folded into eight pages, so that there were only four leaves to turn during the entire exercise—a process barely perceptible. One of these short-hand manuscripts—a much-prized treasure—is now before me, consisting of only eight pages, although it occupied forty minutes in the delivery.

"The power of Chalmers with MS., however matchless in its own way, was, I repeat, impotent compared with the might of his extempore bursts. The difference was early perceived by discerning men. His Memoirs contains a singularly-interesting passage in relation to this subject. The celebrated Andrew Fuller, during one of his Scottish journeys on behalf of the Baptist mission, before Chalmers had become famous, having spent some time with him at Kilmany, labored hard to wean him from the habit of reading. Dr. Hanna, his son-in-law, says:

"'Under the very strong conviction that his use of the manuscript in the pulpit impaired the power of his Sabbath addresses, Mr. Fuller strenuously urged upon his friend the practice of extempore preaching, or preaching from notes. "If that man," said he to his companion, Mr. Anderson, after they had taken leave of Kilmany manse—"if that man would but throw away his papers in the pulpit, he might be king of Scotland."'"

You observe, my brother, that when Chalmers

allowed his naturalness to break the fetters which bound him to his MS., override the trammels of a stiff, unnatural pulpit style, his bursts of eloquence were absolutely overwhelming. Had he adopted and practiced the natural mode of preaching, he would have eclipsed Demosthenes. Mr. Fuller said "he might have been king of Scotland," or what is immeasurably superior—king of pulpit orators.

I have not given a specimen of Wesley's preaching, for his sermons have been so extensively read that I do not consider it necessary. He was a methodical sermonizer, but his system was evidently employed as a means of clearness and efficiency, and not simply for the sake of system. I verily believe that Wesley and his noble band of street-preachers, taking them together as a body of living ministers, conformed, in every particular, to the Savior's model more perfectly than any other body of men since the days of the apostles. Their wonderful success is patent to all.

The early pioneers of Methodism in America conformed to this model in a high degree. Most of them possessed clearness and earnestness, as do most of their successors to the present time.

Many of our fathers, to be sure, had but a limited literary education, but they had a clear religious experience, and clear views of the essential doctrines and appliances of the Gospel. They knew but little about the dead languages, but were familiar with the living language of Canaan. They had but few literary quarterlies, monthlies, and weeklies, but they had the

Bible, Hymn-Book, and Fletcher's Checks. They were well posted in Bible truth—chapter and verse—and in our theological standards. Those who accuse many of them of "murdering the king's English," have, nevertheless, been obliged to admit that the king's English escaped with much less damage than his crimes and his devil. True, some of the fathers carried their "Jerusalem blade" in a rustic scabbard, but they kept it bright and sharp, and frequently mowed down the ranks of the enemy with it like men slain in battle. From the best information I have been able to gather, my opinion is, that though the mass of preachers of the present day have more education and refinement than our fathers in the Gospel, we do not surpass them in clearness and earnestness, and do not equal them in naturalness and literalness. I think this is true as a rule, yet admitting many exceptions on both sides of the question.

I do not say that the ministers of modern days do not equal the fathers in piety and Gospel fidelity; and I believe that, while they are generally exempt from the long, dangerous journeys and privations to which the fathers were subject, their duties are so multiform, extending to so many interests—such as Sunday school, tract, missionary, and other institutions and charities, which scarce had an existence among us seventy years ago—that the mental wear and tear, and perplexing toils of modern ministers exceed those of the fathers; and yet in trying to adapt ourselves to the refinements of modern taste, and have every thing done with critical exactness, though the mass of the people have not demanded it of us, we have laced on to ourselves a strait-jacket of formal sermonizing and stiff, unnatural modes of delivery, which seriously trammel and embarrass our efforts. I think the comparatively new thing of sermon-reading in Methodist pulpits, though generally unpopular with our people, is increasing, while a great many of the regular sermon-reading ministers of other denominations are throwing their manuscripts aside, and betaking themselves to extemporaneous preaching.

The limits of this little work will only permit a brief notice of but a few of the vast multitude of American preachers of the past and present, who have conformed and do conform in a very efficient degree to the model of Jesus.

Jonathan Edwards excelled in clearness, earnestness, and a peculiar pungency of application to the conscience of the sinner.

Jesse Lee, with wonderful clearness and earnestness, excelled in naturalness and literalness—full of incident, sharp wit, and pungent appeal power.

Dr. Fisk, though a man of a different type, was a fine example of the same kind of preaching.

Cookman, combining a noble degree of all the essential elements of the model, excelled in literalness of illustration.

Dr. Olin, I think, excelled in clearness, earnestness, and a majestic power of application. From what I have seen and learned from others, I believe that his ministry was characterized by a great degree of naturalness also.

Bishop M'Kendree, with great clearness, earnestness, and appropriateness, also excelled in naturalness.

Wm. B. Christie, whose praise is in all the Churches of the west, excelled in the first two and fifth characteristics of the model. The same may be said of Russel Bigelow.

John Strange, whose name will live forever in the history of western Methodism, possessed in an unusual degree all the characteristics of the model, excelling most men in naturalness and literalness. He was of the "Boanerges" type. His ministrations were full of striking, telling episodes and overwhelming bursts of surprise power. Brother S., an old presiding elder in Indiana, said to me a few weeks since, "When I was an unconverted young man, I went, in company with a lot of wicked young men, to a camp meeting. We entered within the circle of the tents while John Strange was preaching, and as we passed down the aisle John paused, and straightening up his tall form to its utmost hight, looking right at us, he cried, 'Here they come! Lord God, shoot them! Load and fire again!' Every hunter present understood that. I felt," said brother S., "something like a sharp pain strike right through my body, and for a moment thought I was shot, and every one of us dropped down almost as suddenly as if we had been shot." It was very common under the preaching of

Strange for men to fall prostrate like men shot down with a Minnie rifle.

John Collins possessed an equal degree of naturalness and literalness with Strange, but of a milder type—rather more "a son of consolation." Rev. J. B. Finley bears the following testimony of him: "No preacher had the power of rousing the masses, and holding them by his eloquence and power, to so great an extent as the meek and sainted Collins. Often have we heard him relate the story of the lost child, describing with inimitable tenderness the feelings of the mother, whom he tried to comfort, but who, like Rachel, 'would not be comforted, because her child was not,' and then, when the child was found, with the utmost pathos would relate the joyous emotions of the mother. No tragedian ever succeeded better in transferring the feelings of a character to his audience in his impersonations than did the inimitable Collins. So far was he from falling under the charge made by a tragedian to a minister of the Gospel, of representing fact as if it were fiction, that he became the living embodiment of his theme, and, with a soul on fire, he poured out the living truth till every heart was moved. Often have we seen thousands borne down by his impassioned eloquence, like the trees of the forest in a storm. And it was irresistible. Steel your heart as you might; summon all your philosophy and stoicism; and nerve up your soul to an iron insensibility and endurance, surrounding it with a rampart of the strongest prejudices, the lightning of his eloquence, accompanied by the deep-toned, awfully-sublime thunder of his words, which came burning from his soul, would melt down your hardness, and break away every fortification in which you were intrenched, while tears from the deep, unsealed fountains of your soul would come unbidden like rain. The only way to escape his power was to flee from his presence and hearing." (Sketches of Western Methodism.)

Valentine Cook combined in a good degree all the elements of the model. A glance at his literalness may be seen in the following extract from Bishop Morris's Miscellany:

"Brother Cook, as a preacher, was altogether above the medium grade. His pulpit performances were marked for appropriateness, variety, fluency, and extraordinary force." "While brother Cook was remarkable for solemnity, both of appearance and deportment, there was in his natural composition a spice of eccentricity, sufficient to attract attention, but not to destroy his ministerial influence. On one occasion he commenced his public discourse—in a country place—thus: 'As I was riding along the road to-day, I saw a man walk out into his field with a yoke under his arm; by the motion of the stick, he brought up two bullocks, and placed the yoke upon them. At another place I saw an ass standing by a corn-crib, waiting for his daily provender.' Then he read for his text, 'The ox knoweth his owner, and the ass his master's crib; but Israel doth not know, my people doth not consider.' He was a ready man, had a fruitful mind, and, no doubt, what he had seen on the way suggested the subject of his discourse."

From the sermons of living men, I have, as you have seen, selected but two specimens—Spurgeon and Caughey. I might select from many others more acceptable to the critics, perhaps, did my space permit. Notwithstanding all the objections raised against Spurgeon and Caughey, they combine a masterly degree of the essential elements of power contained in the Gospel model, and their extraordinary success is known to the world.

We have many living ministers of different denominations, who combine, in a very efficient degree, all the characteristics of the model.

Dr. Durbin excels in the first two and last two—and has, withal, when animated, a glowing degree of naturalness.

Bishop Simpson combines all in such symmetrical proportions, that I do n't know that one is more prominent in his ministry than another. He employs a great many historical and scientific illustrations, but they are made natural and simple to the life.

I might multiply cases of mighty men, in different branches of the Church, who conform in a high degree to the Master's model, but I forbear. I will simply add, that I believe there are thousands of men with "one talent," who conform more fully to the great Teacher's model, and hence, in proportion to their natural force and humble sphere, accomplish more than many of the "star preachers."

I think the foregoing examples of pulpit eloquence are sufficient clearly to establish the proposition they were designed to prove and illustrate; namely, that the most effective pulpit orators of different ages, were those who conformed most nearly to the model of the Master, and that their success was proportionate to the degree of their conformity to it; and hence, the presumption is clear, that their success is attributable to the fact of their conformity to the model of Jesus.

LETTER XVII.

MISCELLANEOUS SUGGESTIONS.

My Dear Brother,—I want to tell you a little of my experience in regard to pulpit encyclopedias. After I had been preaching a couple of years, I was prevailed upon, at conference in Baltimore city, to purchase a copy of a new work, containing five hundred sketches of sermons, and all the examples and directions necessary to furnish a man thoroughly unto every good work, and to great efficiency as a preacher, and, moreover, it was pleaded in the argument, that all the preachers were supplying themselves; and so, as I did not like to be left behind entirely, and as I had a sincere zeal for God and souls, I bought the book, and thought I would try and keep up with my young brethren, as a sermonizer, and save as many souls as possible.

I had upward of two hundred miles to travel to my circuit, and on the way I seized every opportunity to examine my new book. I read a number of the sketches, and found that they divided and subdivided the text, till it required a large proportion of the figures of the multiplication table to number the points, and said more about the subject than I had ever thought of, or supposed I ever could have thought of. And now the question in my mind was,

"What can I make of any one of these sketches?" To appropriate and use it as my own will probably expose me to the just charge of plagiarism, and even if my theft should not be detected, it will not meet the honest demands of my own conscience. Again, I want to learn to walk alone, and grow up to be a man, and if I begin by walking on crutches, and borrowed ones at that, I will move very ungracefully, and this will perhaps make an awkward hobbler of me during my whole life." I thought of selecting from different sketches, and fitting the selections on to a new text, and try it in that way, but soon came to this conclusion, "That will be but a hypocritical ruse got up to cover my theft, and I can't consent to such a thing." I found, too, that as the sketch contained every thing that I could think of, as having any connection with the subject, I had, instead of gaining a sermon, lost a text. And having already lost two or three favorite ones, I shut up the book, and the first opportunity I had, gave it away to a local preacher. I believe, my brother, that, while such works contain a vast amount of valuable theological matter, their use, upon the whole, has a bad effect on our young preachers. 1. It presents too strong a temptation to plagiarism. 2. The standard of sermonizing which they furnish is too abstract, too formal, too stiff, and yet, claiming to be supported by the most celebrated authorities in the Church, many young men conclude that to gain a reputation as sermonizers, and not mere talkers or exhorters, they must conform to this standard—that nothing is entitled to the name of a sermon unless it be prefaced with a formal exordium, and then contain at least three regular divisions, and four or five subdivisions, under each head of discourse, then a recapitulation of the whole, and finally an application containing nearly as many divisions as the body of the sermon.

I opened a book of sermons a few days since, from the pen of one of the great modern models, and the first sermon I examined contained forty divisions and subdivisions, all duly numbered.

Now, there is a legitimate order of truth, and if to number the points will in any case add any thing to brevity and clearness of statement, or to efficiency in the application of truth, by all means number your points; but the idea of sacrificing most of the essential elements of pulpit power for the sake of maintaining a false formal standard of sermonizing, is a fallacy deep dyed with the blood of souls. See a man called of God to preach the Gospel delivering a long, systematic, dry sermon. Some of his hearers are stumbling on the threshold of perdition, and are hearing the man of God for the last time. God sees those souls rapidly drifting to the equatorial line between possible salvation and eternal death. Jesus, with yearning heart, stands in the pulpit "with" his embassador, according to his promise. The Holy Ghost hovers over the awful scene, and knocks now at the perishing sinner's heart, and now at the preacher's heart, and brings to his "remembrance the things" that would reach the sinner's conscience. The preacher is almost persuaded to let his arrangement go, or the latter half of it, at any rate, and break forth in earnest appeal, but the thought of his reputation as a sermonizer deters him, and he proceeds with his sermon as before arranged. What does Jesus think of such a man? How does the Holy Spirit feel on such an occasion? How the ministering angels, waiting to bear the victorious war dispatches to heaven, hover and gaze, and wonder at such a spectacle! During the ensuing week a dear neighbor, who attended Church that day for the last time, takes suddenly ill and dies without hope.

In regard to reading sermons, my brother, I need say but little. If, after mastering a subject, as you should always do in a good degree before you attempt to preach on it, you can not retain in your memory what you wish to say long enough to announce it to your people, how can you expect them to remember it from a single hearing?

If your sermon is sufficiently clear, earnest, natural, literal, and appropriate for efficiency, neither you nor your hearers will find much difficulty in remembering it; but if it is made up of dry abstractions, you will have to write it out in order to remember it yourself, and it don't make much difference whether the people recollect it or not, as it does not contain enough of practical power to do their souls much good.

It is improving to the mind to write on any useful subject; but if you wish to write a sermon, you can do it much better after preaching it than before. You will then get into it the flashing touches of the Holy Spirit on the occasion of delivery, with the enlarged ideas to which it led you.

If a man wishes to write sermons for publication for the sake of doing good in that way, or simply to preserve in manuscript form, of course it is all right, and to read or have them read privately or publicly, is appropriate enough; but reading sermons is not preaching the Gospel, and to substitute it for preaching is anti-apostolic, and, in my opinion, very offensive to the Holy Spirit. But reading or repeating a borrowed sermon without giving credit, is not only inappropriate, but dishonest.

One of the most popular pulpit orators in Indiana gave me a little of his experience, a few days since, in regard to plagiarism. "Having to preach on one occasion," said he, "soon after I entered the ministry, in a large town, where I supposed I would have in my audience a great many learned critics, I was afraid to risk one of my own productions, and hence selected and committed to memory one of the best published sermons I could find. It was a masterpiece, and I thought I might make it do a great deal of good, and fixed it indelibly upon my mind. I never thought of the impropriety of such a thing till I got into the pulpit, when it struck me that I had stolen another man's sermon, and was about to pass it as my own, and something seemed to say to me, 'Thief, thief! steal a sermon and pass it hypocritically as your own. Hypocrite, hypocrite, you need not think to escape detection. Many of these intelligent men have read that sermon, and will expose you all over town before the setting of the sun. Thief, thief, hypocrite, hypocrite.' It appeared to me that the devil was let loose to torment me, for 'thief, thief,' rang in my ear till my hair seemed to rise on my head, and the perspiration rolled off me. I could not tell what to do. The hour for preaching had come, and I had no other sermon available. So I got up in that sad plight, and repeated the stolen sermon as best I could. As I came down from the pulpit, the accuser assailed me again, saying, 'Thief, thief, you'll be found out. These men are looking on you with contempt now.' I hastened out of sight, and cried to God with the anguish of a condemned criminal, and said, 'O Lord God, pity me. For Christ's sake forgive me. By thy grace I will never attempt such a thing again as long as I live. Let those men tell it; let them publish my shame to the world. I will tell it myself, and confess my guilt to God and to men, and solemnly promise never to be guilty of the like again while God gives me breath.'"

While, my brother, in the matter of direct appeal to the heart, and an effort to lead souls directly to Christ, we should carefully guard against introducing any thing irrelevant, or calculated to divert attention from the one essential question of a present salvation, it is nevertheless a minister's duty to be well posted on all the important questions of the day, and to throw his influence in favor of temperance, and other important reformatory measures of the times. It is his duty to exercise his elective franchise, and to express his opinions on any subject, when he can by so doing promote the glory of God and the good of society. And yet as an embassador of Christ, sent forth to preach the Gospel, not to any particular party, but, as far as he can, to the world, he should not allow himself to be carried by party excitement and strife out of the line of general acceptability and usefulness as a minister of the Gospel.

The Savior and his apostles witnessed many enormous evils, political and social: organized and legalized, they stood out in the light of day in all their undisguised, iniquitous deformity. Even their own people were groaning under the tyranny of Rome, and expected certainly that Messiah at his coming would break the yoke, and proclaim a grand jubilee to all the oppressed; but the bondage of their bodies was so small a matter, compared with the bondage of their souls, that Jesus went and preached deliverance to the captives, breaking the dominion of sin in their hearts and lives, directing their attention entirely to a kingdom not of this world, and said but little about their oppressions or their oppressors. One thing at a time was as much as people or preacher could then successfully attend to.

I have sometimes got prisoners in a good way of seeking the Savior, when they would get an idea that I would be just the man to get up a petition for a reprieve, and release them from prison. That invariably diverted their minds from the vital question—the soul's salvation—and I could lead them no further in that direction.

The Savior doubtless felt, and always manifested a profound sympathy for the people in their bodily sufferings, whether from personal affliction or civil oppression, but a sympathy for their souls as much greater as their spiritual interests were more important than their temporal; and,

As the purity and moral strength of a nation, or any organization, depends solely on the purity of the individuals composing the organization; and,

As great national sins, and organized forms of iniquity and oppression, could only be effectually undermined, cured, and removed by the individual piety of the people; and,

As the enlightened piety of the people individually was the only thing that could make an easier lot in life a blessing to their souls; and,

As an avowed, direct assault upon organized evils would greatly complicate the already momentously responsible work of his embassadors, draw around them many impure ambitious spirits, and generally divert attention from the great work of their mission—the salvation of the world, by individuals;

Therefore, the Savior, for these, with other reasons, probably was pleased in his wisdom to direct the whole moral enginery of the Gospel, not to the *direct* purgation of corrupt governments, and the conquest of the world *en masse,* but to the personal application of its saving power "to every creature," enjoining, by precept and example, obedience to the "powers that be," till by this individual, regenerating, purifying energy of the Gospel, those powers could be made better.

St. Peter expresses the apostolic view of the subject, saying, "Submit yourselves to every ordinance of man for the Lord's sake: whether it be to the king, as supreme; or unto governors, as unto them that are sent by him for the punishment of evil-doers, and for the praise of them that do well. For so is the will of God, that with well-doing ye may put to silence the ignorance of foolish men: as free, and not using your liberty for a cloak of maliciousness, but as the servants of God." The ground on which they urged submission is not that "the kings" were honest and good, and "the ordinances" just and equitable, for they were most tyrannical and corrupt, but because government itself is a necessary institution of God, and because, though "free," and not in justice bound to submit to unjust laws, yet, for the "Lord's sake," by their meek example, "putting to silence the ignorance of foolish men," and thus further the great ends of the Gospel.

The embassadors were thus sent forth, not with carnal, but spiritual weapons, "but mighty through God in pulling down the strongholds" of sin in all its forms. Such was the direct importance of their message, that they were commanded to "salute no man by the way"—to lose no time in needless ceremony, but run on, proclaiming the jubilant tidings, till liberty shall be proclaimed to "all the inhabitants of the whole earth," and the little Gospel stone shall have rolled on, with increasing size and momentum, breaking down and demolishing every opposing force, individual and governmental, and filled the world, and "bring in everlasting righteousness."

Some Pharisees and Herodians once combined their influence to try to make a political partisan of Jesus, and thus addressed him, "Master, we know that thou art true, and teachest the way of God in truth; neither carest thou for any man"—thou certainly hast opinions on the great political questions of the day, and teaching "the way of God in truth," thou hast right opinions, and art not afraid to express them, for thou carest "not for any man"—no conservative dough-face—"for thou regardest not the person of men." "Tell us, therefore, what thinkest thou? Is it lawful to give tribute unto Cæsar, or not?" They hoped to commit him to one or the other of the great contentious political parties of the nation, and thus "entangle him." "But Jesus perceived their wickedness, and said, Why tempt ye me, ye hypocrites? Show me the tribute money. And they brought unto him a penny. And he saith unto them, Whose is this image and superscription? They say unto him, Cæsar's. Then saith he unto them, Render, therefore, unto Cæsar the things which are Cæsar's, and unto God the things that are God's. When they had heard these words they marveled, and left him, and went their way."

While, therefore, my brother, we should fearlessly reprove sin of all kinds—private sins and public sins, in high places and low places—we will find occasion to use all the wisdom with which, by the exercise of common-sense, and by the enlightening power of the Holy Spirit, God may endow us, to plan and conduct our modes of attack so as to promote and not defeat the cause we seek to serve.

The reformers of the eighteenth century grasped the sword, and the weapons of their warfare became mixed—partly spiritual, and in a great degree carnal. The result is patent to all. The reformers of the nineteenth century used Gospel weapons only. The result was a reformation of individuals, which is reforming nations and governments.

I would like, my brother, to make a few suggestions in regard to the "earthen vessels" to which the Gospel treasure is committed—our bodies. If you wish to keep your head and your voice clear, and your nerves in tune for conveying thought, give attention to your diet, and to exercise in the open air, and keep your system in good condition. Nothing will so quickly affect your voice and nervous action, and disqualify you for efficient service, as constipation. Regulate your system, if possible, without medicine. If you make an apothecary shop of yourself, you will never be fit for much else. Do not on any account deprive yourself of your necessary rest and regular hours for sleeping. Rob nature, and it will pursue you like the tax collector.

An old colleague of mine indulged the habit of ting up to talk to his friends, frequently till two o'clock in the morning, and brought upon him a sleepy disease. He can not now listen to a sermon without going to sleep no more than he can command at will the circulation of his blood, and he frequently takes a small nap of sleep between his opening prayer and sermon while the congregation is singing the second hymn. His robbed and injured nature is constantly dunning and teasing him, demanding payment with restitution, and screwing it out of him by small installments.

In anticipation of a heavy Sabbath day's labor, I have found it very serviceable to take vigorous exercise on Saturday—chop wood, work in the garden, or something that will exercise the whole body as much as possible without exhaustion. Next day preaching five sermons will produce but little weariness, and no hoarseness. If my voice is not entirely free and clear, after preaching two or three sermons, I go out alone, and run a foot-race with myself, till I get up rapid breathing, and thoroughly inflate my lungs.

In San Francisco, for years, after preaching three sermons in the forenoon of each Sabbath, I was in the habit of going out on the sand hills after dinner, and running as fast and far as possible without exhausting my physical force, and then go down on the plaza with a voice nearly as clear as a trumpet, and preach

MISCELLANEOUS SUGGESTIONS. 397

to the city and the representatives of the world generally.

When praying vocally, don't throw your head back. Many thus in trying to look up through the roof of the house into the heavens, causing a heavy strain of the vocal organs by an unnatural stretching of the front muscles of the neck, pray themselves hoarse in five minutes.

If you desire to speak with ease and force, and never to "give out," stand erect when speaking—not stiff, like a post—use as much natural action as you desire, but don't stoop forward; keep your shoulders back, give your lungs as much room as possible, and learn the art of deep breathing. Preaching with half-inflated lungs is very much like blowing a fire with half-inflated bellows—constant labor, chafing, and puffing, but not force enough to raise the sparks and heat the iron. Don't speak with the exhausted breath of the lungs, and occasionally, while speaking, thoroughly inflate them by the longest breath you can draw. You will have plenty of time for that in your emphatic pauses. Speak with the natural force of expiration, using the easy contraction of the muscles of the chest from the abdominal muscles up as bellows power for blowing out the words. The softest and loudest tones are thus produced.

Don't acquire the habit of drinking water while preaching, unless really necessary to allay thirst. It is of no advantage to the voice.

When I feel any chafing or soreness of throat from

excessive labor, I take a sup of molasses before going to bed; when a tendency to hoarseness, I put a small piece of alum in my mouth for a moment. I use no candies or any thing for my throat in preaching regularly from eight to fifteen sermons every week, for months together, besides these simple remedies, and very seldom have any hoarseness.

If you travel through the cold in going to an appointment, and find yourself chilled, do n't go to a stove before preaching, unless suffering greatly from cold feet; instead of that, if you have opportunity, walk or run till you raise the temperature of the body to a comfortable degree.

I have not stopped to give you the philosophy of the simple rules I have stated; that will be obvious to you on reflection.

The law of the Sabbath is adapted to our physical wants as really as to the demands of our moral nature, and can not in relation to either be violated with impunity. As a minister's heaviest labor is on the Sabbath, he ought to observe Saturday or Monday as a day of rest and recreation; but do n't indulge any " blue Mondays."

The reaction of the excitement of Sabbath's labors is so severe with some preachers, that on Monday they are as snappish as a surly cur, and their wives have almost to stand guard at their study doors to keep the children away from them. If you feel the " blues" coming upon you, do n't shut yourself up in your study, nor resort to " old wives' fables," or yellow-covered, farcical trash for entertainment, but perform your devotions, and then go out in the open air, and take a romp with the little boys and girls—take them near to your person and near to your heart, sing them little songs, and tell them pleasing little stories about good boys and girls. Attract them to you and to your Savior, and in return they will impart animal magnetism or electricity to your overwrought nervous system, sympathy and affection to your heart, diversion and entertainment for your mind, and thus recuperate your wearied energies faster than any other specific you can employ.

On the subject of using stimulants before going into the pulpit, my brother, allow me to say, their use is very important.

In former days, especially in England, a little of the ardent was provided and kept in the sanctuary for the purpose.

Some, though perhaps but a few, at the present time in our own country, use opium for that purpose, or a compound of opium and spirits. A thirst is thus created which demands a larger dose each week, and a few cases have come to light where mighty men have been bitten and slain by the serpent thus piously fostered in their bosoms. I have met with several such wrecks in California, and have heard of some in my travels on this side of the continent.

Some get up the steam by smoking a cigar before going into the pulpit, and after a while a couple are necessary to produce the same effect; and it is well if they are not induced to resort to something stronger to secure the same pious end.

A great many men of unquestionable piety and usefulness use the weed, but it is a question whether it is exactly appropriate to stink up "the temple of God"—their bodies—with the fumes of tobacco. I do not know certainly whether they constitute a "sweet-smelling savor to the Lord" or not; but I know they don't smell so sweet to a poor mourner on whom they are breathing the words of consolation. I will give you, my brother, a prescription for a stimulant, both wholesome and efficient.

1. A consciousness that you are going before your people with something that will stir their souls, and by reflex sympathy increase the stimulating tide in your own bosom. "See a man wise in his own conceit; there is more hope of a fool than of him;" but a just appreciation of the power with which God has endowed you, and of the power of the good "old Jerusalem blade," bright and sharp, is necessary to efficient action.

Elihu felt the power of this kind of stimulus when he said, "I also will shew mine opinion. For I am full of matter; the spirit within me constraineth me."

2. The baptismal fire of the Holy Spirit is the best stimulant for a preacher in the world.

3. It will be serviceable, as you have opportunity, without wearying your vocal powers, to talk a little to some dying Christian, or direct some trembling sinner to the cross, visit a class, or say a few words to the

children in the Sabbath school, before going into the pulpit. If you have mastered your subject, and if your sermon has enough of literalness in it to make it tell on your hearers, there is no danger of driving it out of your mind by the kind of conversation I have prescribed, but light, commonplace talk operates injuriously. In San Francisco I used to visit the patients in the hospital in the morning, and preach to as many of them as were able to assemble in one room. That constituted a stimulant which brought out the sympathies of my soul, quickened nervous action, and prepared me for the labors of the day.

4. When you get into the pulpit, reassure yourself of your call to be an embassador of Christ, and that you are about to "teach your hearers to observe all things whatsoever he hath commanded," and then by the promise, "Lo, I am with you always," realize by faith that the world's Redeemer is in the pulpit with you, as really present as though you saw him with your eyes—present in his spiritual nature, in his essential divinity, in all the fullness of his saving power. A faithful application of this prescription, my brother, will supersede the necessity of any other, and always operate with satisfactory success.

Whether your inspiration be much or little, my brother, do not preach long sermons. From thirty to fifty minutes is long enough for a sermon, unless the occasion is much more than ordinary. That is the rule—this the exception. Many a suit at law has been lost because the advocate covered too much ground, introduced too much testimony, and made too long a speech to the jury. All he needs are a few clear, apposite points, well sustained by unquestionable evidence, summed up with such brevity and force as to carry the judgment of the court, interspersed with surprise power enough to wake up a lively interest, and arouse the sympathies of judge and jury.

It is said of Sir John Scarlett, a celebrated English barrister, that he never occupied more than from twenty-five to thirty minutes in addressing a jury, for the reason that all the time he could subsequently occupy would only force out of the heads of the jury what he had put in during the first twenty-five minutes.

Often, when a preacher has driven a nail in a sure place, instead of clinching it, and securing well the advantage he has gained, he hammers away till he breaks the head off or splits the board, or, in other words, diverts attention from the effective point already made, to what he has yet to say, but fails to drive another such nail that day.

Never introduce yourself to an audience by a string of apologies; they are poor things, and never converted any sinners. Never preface your sermon with an introduction merely for the sake of having one. I once knew a preacher that generally introduced all his sermons with the same exordium. If you find an introduction necessary, use it; but if you can strike the key-note of your subject in your first sentence, all the better. In your expositions of

Scripture, try to find out the meaning of the Holy Spirit, and convey the Spirit's ideas and your own in the fewest words consistent with clearness, and in the most simple, literal words suited to the subject. Never use words simply for the sake of sound, or to fill up your sentences. Words are designed as the vehicles of ideas, and not substitutes for them.

Learn all you can from books, but select your preaching matter mainly from God's books of inspired truth, of nature, and of providence. Many men spend nearly all their time in their studies, plodding along in the path of other thinkers, stuffing memory with their thoughts, till they take intellectual dyspepsia; whereas, if they would just go out into God's fields of original truth, they could dig up the virgin gold from the mine with greater success than many of the men they read after; and then it would be fresh and original, and all their own, and the exercise, developing equally all their powers, mental and moral, would be most healthful and invigorating. The knowledge thus gained is much more available and effective.

THE END.

www.ingramcontent.com/pod-product-compliance
Lightning Source LLC
Chambersburg PA
CBHW051243300426
44114CB00011B/875